ACTION CHICKS

ACTION CHICKS

New Images of Tough Women in Popular Culture

Edited by

SHERRIE A. INNESS

ACTION CHICKS
Copyright © Sherrie A. Inness, 2004.

First published 2004 by
PALGRAVE MACMILLAN™
175 Fifth Avenue, New York, N.Y. 10010 and
Houndmills, Basingstoke, Hampshire, England RG21 6XS.
Companies and representatives throughout the world.

PALGRAVE MACMILLAN is the global academic imprint of the Palgrave Macmillan division of St. Martin's Press, LLC and of Palgrave Macmillan Ltd. Macmillan® is a registered trademark in the United States, United Kingdom and other countries. Palgrave is a registered trademark in the European Union and other countries.

ISBN 1–4039–6403–3 hardback
ISBN 1–4039–6396–7 paperback

Library of Congress Cataloging-in-Publication Data

Action chicks : new images of tough women in popular culture / Sherrie
   A. Inness, editor.
      p. cm.
   Includes bibliographical references and index.
      ISBN 1–4039–6403–3 (cloth) — ISBN 1–4039–6396–7 (paperback)
      1. Women in mass media. 2. Mass media—United States. 3. Popular
   culture—United States. I. Inness, Sherrie A.

P94.5.W652U614 2004
791.45'652042'0973—dc21   2003050906

A catalogue record for this book is available from the British Library.

Design by Newgen Imaging Systems (P) Ltd.

First edition: February 2004
10 9 8 7 6 5 4 3 2 1

Printed in the United States of America.

For Julianna A. Buchsbaum

Contents

Part II   New Images of Toughness

Acknowledgments

I wish to thank all the people who helped make this book possible. My contributors have done an excellent job of keeping deadlines. They tackled repeated drafts of their work with great cheer and were models of what contributors to such a project should be. I want to thank all the individuals, including Hallie Bourne, Claudia Herbst, Theresa Hurst, and Whitney Womack, who have read parts of the manuscript before its publication. Their input was invaluable. Hallie's skills as an editor are impeccable. All the people at Palgrave Macmillan who made this book possible also deserve my sincere appreciation for their fine work, especially Amanda L. Johnson, Michael Flamini, Donna Cherry, Jen Simington, and Matthew Ashford.

I appreciate my friends, including Hallie Bourne, Julie Hucke, Michele Lloyd, Debra Mandel, Marla Mayerson, Heather Schell, and Liz Wilson. I cannot express what encouragement they provide to me. They are also always willing to take me away from my writing when I need a break. I thank my colleagues at Miami University for their support. I am grateful to some especially important people in my life, my mother and father, Ruth and Lowell Inness.

Finally, this book is dedicated to Julianne A. Buchsbaum, someone I cherish.

Introduction

"Boxing Gloves and Bustiers": New Images of Tough Women

Sherrie A. Inness

"Ladies, get out your boxing gloves and bustiers," Jennifer Steinhauer writes in a 2000 article from the *New York Times*. "This year's heroines of prime time and the big screen are muscular and trained in the martial arts, and they have no compunctions about slapping, immolating, and kicking their way through life. . . . They are restoring world order and ending bad dates with swift, punishing blows."[1] Recent years have witnessed an explosion of tough women in the popular media—including films, television shows, comic books, and video games.[2] Along with Steinhauer, other commentators have noted this phenomenon.[3] In 2000, Lorraine Ali comments in *Newsweek*:

> The petite actress Zhang Ziyi in Ang Lee's new movie "Crouching Tiger, Hidden Dragon" slays several men twice her size while drinking a cup of tea. In "Charlie's Angels," Drew Barrymore manages to pulverize her captors with her feet bound to a chair. And then there's "The Matrix's" Carrie-Anne Moss, who, even in a skintight bodysuit, manages to flip her enemy like a flimsy omelet. Across the country female moviegoers no longer dream of being saved by Jean-Claude Van Damme but of kicking and chopping the bad guys till they cry for mercy.[4]

Similarly, in 2001, Stephanie Mencimer writes for the *Washington Monthly*, "This year, the muscle-bound stars of action-film block-busters of the '80s and '90s have found themselves ungraciously drop-kicked out of the genre by, of all things, a bunch of girls. Girl-power flicks like *Charlie's Angels*, *Crouching Tiger*, and *Tomb Raider* are topping the $100 million mark once dominated by men like Schwarzenegger."[5] Does the trend identified by Steinhauer, Ali, and Mencimer have a far-reaching impact on popular culture? What has happened to make these tough females so popular? Do they represent greater freedom for women from gender stereotypes? What do these figures suggest about changing societal roles for women and men?

It is difficult to escape the onslaught. We turn on the television and find numerous shows, including *La Femme Nikita, Xena: Warrior Princess, Buffy the Vampire Slayer, Alias*, and *Dark Angel*. In the movie theater, we find *Tank Girl, Girlfight*, and *Barb Wire*. In video games, Lara Croft dominates, but there are other games, including Parasite Eve, Resident Evil, Bloodrayne, and Tekken III, that feature similar tough women. Even children's television has joined the tough girl craze with the Powerpuff Girls.[6] Popular culture cannot seem to get enough of tough females. Of course, they are not an entirely new phenomenon. The United States has had a tradition of such women. Steinhauer observes, "Physically strong and super-naturally enhanced women have a long history in American pop culture: think back to Rosie the Riveter and Wonder Woman."[7] The tradition stretches back to even earlier figures, including Calamity Jane and Annie Oakley, who were portrayed in 1800s dime Westerns; although they were based on real women, they became larger-than-life heroines in fiction. Many other tough females, including Wild Edna, the Girl Brigand, and the Detective Queen, were also featured in the dime novels. Numerous tough women followed those early figures. In the 1930s, a number of female detectives appeared in pulp novels, including Carrie Cashin, Violet McDade, and Aevada Alvarado. All three showed that they were tough enough to survive in this male-dominated universe. In the pulp magazine *Weird Tales*, C. L. Moore's action-adventure female Jirel of Joiry appeared, as did Robert E. Howard's Red Sonya, Conan's sidekick. Sheena was a heroic queen of the jungle in comic books; she debuted in the United States in 1938 and flourished until the early 1950s. Her success led to the popularity of other heroic jungle girls in the comics. In hard-boiled detective novels, a few tough women appeared, including Mike Hammer's secretary Velda, who was also a private investigator and packed her own gun.

More recent decades have had their share of tough women, too. The British television show *The Avengers* was popular in the states in the 1960s. It featured Mrs. Emma Peel (Diana Rigg) as a tough woman who was more than capable of taking on any man, although she did have a male partner. Another sixties British import was Modesty Blaise of comic book and novel fame. Equally tough were Pam Grier, Tamara Dobson, and other heroines in 1970s Blaxploitation films. *Charlie's Angels* and *The Bionic Woman* appeared in the mid-1970s, and both television shows were popular, demonstrating that there was an audience for tough women, albeit beautiful, slender, heterosexually desirable ones. Other tough women followed during the last decades of the twentieth century, including, most importantly, the hero of *Alien* (1979), Lieutenant Ellen Ripley (Sigourney Weaver), one of the toughest females to appear in the mainstream media. *Alien* and its sequels showed that millions of audience members "of both sexes could connect powerfully to the image of a . . . heroine getting sweaty and bloody in brutal physical combat with a monster."[8] Ripley demonstrated that women did not have to look as though they stepped directly from a beauty parlor when they battled foes. Following her lead, Linda Hamilton, as Sarah Connor starred in *The Terminator* (1984) and *Terminator 2: Judgment Day* (1991). A buff figure in the second film, she showed that women could compete with men as action-adventure heroes. Ripley and Connor's success led the way for the large number of tough female characters who appeared in subsequent years. Strong women characters have always existed in the American mythology. What has changed are the sheer numbers.

Tough women are appearing not only in the popular media but in real life, too. In the gymnasium, women are taking up boxing and other sports typically considered in previous years to be just for men. Weight lifting has also grown in popularity. In the weight room, some women strive for muscles reminiscent of Sarah Connor's in *Terminator 2*—a change from previous years when young, fashionable women did not want too-visible muscles and worried that weight lifting would make them overly muscular. Now, these same women lament if their biceps do not bulge or they do not have six-pack stomachs. They are willing to spend hours in the gym to obtain such figures. Many women are content just to be toned; however, there is a higher threshold for what counts as toned. They want to have a look that is more muscular than earlier feminine body ideals—they want buns of steel and abs of iron.

The craze for a tough appearance has also struck Hollywood. Stars such as Madonna, Sarah Jessica Parker, and Janet Jackson give detailed reports of the fitness routines that led to their impressive biceps and muscular stomachs. For her "six-pack abs," Jackson pursued a workout routine that included "three days of abs, five to six days of cardiovascular, and two days of upper body and legs."[9] Angelina Jolie took intensive Body Pump weight-training classes for the lean, mean look she sported in the film *Lara Croft: Tomb Raider*.[10] Demi Moore relied on "a personal trainer, a yoga instructor, a chef, and an exercise trailer" to "sculpt her body into shape for tough roles such as *G. I. Jane*."[11] If female stars do not begin with impressive physiques, they are forced by media pressure to gain them by pursuing grueling routines worthy of the Marines. As a commentator for Fox News observed, "Lithe and little just doesn't cut it for some superstar women these days, as top-name celebs . . . build their bulging biceps, killer calves, and washboard abs."[12] Stars want "to be cut" and "body-builder ripped."[13] One writer, Bryan Williams, enthused, "There is just something intriguing about a woman who looks like she could kill you."[14]

In addition to the gymnasium and Hollywood, tough women also crop up in the toy store. Barbie has some new challengers, and they "aren't the typical Barbie clones notable for their wardrobes and tresses. Instead, a new group of gals is trying to turn heads with career focus, athleticism, and kick-butt attitude."[15] Get Real Girls is a group of six female athletes, complete with muscle definition. The G.I.R.L Force line from Jakk's World Wrestling Federation features athletic female characters who can "twist, bend and hold a pose unlike any other fashion doll."[16] Julz Chavez created the Get Real Girls, including "snowboarding Skylar, basketball-playing Nakia, and hiking Nini."[17] The emergence of such figures, no doubt, has Barbie hiring a personal trainer and heading to the weight room. Before we know it, the beleaguered blonde will be appearing as Karate Barbie with muscle definition, easily able to throw Ken over her shoulder. As in the larger world, something is changing in the land of the dolls.

A whole new tough aesthetic is emerging for women, one in which it is praiseworthy for them to be more muscular and aggressive than in the past. In the *Sun-Sentinel* in 1998, Lisa Shroder asks in her article "Macho Macho Femme":

> When did women start comparing muscles? Recently, ordinary women have appeared wearing muscles on the streets of South Florida, while women warriors have shown up in movies and on TV, from Xena to Buffy to Nikita to Sigourney Weaver in the *Alien* movies and Demi Moore in *G. I. Jane*. Is this simply a new aesthetic— a healthy switch from the anorexic model look? Is it a step forward in feminism, that women are gender bending with bodies that defy stereotypical femininity?[18]

Do the new styles and behaviors show, as Gerard Jones argues, a profound shift in the "relationship of women, to power, sex, and aggression"? He believes that rather than being just the latest fashion trend, these images reflect the fact that women are challenging the male monopoly on power and aggression, a shift that has broad ramifications for how gender is constructed.[19]

In order to understand the roots of this aesthetic, one needs to recognize how second-wave feminism rippled through American society in the last few decades, changing women's roles on all levels of society. Feminism questioned the notion that women are "naturally" not aggressive, incapable of handling the same challenges as men. Feminism also taught women to question the gender status quo. What emerged were women who pursued many different roles previously held almost exclusively by men. In the workplace, women demonstrated that they could be tough and aggressive. They became soldiers, police officers, fire fighters, and construction workers—all jobs that had been considered too rough for "ladies." In addition, women demanded more authority and power in the workplace; they wanted to demonstrate that they were tough enough to handle even the most stressful and demanding jobs, from

CEO to Congress member. On the sports field, too, women's roles changed due to feminism. Title IX of the Education Amendment of 1972 mandated that publicly funded schools provide equal opportunities and funding for females and males in curricular and extracurricular activities. Enforcement of the amendment led to many more opportunities for girls and women in sports, sometimes leading them to participate in football and wrestling, which were formerly considered to be too physically demanding for the fairer sex. Everywhere from the workplace to the sports field, the feminist movement created a new vision of womanhood, one tougher than before. This cultural shift helped create an environment where women could adopt more aggressive roles than those that they had been able to have in the 1950s and earlier decades.

With changes in women's real lives came changes in popular imagery. No longer could women be represented in the same stereotypical ways as they had been in the past. Something had to change. The rise of the female action heroine was a sign of the different roles available to women in real life. Yvonne Tasker writes, "At one level the action heroine represents a response of some kind to feminism, emerging from a changing political context in which images of gendered identity have been increasingly called into question through popular cultural forms."[20] She continues, "In responding to feminism, image-makers sought to present women as active and as powerful, mobilizing already existing types and conventions, images that were an established part of popular culture, such as the leather-clad dominatrix."[21] Tasker points out that the evolution of women's action roles needs to be studied because it reflects the change of real women's roles in society. It is also important to be aware that these new heroines can stem from sometimes stereotypical roles, such as the dominatrix. Thus, these figures can be rooted in stereotyped female roles but can simultaneously challenge such images.

Action Chicks in Context

A number of scholars have studied the cultural and social impact of tough women in the popular media; the researchers, however, have typically analyzed influential early films and television shows. For example, my book, *Tough Girls: Women Warriors and Wonder Women in Popular Culture* (1999), focuses on many earlier tough women, including Sarah Connor and Ripley.[22] Similarly, Martha McCaughey and Neal King's anthology, *Reel Knockouts: Violent Women in the Movies* (2001), includes essays on films such as *Thelma and Louise* (1991), *Basic Instinct* (1991), *The Silence of the Lambs* (1991), *Terminator 2* (1991), and *La Femme Nikita* (1991).[23] In addition, Elizabeth Hills's influential essay "From 'Figurative Males' to Action Heroines: Further Thoughts on Active Women in Cinema" (1999) discusses the *Alien* series and Ripley.[24] Instead of focusing on such early images, *Action Chicks* analyzes more contemporary examples of tough women in popular culture, studying how such images have changed.

Do the most recent tough female characters reflect a change in how popular culture depicts women? The essays in *Action Chicks* explore this question from a variety of perspectives. Some chapters praise the new tough, autonomous female image. Popular culture's new tough women do not need men to rescue them from peril. Even though many of these women might be attractive and feminine, they do not graciously accept their places in society. Many of *Action Chicks*'s contributors share McCaughey and King's opinion that popular culture's tough women—no matter how traditionally feminine and beautiful they might appear—offer insights into how women are fighting to escape conventional gender role expectations that, in the past, have kept them from being aggressive, whether in real life or the media. McCaughey and King write that violent women are "pop-cultural players shaped by fights over race, class, and family values in a vital game of sexual politics. They disrupt dreams of women's gracious acceptance of all that men hand them. . . . [They are] possible tools in the liberation of women from racial, class, gender, and other political constraints."[25] Thus, researching how the media portray tough, aggressive women offers insight into potential new role models for real women.

Other authors in *Action Chicks* focus on how the new tough women are subversive in a variety of ways. These characters not only rebel against traditional gender roles but also call into question the duality of gender. Hills writes:

> Female action heroes confound binaristic logic in a number of ways, for they access a range of emotions, skills, and abilities that have traditionally been defined as either "masculine" or "feminine." As female characters who take up the central spaces in the traditionally "masculine" genre of action cinema, they derive their power from their ability to think and live creatively, their physical courage, and their strategic uses of technology.[26]

For Hills, not only does the action heroine demonstrate that she can perform the same tasks as a man in an action-adventure narrative, but she also challenges the entire gender system based on the binary male–female relationship. She creates a new gender system in which she can enact "woman" in nontraditional ways, as does Ripley and other action figures. A number of the authors in *Action Chicks* demonstrate how action heroines question notions of conventional gender roles and, as Hills suggests, create a whole new gender system for women (and men).

Tough-women characters, however, do not entirely escape traditional gender role expectations, and chapters in *Action Chicks* also focus on how these females adhere to gender, sexual, racial, ethnic, and class stereotypes. For example, the characters are predominantly white, upper or middle class, attractive, feminine, and heterosexually appealing. The freedoms that these figures suggest frequently lie within a narrow set of prescribed social boundaries. Mencimer is skeptical about whether such figures offer a real challenge to stereotypical gender roles, observing, "No doubt our action heroines have come a long way since Wonder Woman, but the feminist critics are right: Women are still only allowed to be violent within certain parameters largely proscribed by what men are willing to tolerate."[27] Most men do not want women who are too violent, too tough, or too masculine in films. "To achieve box-office success," she observes, "the new action babes have to celebrate women's power without being so threatening that men would be afraid to sleep with the leading lady."[28] Like Mencimer, several of the authors included in this anthology are dubious about how revolutionary the tough woman is. They focus on two issues that need to be considered when analyzing tough women in the media. First, are they sex symbols developed primarily for a male audience? Second, how much is their power lessened by making them appear feminine and beautiful? Both of these are important concerns because the mainstream media remain cautious about how tough women are depicted. *Action Chicks*'s authors examine how tough women are frequently toned down to make them more palatable to a mass audience.

From Lara Croft to Aeryn Sun

The chapters in the book's first section focus on changing images of action heroines over the last decade. The writers, however, are also cognizant of how such generic figures have resisted change. Action heroines might be tougher than in the past, but they also adhere to various stereotypes about how they are supposed to look and behave. This section teases out the complex, sometimes contradictory, strands that make up the modern action heroine.

The first chapter focuses on an action heroine who seems to offer a new image of womanhood but who, Claudia Herbst argues, is a more reactionary figure. The video game character Lara Croft is held up by those who promote "grrrl power" as representing a powerful new image of womanhood. Herbst offers a more disturbing interpretation: Croft is an oversexualized stereotyped character who appeals primarily to males. To understand Lara's image, one has to recognize that she and other similar figures stem from computer technology connected to warfare. Herbst suggests the importance of acknowledging the computer industry and visual imaging technology that make Croft possible. Only by doing so will we recognize how closely connected to war technology she and other similar video heroines are. There is a small shift from her world to the world of warfare.

Jeffrey A. Brown is also interested in the hyperbolic, over-the-top sexualized females found in video games and comic books, as he examines the role of "bad girls" in comic books and in recent movies, especially *Barb Wire* (1996). He argues that the film challenges the typical bad girl story, since the central figure, Barb Wire (Pamela Anderson), is a tough killer only so that she may defend other women, particularly when odious men threaten them. She must act because no one else will defend women against such male predators. Brown suggests that *Barb Wire* creates a new vision of toughness in which bad girls are not merely eye candy. In this fashion, he demonstrates the importance of recognizing that tough images of womanhood, which are sometimes dismissed as appealing solely to male fantasy, deserve more scrutiny as offering, potentially, a more libratory message to women.

Like Herbst and Brown, Sherrie A. Inness focuses on tough female action heroes and how they have changed in the last decade. Analyzing the female action figure toys that are spun off from many films and television shows, she suggests that these toys model for children how to behave as gendered individuals. Toys teach the socially acceptable roles for men and women, including who is supposed to be the hero. Traditionally, this role has been allotted to males, so the overwhelming majority of action figures are male. Over the last few decades, particularly the last ten years, more females are joining the ranks of action figures. This change must be understood within the larger context of a society in which women are increasingly allowed to be heroes in a variety of contexts. Despite this change, toy-store heroes are still predominantly male.

The next three chapters, by Charlene Tung, David Greven, and Sara Crosby, focus on changing images of the female action hero on television, an especially interesting medium to study because many of the most popular recent tough females have appeared there. Television is willing to take more risks with female gender roles than mainstream films. With television, it is easier for producers to experiment with different roles for women, although these roles are still limited. It is less costly to experiment with one episode of a series rather than experiment with a major film. Also, because of television's omnipresence, its tough women have a major impact on the American cultural imagination. Charlene Tung analyzes the show *La Femme Nikita*, examining the complicated relationship between viewing pleasure and cultural critique when considering intersections of gender, race, and sexuality. Nikita, the heroine, both challenges traditional notions of women's bodily comportments and reinforces existing constructions of white womanhood. She breaks down stereotypes about how women are supposed to act physically by presenting a new image of them as aggressive and physically in control. Yet, at the same time, Nikita is white and heterosexual as is typical of television heroes. *La Femme Nikita* has a troubling adherence to a racial ideology about who best embodies a heroine (or hero). Nonwhite women are rarely depicted, and when they are, they are seldom shown as heroic. The show supports a world in which the "natural" heroine is white, suggesting that women from other races fail to qualify.

The next chapter analyzes the television show *Witchblade*. David Greven explores how Sarah Pezzini, a tough New York City police detective, combines toughness and tenderness. He examines how the show focuses on the difficulties of negotiating between these antipodes, and that what emerges is a particularly powerful, complex hero. The show, however, perpetuates some disturbing stereotypes: Sarah Pezzini, at least according to the show's logic, is a hero only because she is the descendent of a long lineage of females who have wielded the Witchblade, an essentialist argument that has troubling ramifications for women. In addition, despite her initial portrayal as a lesbian, Sarah is ultimately shown destroying homosexuals and the threat they pose to the mainstream heterosexual order.

Like Greven and Tung, Sara Crosby is interested in how the media create powerful female heroines but subsequently curtail their power when those women are found to be too subversive of the dominant social order. The shows *Dark Angel*, *Buffy the Vampire Slayer*, and *Xena: Warrior Princess* created particularly powerful tough women, characters so powerful that they threatened the patriarchal status quo. Thus, their lives had to be snapped short by death. Crosby shows how such a trajectory is historically typical. When a woman who is too powerful and tough appears in the American imagination, her life is invariably cut short, reminding the audience of the threat posed by such women. After tracing this cultural pattern through American history, Crosby discusses how the same pattern is present in many of today's television shows about tough women.

The chapters in the second section question the media's standard constructions of female toughness and suggest different forms that toughness can take. The popular media have created certain predictable images of toughness. The tough woman in action-adventure narratives is likely to be muscular but not too muscular, and she is also apt to be independent, not requiring any support. The tough woman is typically not as tough as the males around her. For instance, Sarah Connor was relatively weak and benign when compared with her partner, the muscular Terminator, played by Arnold Schwarzenegger. One of the fascinating developments in the media is that now these stereotypes are being questioned. Increasingly, it is possible to discover women who create new notions of toughness. Such characters also bring into question what it means to be gendered as a woman.

The stereotypical female heroine can be muscular but not so much so that she presents a threat to the males with whom she stars. Her muscularity might be impressive for "a girl," but she is no challenge for the "boys." This stereotype is questioned by Dawn Heinecken, who argues that the wrestler Chyna of the World Wrestling Federation creates a new image, one of a woman who is extremely muscular but also sexually desirable. Ultimately, her image, which is too transgressive, too dangerous, and too masculine, is toned down and given a more feminine appearance. For instance, she has breast implants. Chyna challenges traditional feminine beauty standards while also attempting to adhere to them. Still, her appearance does represent a step forward in depicting muscular women as sexual and desirable, according to Heinecken.

(Yet another typical characteristic of the tough female character is that she is childless. If she does have a child (like Sarah Connor), her aggression is shown as only a manifestation of her desire to save him or her.) Marilyn Yaquinto focuses on a new depiction of the violent, aggressive woman who is also a mother. Yaquinto explores how Carmela Soprano, in the television show *The Sopranos*, creates an image of a tough woman who is married with children but who is also a partner in crime with her husband. This is an important shift in the media that demonstrates how women's toughness can be conceptualized in new ways, including exploring how toughness and maternity can go hand in hand. Yaquinto also studies the other tough women who hang out with mobsters: the molls, who are caught in the space between wife and criminal partner. As with Carmela, their toughness ensures their survival within the male domain of the underworld. Whether Soprano wives or molls, such women suggest new ways that gender and toughness can be combined.

(Another stereotypical characteristic of the tough action heroine is that she typically acts independently, requiring nobody's support.) Sharon Ross finds exceptions to this pattern in two television shows that create powerful female communities to help the heroes, showing that heroism can be shared. Both Xena and Buffy challenge the traditional notion of the hero as an independent, autonomous loner. Instead, they have communities of women that are involved in the heroic action. Because Xena and Buffy are not the only heroic figures in their shows, their behavior and actions do not appear to be unique. This makes heroism seem as though it is something that any woman can perform, especially when a female community enters into that heroism, creating a new idea about who can be a hero.

Finally, Renny Christopher questions a typical characteristic of the action heroine. She can be tough and aggressive but not enough to make men nervous, since they might question their own masculinity if she were too tough. This last chapter moves to an appropriate new location: outer space. It is here, Christopher argues, that women's toughness can be reimagined most dramatically. A television show that creates a particularly revolutionary image of toughness is *Farscape*. One of the lead characters, Aeryn Sun, is originally from a planet where both males and females are entirely equal; no assumption exists that either men or women are the superior sex. It is assumed that both are tough and aggressive, and both serve as interplanetary space police. Sun is a new tough image of womanhood, one that does not yet exist on earth. Her relationship with human astronaut John Crichton is a major focus of *Farscape*. This relationship creates a new vision of gender roles in which traditional gender stereotypes are turned topsy-turvy. She is the more masculine partner, which is viewed as sexually acceptable in this alternate universe. More radically, he is depicted as the more feminine partner, and this does not diminish his attractiveness. No attempt is made to indicate that this relationship is abnormal; instead, it is viewed as completely normal. The show creates a new vision of gender, one not available to people on Earth.

Where the Heroines are Headed

Xena, Lara Croft, Buffy, Barb Wire—these characters and the others in (*Action Chicks* are creating new images of womanhood.] The authors reveal the complexity of understanding such tough women. Although there is no doubt that they are appearing in greater numbers, what is open to question is what cultural role they play. Do these characters offer a more powerful vision of womanhood than that afforded to women by the media in the past? Or are they merely the newest trend in beautiful women fighting crime, following in Charlie's Angels' footsteps, doing little to challenge or question gender stereotypes? As the authors of this anthology demonstrate, both are correct. Some of these tough women do follow in the same footsteps as the Angels and a host of other beautiful women who battle the bad guys but whose fundamental purpose seems to be to function as eye candy. Such characters have a long tradition in American popular culture, and the authors delineate the ways that some tough women continue to be designed to appeal to a primarily male audience. Tough women are still expected to be feminine, attractive, and heterosexually appealing.

But the authors also show that these characters cannot be viewed as *only* eye candy. Like Buffy, Barb Wire, and Sarah Pezzini, many of the new tough women are attractive, feminine, and heterosexually appealing but they also challenge the patriarchal social structure by defending women and acting against the men who threaten them. This is a particularly interesting shift suggesting that women can be the heroes. Traditionally, this role has been allotted to men, both in real life and the media, so having women assume these roles shows that females can handle the heroic roles that, in the past, were regarded as too challenging. In addition, these tough women heroes do not require men to help them, a shift that removes women from their stereotypical role as men's helpers.

These tough women also challenge stereotypes about how the media construct the female body. In the past, females have rarely been depicted as physically aggressive, even in action-adventure narratives. For example, the 1970s Charlie's Angels depended on their wits or their guns, which they rarely fired. Today, tough women have changed from original Angels and other similar figures and can depend equally on brains and brawn. Now, women are apt to be as physically aggressive as men. This change suggests new models for female comportment. Even though the female body is still likely to be feminine, slender, and attractive, the body challenges some traditional notions about what it means to be a female.

Xena, Aeryn Sun, and other tough women studied in this book are shaking up women's roles beyond American popular culture. Such figures also show their female audience members that they can challenge generations-old stereotypes about what it means to be a woman. For centuries, women have been taught to be physically and mentally nonaggressive if they wish to be accepted by society. They were also expected to wait for men to save them. Now, the media's tough women are teaching real women dramatically different ideas about what it means to be female. For example, being aggressive is desirable, and women should not wait for men to save them. Such changing celluloid notions about what it means to be a woman are influencing real life. We have yet to discover in this new millennium where these new notions will take us.

Notes

1. Jennifer Steinhauer, "Pow! Slam! Thank You, Ma'am," *New York Times*, November 5, 2000, sec. 4: p. 5.
2. For other articles that discuss the burgeoning number of tough women in the popular media, see Shone Buswell, "Babes in Boyland," *Premiere* (January 2001): 33; Sandra L. Calvert et al., "Young Adults' Perceptions and Memories of a Televised Woman Hero," *Sex Roles* 45, no. 1/2 (2001): 31–52; Christopher Goodwin, "Women Kick Butt at the Box Office," *London Times*, 29 June 1997, 1–2; Steve Payne, "Women Flex Their Muscle: Observers Split Over Effect of TV Toughs as Role Models for Children," *Toronto Sun*, April 16, 1999, 77; and Jeff Simons, "Chicks Kick Butt TV: A Leg Up on the Competition," *Buffalo News*, February 17, 2002, TV2.
3. Similarly, writing for *The Toronto Sun* in 2000, Sandy Naiman observes, "Where are women now? With the feisty trio of Charlie's Angels, tough, titillating women martial artists seem to be spiking interpersonal relationships with their macho male counterparts. Add Michelle Yeoh, the female fighter who stars in *Crouching Tiger, Hidden Dragon*, Laila Ali, Muhammad's boxing daughter, and . . . *Girlfight*, and it seems women are sliding into the driver's seat of their relationships." See Sandy Naiman, "Pow! Bam! Today's Women Aren't Afraid to Kick Butt On- or Off-Screen," *Toronto Sun*, November 23, 2000, 83. Writing for *USA Today* in 2001, Patricia Pearson describes Lara Croft's ascendancy as a cultural icon, observing, "[She] kicks butt. . . . Croft is a regular punch-throwing,

butt-kicking Indiana Jonesette, with a huge following of swooning boys and applauding girls." Pearson continues, "In her muscular display of modern girl power, Lara Croft is part of a distinctive new trend. She joins Charlie's scrappy, gun-slinging Angels, . . . and the sword-wielding Xena . . . in a newly burnished hall of fame for women who, well, kick butt." See Patricia Pearson, "Women Get Tougher, on Film and Off," *USA Today*, June 28, 2001, 15A.

4. Lorraine Ali, "Coming to a Gym Near You," *Newsweek*, December 11, 2000, 76.

5. Stephanie Mencimer, "Violent Femmes," *Washington Monthly* (September 2001): 15. Yvonne Tasker writes about the supremacy of the muscular male action star in the 1980s: "The image of Sylvester Stallone as Vietnam veteran John Rambo, brandishing a rocket-launcher whilst parading his musculature, became an icon of American masculinity in the mid-1980s. As the decade went on through, Stallone was displaced in popularity by the even larger figure of ex–Mr. Universe Arnold Schwarzenegger." See Yvonne Tasker, *Spectacular Bodies: Gender, Genre, and Action Cinema* (London: Routledge, 1993), 1. Now, a new tough figure has risen to superstardom, and it represents a challenge to traditional notions of the action hero. Popular culture is chock full of women who would be a match for the muscle-bound Rambo. For a study of tough men in the media, see Susan Jeffords, *Hard Bodies: Hollywood Masculinity in the Reagan Era* (New Brunswick: Rutgers University Press, 1994).

6. For an article that describes the growing popularity of the Powerpuff Girls, see Mike Flaherty, "Girl Power," *Entertainment Weekly* (June 16, 2000): 23.

7. Steinhauer, "Pow! Slam!," 5.

8. Gerard Jones, *Killing Monsters: Why Children Need Fantasy, Super Heroes, and Make-Believe Violence* (New York: Basic Books, 2002), 150.

9. Amy C. Sims, "Female Celebs Flex More Than Their Star Power," Fox News on the web, January 3, 2003, available at http://www.foxnews.com/printer_friendly_story/0,3566,47772,00.html.

10. "Get the Laura Croft Look," Stars Online 2002, January 3, 2003, available at http://www.stars.com/style/99890862484542.htm.

11. "The Making of Hollywood's Hottest Bodies," Ivillage on the web, January 4, 2003, available at http://www.ivillage.co.uk/print/0,9688,529340,00.html.

12. Sims, "Female Celebs."

13. Sims, "Female Celebs."

14. Quoted in Sims, "Female Celebs."

15. Michelle Healy, "These Dolls Got Game and a Whole Lot More," *USA Today*, December 20, 2000, 8D.

16. Healy, "These Dolls," 8D.

17. "Sporty Girl Action Figures Inspire and Entertain," *Amsterdam News*, June 28, 2001, 22.

18. Lisa Shroder, "Macho Macho Femme," *Sun-Sentinel*, August 10, 1998, 1D.

19. Jones, *Killing Monsters*, 149.

20. Tasker, *Spectacular Bodies*, 15.

21. Tasker, *Spectacular Bodies*, 19.

22. Sherrie A. Inness, *Tough Girls: Women Warriors and Wonder Women in Popular Culture* (Philadelphia: University of Pennsylvania Press, 1999).

23. See Martha McCaughey and Neil King, eds., *Reel Knockouts: Violent Women in the Movies* (Austin: University of Texas Press, 2001). Other studies of how tough women are depicted in popular culture and the media include Pamela A. Boker, "America's Women Superheroes: Power, Gender, and the Comics," *Mid-Atlantic Almanac* 2 (1993): 107–18; and Lynda Hart, *Fatal Women: Lesbian Sexuality and the Mark of Aggression* (Princeton, NJ: Princeton University Press, 1994).

24. Elizabeth Hills, "From 'Figurative Males' to Action Heroines: Further Thoughts on Active Women in the Cinema," *Screen* 40, no. 1 (1999): 38–50.

25. McCaughey and King, *Reel Knockouts*, 20.

26. Hills, "From 'Figurative Males', " 39.

27. Mencimer, "Violent Femmes," 18. Similarly, Sandy Naiman asks: "Are they the latest incarnation of . . . the mythological Amazon female warrior or surfacing symbols of some new societal/cultural archetype? On film, men love their jiggling breasts, their cinched-in waists, their silken limbs, their flipping tresses and their supreme strength. . . . But what do they say about women?" ("Pow! Bam!," 83).

28. Mencimer, "Violent Femmes," 18.

Part I

Changing Images of the
Female Action Hero

Chapter 1

Lara's Lethal and Loaded Mission: Transposing Reproduction and Destruction

Claudia Herbst

In 1962 a young computer programmer at MIT designed the first computer game, called *Spacewar*. By the mid-sixties, when computer time was still very expensive, *Spacewar* could be found on nearly every research computer in the country. The title and content of the game are appropriate, because much of gaming technology, and most of today's imaging technologies with which games are created, originate in projects funded by the military. Rosanne Stone links the close relationship of war and games to companies like Atari (producer of the once–highly popular game Pac-Man), which recruited talents from defense-based companies, such as Lockheed Martin and McDonnell Douglas. Stone recounts, "Soon Atari had project managers who drank coffee out of personalized Cruise Missile mugs directing interactive entertainment software projects. The skills they brought to the game market were acquired by designing missile launchers and tank guidance controls. They saw no particular difference between missile software and interactive games."[1]

The traces of this war heritage are visually and linguistically present in today's technology and the many products resulting from their application, most notably games. The name "Atari," for example, comes from a Japanese expression that means, "I am going to attack you."[2] While the visuals of computer games and of digitally enhanced imagery such as those seen in Hollywood films have become increasingly more sophisticated, their content has developed remarkably little. As *Spacewar* did decades ago, the theme of most computer games, many contemporary digitally enhanced films, and other computer graphics–related products revolves around disaster, mayhem, and war. The computer game *Kingpin: Life of Crime*, for example, advertises that the player can "target specific body parts and actually see the damage done— including exit wounds" and allows for "multiplayer death match for up to 16 thugs."[3] Other gaming titles such as *Battlezone*, *MechWarrior*, *Doom*, and *Mortal Kombat* are equally revealing. As in real war, the ability to kill is rewarded. The player is trained to perceive anything that moves as hostile, to target it, and to shoot it at rapid speed. Bloodshed is not a byproduct of these games but their sole purpose; throughout the game there is no interruption or variation of the graphically depicted violence. As computer graphics technology becomes ever more sophisticated, gaming companies can boast greater realism in their games. This has not gone unnoticed. In 2002 the United States Army unveiled two games designed to appeal to a media-saturated and tech-bombarded generation for the purpose of recruitment.

Into this land of war and violence has stepped a new figure, Lara Croft. The virtual heroine of the computer game *Tomb Raider* made her debut in 1996 and reportedly is her designer's idea of a dream woman.[4] Lara's existence is well documented, in cyberspace as in real life; a search on the Internet using the keywords "Lara Croft" returns thousands of entries. Lara, it has been pointed out before, exemplifies changing definitions of gender. Technology allows for a stylized representation of the female and permits her to be placed in the context of toughness and heroism that traditionally has been reserved for men. She adopts male forms of behavior but is unmistakably female and highly eroticized; in a discussion of Lara, the question of gender is inevitably involved. She spans ideological ground ranging from entertainment to politics. British Science Minister Lord Sainsbury of Turville declared,

"I want Lara Croft to be an ambassador for British scientific excellence."[5] The avant-garde filmmaker Peggy Ahwesh recently was featured in the Whitney Biennial 2002 with her video titled *She Puppet*.[6] Ahwesh used re-edited footage of the game *Tomb Raider* and dealt with the preprogrammed "mission" of its heroine and with female identity in virtual space.

Lara is also no novice to feminist critique and analysis, and there has been much written discussion of her.[7] My inquiry into the meaning of Lara Croft as an intermediary in the promotion of an increasingly popular new image of women provides a fresh look. The amount and range of attention Lara Croft has received is an indication that she exemplifies more than a visual phenomenon or a fleeting trend in the representation of the female. Lara's role outside of the erotic and violent spectacle she provides for the sake of entertainment is worth investigating as her internationally recognized and discussed presence suggests a greater cultural relevance than thus far acknowledged. On the virtual terrain of war-inspired computer games, the female, biologically inescapably tied to the processes of reproduction, is represented in an unprecedented display of eroticism and violence. Beyond questions of female empowerment and female representation in virtuality, the phenomenon Lara Croft begs the question: What are the driving forces and eventual consequences of extreme forms of sexualized aggression?

I will be concerned with Lara's role in the contemporary technology-inspired shifting notions of life and death and will be addressing the link of these gender definitions to imaging technologies, a link indisputable in the twenty-first century. War, the industries delivering the simulation of violence for the sake of entertainment, and reproductive technologies are male-dominated disciplines that heavily rely on imaging technologies. These technologies are presently altering our interpretations of gender as they are applied in the visualization of processes such as reproduction and destruction. Lara Croft and other digitally generated heroines are the sexy messengers announcing a shift in the definitions of gender, and therefore a shift in the definitions of power, informed by state-of-the-art imaging technologies.

Lara may be virtual, but many a website makes reference to her "vital statistics." Not only are her measurements given but also her date and place of birth (Wimbledon, London), as well as her blood type (AB negative). She is the daughter of Lord Henshingly Croft, and while paternity is established many times over, there is no reference to her mother.[8] Listed among her "dashing features" is a 9 mm handgun; another place makes reference to a fully loaded M-16 automatic rifle. She is also said to be skilled with a Remington 12-gauge shotgun, an Ingram 8 mm submachine gun, a Heckler and Koch grenade launcher, a SOLA harpoon gun, an OSS assassination crossbow, and a variety of other lethal weapons.[9] Lara's hyperviolent design is as much a product of the game industry as it is a response to an audience demanding the excessive use of firearms and to a larger audience endorsing such a use. An anonymous *Tomb Raider* fan suggests, "Lara should have a .50 AE Desert Eagle, M2.50 caliber mounted on her jeep, a 7.62 mm minigun, Franchi SPAS 12 shotgun, M-79 grenade launcher, M-16 assault rifle, Heckler & Koch MP5 9 × 19 mm, hand to hand combat, high explosive grenades."[10] Another fan is equally specific as to the weapons Lara should carry and comments, "I think Lara should have a silenced pistol. Also, she should have all her weapons at her house to kill the butler in style. Desert Eagle silencer equipment, .22 pistol, Magnum revolver, Uzis, long barrel Mac10 (more spray than a precise shot weapon), shotgun twin barrel."[11] The list goes on.

Lara may be as lethal as much of her audience expects her to be, but as the daughter in an aristocratic family, she is also cultured, has attended a Swiss finishing school, speaks several languages, and, last but not least, is a good cook. According to her designer, Toby Gard, Lara's initial biography included that she likes to work with underprivileged children and the mentally disabled and that she has a degree in needlework.[12] Over the course of her evolving design, these kinder traits have been replaced by enhanced combat capabilities.

Lara has been a sexy sales figure for a booming industry composed of many products. Merchandise featuring her image includes t-shirts, mouse pads, calendars, watches, and candy bars. Her character has also been employed internationally in advertisments to sell products such as cars, game consoles, lemonade, and magazines.[13] Lara's image is often used for her sexualized design; many advertising campaigns have focused on her apparent eroticism. She is a sex symbol and is openly exploited as such.

In 1997, for the release of *Tomb Raider II* in the United Kingdom, a "washroom-campaign" was started for which pictures of Lara were placed in men's bathrooms.[14] In a German advertisement campaign, Lara states, "You can move me into 2000 different positions. Try that with your girlfriend!"[15] Sex is often the underlying message in advertisements, although in mainstream imagery, it is seldom this blatant (or quite this offensive) or, based on placement, content, and tone, so clearly directed toward male audiences. An unofficial "Nude Raider Patch," which allows a player to watch Lara fight her way through the different levels of the game naked, exists for *Tomb Raider II* and can be downloaded from the Internet.[16] On the Internet, countless other unofficial images of her (more often than not in an overtly sexual context) exist. Lara is an international star and has attained cult status far beyond the game industry. Stardom and visual representations are interconnected. John Belton comments, "Stars become stars when they lose control over their images, which then take on a life of their own."[17] By all definitions, the Lara phenomenon has taken on a life of its own. Through images, stars are popularized and worshiped. In the digital age, the production of images has a unique meaning because, today more than ever, the eye rules all other senses.

Technologically Mediated Male Desires

Technologically advanced cultures value visual representations.[18] Of the five senses, vision is the most preferred sense of Western culture, a circumstance enhanced by the abundance and expansion of modern imaging and surveillance technologies. Paul Virilio speaks of the automation of perception and notes that the importance of sight is illustrated by the industrialization of vision and the need for synthetic perception, particularly in the context of the battlefield.[19] In war, vision technologies are crucial because of the necessity to visualize, observe, and track the enemy. Virilio quoted a former United States state under-secretary of defense who beautifully summarized the role of vision in the process of twenty-first century technology-based destruction: "I'd say as soon as you can see a target you can hope to destroy it."[20]

The gratification and pleasure of the gaze in the context of war and eroticism are closely related. The female is sought after with the intent of procreation (or the act leading up to it); the enemy, inversely, is chased with the intent of destruction. Possibly that is why the new images of women currently permeating popular culture are a composite of sexualized aggression; in computer games and films today, the continued objectification of women is the offspring of the process of visualizing sex and death, humanity's most frequently depicted spectacle. The visually stimulated objectification of women in Western, male society takes on new forms when coupled with contemporary, war-based imaging technologies. In the countless virtual worlds of military-inspired computer games, the representation of the female body is pushed to new extremes. Hyper-realistic productions of sex and death reduce the female to a territory of lust and deadly menace. Based on Lara Croft's appearance, actions, and equipment, she is a fine example of this trend.[21]

Laura Mulvey notes, "Women displayed as sexual objects is the leitmotiv of erotic spectacle: from pin-ups to striptease, from Ziegfeld to Busby Berkeley, she holds the look, plays to, and signifies male desire."[22] It is only when the player of a computer game starts the game and interacts that Lara gains her virtual existence. It is at the moment of objectification, as the female character is electronically made visible and the player (also referred to as the "user") decides to manipulate her actions, she begins to exist. Once the player tires and the game is over, game and female alike conveniently disappear into electronic vapor. Lara offers a sexy identity void of demands and stipulations. The terrain of computer games has become the site of erotic spectacle; in it the virtual heroine, as Mulvey described, plays to the male, holds his gaze, and is utterly and completely in his control.

Lara's design reflects masculine desires. On the one hand, her action-figure design puts G.I. Joe to shame; on the other, with a body exuding hypersexuality, she looks like a pin-up girl par excellence. Lara originates from a male-dominated industry and gaming culture. The virtual worlds in which she makes her appearances are designed and implemented by men in their teens and twenties, focusing on the topics young men tend to focus on.[23] This hormone-infused group remains behind the layers of the interfaces of virtual worlds but describes and codes the way bodies are represented in virtual spaces.[24] Possibly this is why, as Patti Miller points out, virtual heroines have the disturbing habit of sighing as though they are experiencing sexual pleasure during violent battles.[25] It could not be more obvious: Lara has been designed to please male urges. Mulvey notes, "In a world ordered by sexual imbalance, pleasure in looking has been split between active/male and passive/female. The determining male gaze projects its fantasy onto the female figure, which is styled accordingly."[26] Not only is Lara subject to total control, the virtual space in which she was created allows for an entirely fantasy-based design as the virtual body can take on any proportions and abilities unhindered by the limitations nature presents. In response to Lara's appearance, a *Tomb Raider* player remarks, "She is so beautiful and has these incredible breasts but still she is totally under my control. Whenever does this happen in real life?"[27]

Lara Croft is the virtual sex symbol of the digital age. The idea of cybersex has tickled the popular consciousness for some time now. Even *Playboy* magazine published an issue on "Cybergirls." Virtual heroines make room for sexual fantasies that are often impossible to experience elsewhere, or illegal.[28] Additionally, cybersex delivers a sense of safety as many fears associated with sex, from pregnancy to HIV, do not exist in virtuality. The sense of safety associated with virtuality is superimposed onto the characters originating in cyberspace. Lara offers risk-free excitement.

Virtual female characters, such as Lara, have become hyper-real versions of a female persona. The virtual body is entirely synthesized, an exaggerated version of flesh and blood, and delivers what the real cannot: It omits all human imperfection. Lara combines extreme sexiness and aggression with virtuality; she has surpassed the real and is hyper-real. For Jean Baudrillard, the imaginary is surpassed by the hyper-real, which represents a more advanced stage as it manages to efface the contradictions between the real and the imaginary.[29] It would be tempting to dismiss Lara's significance. After all, she is a game-based character, not a real person of influence or power. However, the fact that Lara's eroticized body does not exist only increases her desirability; her virtuality gives her existence more, not less, credence.

Hard Females, Morbid Fantasies

The image of Lara has been employed in the promotion of female empowerment. Because she is born out of a male fantasy and so clearly caters to male desires, it is ironic that she has also become a poster girl for a new brand of feminism, recognized under the headings "cyberfeminism," "cybergirlzzz," and "girrrlpower." Women are supposed to ignore that the image of Lara was created neither by them nor for them.

Powerful female characters are not exactly new to the screens of entertainment; their appearance and meaning has been examined before.[30] It would be an overstatement to claim that digitally created heroines such as Lara Croft present the audience with an entirely novel interpretation of a tough female character. Rather, she represents an excruciatingly exaggerated version of the female as tough. She is as fearless, as aggressive, and as oversexualized as none before her. In many computer games, sex has moved from the periphery to center stage.[31] Lara signifies excess; at the site of her body an ongoing exchange takes place between sex and violence, one leading to and allowing for an amplification of the other. Lara's gun grows more acceptable in the presence of her overt sexuality; the display of overt sexuality in turn appears strangely justifiable by the simultaneous potential for violence. Lara and her peers[32] are noteworthy not because they offer a radically new version of the tough female, but because they represent *extreme* versions of the sexy, tough female.

The new class of female characters that Lara represents generally carries a variety of conspicuous guns combined with attire that reveals much of their virtual and biologically impossible bodies (see figure 1.1). Virtual females such as Lara negotiate the loopholes of the provocatively acceptable. Her measurements, at times verging on the obscene, at times on the absurd, defy not only nature but also the properties of silicon. The image of Lara borders on the pornographic; what barely legitimizes her design is the context of games and play.

Figure 1.1. The virtual heroine

Lara's exaggerated design pays homage to an old-fashioned notion. The Victorian era favored tiny waists, achieved by the tight lacing of corsets. At the expense of vital organs, women's waists were squeezed to a minimum (see figure 1.2). Lara does not need to wear a corset. Her waist needs no forceful strapping in as her body appears even harder than the wires of a corset and always stays in the desired shape.

The Victorian era was also one marked by high death rates, especially among infants and children. Lara exists in an environment in which death is an expected and frequent occurrence. In the digital as in the Victorian era, when death looms, feminine beauty ideals tend to focus on the waist. A tiny waist, such as Lara's, is considered seductive because it indicates she is not pregnant and thus "available" for the act of procreation.

She reintroduces the agonizingly small waist of the nineteenth century and is similarly restricted in her movement, not by wires and laces but by the limitations of her preprogrammed actions and the instructions of the player. The tiny waist, formerly achieved by

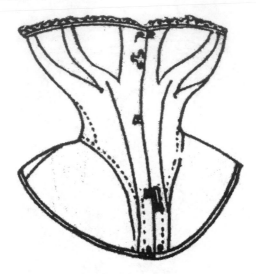

Figure 1.2. Women's corset, ca. 1860

corsets, has an erotic appeal and also suggests constriction and pain.[33] Lara's exaggerated hourglass figure signifies the forceful manipulation of the body, a practice nowadays mostly associated with sadomasochism. Her sexuality is emphasized by portraying her as a dominatrix. She is often staged so that she is looking down on us. Her stance is usually rigid, her legs apart, her arms resolutely planted on her hips or, alternatively, pointing her guns at us. One eyebrow is typically raised, and her expression is angry, though her mean grin suggests she is enjoying her superiority. The real-life models representing Lara's character often wear her trademark green rubber tank top, a material rarely paired with hiking boots but commonly found in the wardrobe of a dominatrix. Because of the manner in which she is depicted and the danger of violence (and thus pain) she represents, it is difficult to address the eroticism linked to her outside of the context of domination.

Moreover, the sustained illusion of power and control is a key ingredient in the context of sexual domination. In *Tomb Raider*, the camera, the player's cinematic view, plays a decisive role in how Lara is perceived. Most other computer games are experienced through the eyes of the protagonist (in these "first person" shooter games the player is often represented by a gun that appears on the lower half of the screen, a phallic symbol perpetually protruding into the field of vision). *Tomb Raider* belongs to the genre of "third person" shooter games, in which the virtual world is seen through the "eyes" of a third person. The camera, and thus the player, continuously follows Lara. While the player controls her every move, cinematically she is depicted as though she is the leader and in charge. Lara is perceived to be the tough fighter, the one in control, kicking and shooting, when in actuality she is granted no autonomy whatsoever.

Unusual for mainstream images of women, the virtual female as a composite of sexualized aggression radiates a morbid type of sexuality, one more closely related to death than life (see figure 1.3). Lara's sexuality is indistinguishable from the deadly danger she represents. Her body signifies femaleness in an overwrought way while her attitude emulates combat sensibilities.

Lara continuously runs, jumps, climbs, swims, and shoots. Her activities are neverending; her hyperfunctionality exemplifies military ideals. Like that of a trained soldier, her body resembles a stylized killing machine more than it represents womanly flesh. This appearance is enhanced by the aesthetic of low-resolution computer game imagery. Her body appears "blocky" and especially hard due to the pixelated nature of her rendering.[34] Her annihilation impulses and her hard exterior recall fascist ideals of the male soldier extensively researched by Klaus Theleweit, only this time the rigid body in question is female.[35] Lara's designer admitted that at one point he felt she began to look too "Nazi-like."[36]

Lara is no sissy, the dread of the fascist soldier as outlined by Theleweit.[37] She shows no weakness, and there are no variations to her obedience. In accordance with fascist ideals, Lara has no alternative but to follow each and every command precisely as ordered. All of her actions are in response to the player interacting with her, and to the actions assigned to her by the computer programmer who gave the game its functionality. Lara's actions are always in response to a command. Her compliance is guaranteed. She is not just a tough girl; cleavage aside, she embodies fascist ideals of obedience and hardness. In many ways, she is a composite of traits that are the exact opposite of those traditionally identified as desirable in a woman; she is the antithesis of a caretaker.

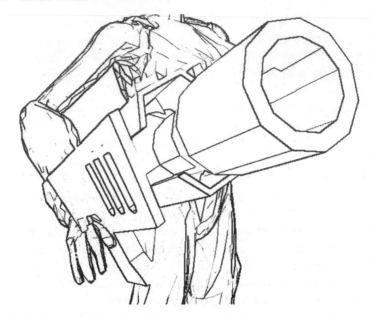

Figure 1.3. The virtual heroine and her gun resemble fascist ideals of hardness

Interior: Exchanging Life for Death

Lara has banished the fearful notion of nurturing, of love, of the all-engulfing mother. Reproductive potential *is*, however, part of women's biological identity, and women have been both feared and worshiped for their reproductive powers throughout history. Lara as the hardened and oversexed female appears strangely infertile in contrast; her midsection is so small her body could not possibly accommodate reproductive organs. Scott Bukatman observes that in science fiction the nemesis-monster is almost always presented as flowing, gooey, and slimy (characteristics generally identified with the female reproductive system), whereas the female is portrayed as hard.[38] Nothing about Lara is wet or soft; there is nothing to be fearful of other than her gun. It is as though we know her computer-generated, virtual body contains no messy reproductive system. Her presence seems to deny the very question of menstruation, much less pregnancy and the potential for motherhood. Void of the dark, soft, and mysterious vagina, her body has become a hard instrument. Lara and her peers are perpetually pristine, her exterior and presumably her interior are parched and clean.

Lara wears a garter-like contraption that holds a gun. The gun, at once object of destruction and phallus, is carried on her thighs, just below her tiny waist, close to where her reproductive system would be located were she real. The presence of life-threatening weapons in proximity to the female reproductive system has traditionally been viewed unfavorably. In the past, communities tended to protect the source of their progeny, with the womb representing the continuation of a community's existence. Historically, women have been excluded from organized violence in large part because of the conflict induced by the sight of a potentially life-bearing body in proximity to violence and death. In Lara, however, the apparently fake, simulated reproductive potential—as marked by her exaggerated lips, breasts, waist, and hips—as well as the obvious potential for destruction appear no longer to be contradictory.

As Nancy Hartsock and others have pointed out, an important argument against women in combat was that war was men's business, and the presence of women would threaten the male exclusiveness of the role of the soldier, and thus men's identities.[39] Hartsock further states, "In our culture the masculine self, at least as a cultural norm, must be defined by a fascination with death."[40] When women are identified with death, rather than life, this "cultural norm" is changed drastically, and men's exclusive right to battle is challenged. Lara's body is designed to trigger sexual impulses leading up to reproduction but biologically she is clearly not capable of reproducing. Presumably male identity is less threatened and the need for exclusiveness reduced if the female body is no longer the mysterious and powerful place from which life springs.

Hartsock also reminds us that despite this male exclusivity, women have been combatants in every war in the twentieth century and that women serve in modern militaries.[41] What has changed is the embrace of female presence at the site of violence. Mere tolerance of women's (limited) involvement in war in the past has been replaced by an open invitation to participate. It is women's welcome partaking in war's organized killing and slaughter that Lara is making palatable.

In an unprecedented way, Lara and her peers become sex and destruction symbolically unified. In this sense, the new version of the female, as it is promoted through digital media such as computer games, breaks with a tradition as old as humanity itself. In the past, women's reproductive powers and the bodily processes associated with them have been safeguarded as well as feared. For example, in the Dark Ages, it was believed menstrual blood could turn sharp steel dull and cause iron to rust.[42] Now, these metal-related, mythic powers that were attributed to the natural powers of the female body have been replaced with a shiny gun. Dullness and rust speak of a threat to the phallus as hard; the gun suggests the undiminished erection. The earlier power association is connected to fertility; the gun inescapably implies death. At the site of the virtual female body, birth and death have been transposed.

Lara puts an end to long-held convictions about the female in the context of organized violence. Imaging technologies are applied in many culturally defining disciplines. Progress in the field of reproductive technologies, for instance, is intricately linked to the ability to visualize the female reproductive system of which ultrasound images were only the beginning. The link between reproductive technologies, imaging technologies, and gender is a crucial one and has been recognized before.[43] Throughout history and across cultures, reproduction has been associated with the womb. It was understood that the female body had to be present in all of the processes associated with the creation of life. This has changed as the capacity to visualize the womb and its processes has led to the capability to create life in the absence of the female. Cloning, for example, is a process that involves the visualization of the mother's egg and the fusion of cells. Because the creation of life has become feasible outside of the context of the female body, the representation of the female and the meaning of gender have changed.

The portrayal of the female and the biological processes associated with her have been altered by the rise of technology that at once gratifies male erotic visual pleasure and facilitates virtual and real destruction. It is improbable that virtual heroines such as Lara Croft would be conceivable and placed at the site of carefully constructed scenarios of violence if reproductive powers were still exclusively linked to the female body. Never before has the female body been depicted in a climate so saturated with violence and danger. She has not been placed there by accident or with the intention that she will be rescued later. The female has been placed amidst violence with the objective to watch her fight her way through and around the obstacles put before her. Reproduction has become independent of the body, and the ensuing shift in the depiction of the female is drastic. Characters such as Lara have been designed without consideration for the female reproductive organs. Lara belongs to a collection of futuristic females who will no longer need to reproduce; her womb has been substituted with technology. The potential for new life is no longer associated with her body. Physically as well as psychologically, she is depicted in new and unfamiliar ways.

As giving birth, a power historically identified as female, is no longer solely linked to the female body, the closed-off terrain of the battlefield, once marked as exclusively male and vehemently defended as such, has opened up. Neither reproduction nor destruction is considered exclusively male or female anymore; definitions of gender are reinterpreted. Despite the fact that Lara is represented as an empowered female, she appears to have lost something quintessentially female. Men may interpret her toughness and her tiny waist as sexy. Many women find her figure disturbing and respond negatively to the nature-defying design of her body. Perhaps what women are responding to is that biological femaleness as we have identified it in the past has simply been denied in Lara's design. A woman may sense that an important element of female life-generating identity has been rejected and that this will cast a shadow on the value of all life, her own as well as that of others. The moment the body ceases to be the essential vehicle in the creation of life, its loss becomes more tolerable. In part due to reproductive technologies and in part due to the new virtual heroine, the womb—and therefore to a degree the female—is portrayed as expendable.

The Expendable Female: Virtual and Real

It cannot be overemphasized that the genre that Lara is part of is created with war-related imaging technology. No other medium has resulted in as many images of the female as destructive as have military-inspired technologies. War affects women differently than men, and this differential treatment is likely to be mirrored in the representation of women by war-related technologies. War's heritage leaves its mark in the visuals resulting from the application of these technologies. A degree of violence is inherent in modern imaging technologies, a factor that certainly plays into why so much violent content is created through their application.

In the late 1990s, the company Alias introduced software for the generation of visuals such as those used in computer games.[44] The software allows the user to interactively paint on three-dimensional objects in virtual space. In a glossy advertisement, three images illustrate the progressive application of the software: The first image features the computer-generated head of a woman; in the second, the woman wears make-up; and in the third image she appears bloodied and bruised. Out of the infinite possibilities available to demonstrate the tool's effectiveness, the abuse of a woman was deemed appropriate and compelling. Similar technology is applied in forensic science. In a recent crime reconstruction, the brutal murder of a woman is visualized using computer graphics. A courtroom spectator comments, "When you see her shot in the back and then down on her knees, that brings it to life."[45] Digitally generated images, especially three-dimensional graphics, such as those employed for the creation of *Tomb Raider* and other games, are utilized in the search for truth. In the military and in entertainment products, in the sciences and crime reconstruction, digitally created scenarios aim to reflect reality with their ability to mimic real-life objects and actions. Mary Flanagan points out that products created with 3-D software are perceived not as mere "representations" but as depictions of the world as it *really is*.[46] Lara's three-dimensional representation as tough and sexy is understood not as fiction but as fact. The illusion of reality becomes more convincing as programming power steadily increases.

Through modern imaging technologies, so often applied in the real and virtual production of death, the abuse of female characters gains entertainment value. Such abuse is not entirely new; the threat of violence directed against women has long been a device employed by the entertainment industry, and the tension created by such violence has been considered titillating by many. Only now, encouraged by the illusionary safeness of the virtual world of pretend, have threats against the female turned into the most direct and forceful assaults formerly reserved for the male. The violence that the female is subject to in virtuality and the images inspired by it, is a question of degree. More than ever, overwrought sexiness is inseparable from the violence and aggression amidst which the female is placed. As though sex appeal was a prerequisite for danger, the female characters kick and kill in outfits more suitable for seduction than combat.

But not only entirely synthetically generated images support violent treatment of women. The world of film and television also offers a variety of examples. On the screens that inescapably occupy our surroundings, women these days are at the receiving end of bone-shattering blows. In addition to the battle scenarios of the world of gaming, digitally enhanced movies, such as *Brotherhood of the Wolf, The Matrix*, the *Alien* series, *The Fifth Element, Hardware*, and countless others, depict women getting hit and kicked until they spit blood. Women are thrown about rooms and smashed against furniture and walls, wearing their bruises like badges of honor. With the application of computer graphics technologies that originate in war, women's bodies are misrepresented as super tough and indestructible. Women are depicted as combatants, enduring and casually dismissing grave injury. The depictions of women and soldiers used to bear little resemblance; what was acceptable for soldiers was unacceptable for women. Because women have been invited to join the ranks of soldiers, their treatment as combatants is permissible.

When the world of the virtual spills over into reality, the violence-endorsing mechanisms at work appear particularly dramatic. As a virtual heroine, Lara is invincible. Her environment offers a simulated reality in which no action has any lasting consequences; characters are reborn with each new game. The real world looks different but is informed by the fantasies of virtual reality. In the summer of 2001, Lara Croft turned flesh and blood in the motion picture *Lara Croft: Tomb Raider*, rated PG-13. The virtual fantasy of Lara was incarnated by Angelina Jolie, giving credit to the idea of the unrealistically hyperpowerful female. The following year, the virtual female heroine of the game *Resident Evil* came to life on the big screen. When viewed in the flesh, the ability of these characters to deal with violence appears even more disturbing. Only minutes into the movie *Resident Evil*, a female character suffers death when a falling elevator crushes her head. Moments later, the second female lead (played by Michelle Rodriguez) appears in fighter gear. For the duration of the film, she aims an automatic weapon at anything that moves. After shooting another female, she coldly states, "The bitch is not walking anymore." In the end, she, too, suffers death as the film's lead, played by Milla Jovovich, shoots her at close range.

The design of the virtual female makes distinct reference to masochism, the treatment of women on the big screen, equally eroticized, is unequivocally sadistic, especially in these game-based films. For Georges Bataille, this link of eroticism and death is not paradoxical. "The excess from which reproduction proceeds and the excess we call death can only be understood with the help of the other."[47] Lara's design is not only overtly sexual; her guns are a constant reminder of deadly violence, and the title of the game places her in the context of tombs and graves. It is the continuously visualized simultaneous transgression of the sex and death taboos that is utterly exhilarating and during which the female suffers so intriguingly. Her suffering, depicted as safe and without consequences, particularly in games and in the films inspired by them, satisfies a sadistic appetite.

Aggressive, pristine, and unsympathetic, Lara exemplifies fascist fantasies of hardness and toughness typically projected onto the male body. Theleweit discusses the hatred male soldiers exhibit for the female, a hatred that arises out of the context of battle that is simulated in computer games.[48] Theleweit states that male soldiers want to reduce the female to a "bloody mass." The hatred for women is deeply rooted in and results from extreme states of conflict such as war. Because the female has joined the ranks of combatants, terrain clearly marked for the demonstration of violence, the hatred directed against the female, according to Theleweit, is represented as justifiable. The fact that she is now a soldier legitimizes her as a target. The actions on the screen instruct us that the hatred and dread of women no longer needs to be repressed but can be discharged with fury.

Though we tend to think of war as the exception, virtual heroines like Lara exist continuously and exclusively in states of conflict and are portrayed in settings that ignite hatred against them. In this context, it should be remembered that war and sexual violence against women are inseparable. The accounts of assault against women during war, particularly against their reproductive systems, including rape, forced sterilization, and sexual slavery, are as horrifying as they are endless.[49] Outside of war, violence and rape remain interconnected. Based on statistics, Deborah Blum concludes more-violent cultures show greater inclinations to rape because rape is aggravated by violence.[50] The depiction of violence on the screen, especially when it is presented as seductive and exciting, potentially promotes violence in real life as young audiences tend to reenact behavior seen on the screen. Because violent behavior and rape are interrelated as the frequent occurrence of rape during war suggests, and as Blum concludes, the promotion of violence on screen may also lead to an increase of rape in real life. This is especially true when the female is represented as invulnerable. For the female, such as Lara, being depicted in settings offering no alternative to violence can hardly be interpreted as advantageous.

As the newfound female invincibility breaks with the previously prevalent images of incompetence and weakness, women and men, for different reasons, have embraced women's latest, tough identity. The representation of women's behavior has changed. What consequently is considered acceptable treatment of women has taken on new forms as well. In technologically enhanced images of popular culture, women are encouraged to turn violent against men, against each other, and to be indifferent about the violence directed against themselves. In reality, women are far more likely to be the target of an assault because they tend to be physically weaker than their aggressors. Amidst the rhetoric of empowerment, it is often overlooked that damage done and hurt inflicted on this side of the screen is real. Women's onscreen ability to survive serious physical assault largely unscathed inadvertently implies tolerance of violence against women.

The heroines of the digital age have surrendered the powers of reproduction and instead are invited to partake in scenarios of organized violence. On screens large and small, women have been assigned the powers of destruction and at the same time have been depicted as expendable, their loss rendered inescapable if not necessary. This is a sacrifice no culture was willing to make in the past. In the history of war and violence, it was men who were expected to risk their lives in battle; now it is women.

Definitions of Power

Definitions of power may be flexible, but they are invariably formalized by those in power. In the past, killing has been defined as the ultimate power, a power generally attributed to men. In the new images portraying women as tough, this formerly exclusive power is quite suddenly generously attributed to the female. Ultimately, the meaning of power depends not so much on the act historically defined as empowering but on the interests of those in power who define the meaning of power. Once the transferal of the creation of life has successfully been shifted from the female womb to the laboratory, it is likely that the generation of *life* not death, will be interpreted as the absolute expression of power.

This shift in the definitions of power is a profound one, especially since life and death, as well as their production, are commonly thought of as opposites. Wars, and their simulation for the sake of entertainment or deterrence, have been and will continue to be highly profitable products, as is illustrated by enormous defense budgets.[51] Similarly, the technology-driven industrialization of reproduction is already a thriving business the world over. While Donna Haraway offers that the corporatization of biology is not a conspiracy and that it would be a mistake to assume all of its effects are necessarily dire,[52] its potential affects on the female psyche should not be underestimated. Tapping into the source of women's biological identity will eventually bear consequences for women psychologically. Likewise, women's social and cultural status can be expected to be transformed based on their changing biological role.

State of the art imaging and visualization technologies are finalizing this death/life transference of power while at the same time generating the imagery promoting the acceptance of the inevitable gender role reversal through icons like Lara Croft. Because she and other similar figures, such as the heroines of the games *Parasite Eve*[53] and *Bloodrayne*,[54] are interactive and marketed for the young and impressionable, their world of sexiness and ceaseless spectacle offers what should be counted among the most intriguing and effective propaganda to date. The newest weapon technologies, so-called smart weapons, require skills similar to those learned in the playing of computer games.[55] For instance, through computer games, eye–hand coordination (point, aim, and shoot), indispensable during combat, is interactively optimized from an early age.

Some arguments made in the name of women and regarding violence tend to ring hollow. For example, the argument of equality is often applied when women are invited to join not only virtual battlefields but also real front lines. Equality, in order to be cultivated, requires and is dependent upon an established political system or structure, such as democracy. The prevailing milieu in most game environments, however, is best described as anarchy. Even Lara's most basic of human rights, survival, is challenged continuously. Like a gladiator, she knows no other form of existence than to defend her own life and to take the lives of others. She has no rights or options; her world is not one of empowerment but one of desperation. The potential for violence and equality should not be equated as violence undermines the structure necessary for equality to flourish. Scenarios damaging to the foundation of equality cannot simultaneously advocate equality.

The new image of woman that Lara signifies proliferates at a breathtaking rate; few body ideals before her have been disseminated so widely and so quickly. Since their premiers, the games *Tomb Raider I* and *II* have sold over six million copies and, according to the company Eidos, Lara has been featured on more than 80 magazine and newspaper covers around the world.[56] Her notoriety should be interpreted as an indicator that ideas promoted by computer games and digitally enhanced films are far reaching.

Whereas, until recently, we were supposed to be alarmed by violence, we are now encouraged to glorify it. Over the course of a few short decades, the previously unthinkable hyperaggressive, gun-laden action heroine has made her way into entertainment products and thus into the consciousness of our image literacy. It took four short years for the virtual Lara to turn flesh and blood and to make her first appearance in a movie. The images of the virtual, violent female will at least facilitate, if not ensure, her

physical manifestation. While these trends can be expected to pro-
foundly affect women's lives, they scarcely reflect women's perspectives or interests. The current transformations in gender and
power definitions originate in the military and the sciences, the
male cornerstones of computer technology. As long as technology
remains firmly rooted in these disciplines, it is unlikely to be
applied in the creation of a positive female role model. Lara's international fame should also be read as an indication for how starved
the digital era is for a strong female character. For now, Lara may
look like a sexy and powerful messenger; nevertheless, the voice of
the female remains suspiciously absent from her mission.

Notes

1. Rosanne A. Stone, *The War of Desire and Technology at the Close of the
   Mechanical Age* (Cambridge: MIT Press, 1996), 129.
2. Judith K. Larsen and Everett M. Rogers, *Silicon Valley Fever* (London: Unwin,
   1986), 261.
3. *Kingpin: Life of Crime.* Available from Xatrix. 1999
4. The *Tomb Raider* series is available from Eidos. *Tomb Raider* was first released
   in 1996.
5. BBC online network. "License to Thrill," December 1998, available at
   http://news.bbc.co.uk/1/hi/sci/tech/225615.stm.
6. *She Puppet*, prod. and dir. Peggy Ahwesh, 15 min., 2001, videocassette. Featured
   in the Whitney Biennial 2002.
7. Useful references include Mary Flanagan and Austin Booth, eds., *Reload,
   Rethinking Women and Cyberculture* (Cambridge: MIT Press, 2002); Claudia
   Springer, *Electronic Eros: Bodies and Desire in the Post-Industrial Age*
   (London: Athlone, 1996); and Anne Balsamo, *Technologies of the Gendered
   Body: Reading Cyborg Women* (Durham, NC: Duke University Press, 1996).
8. It is noteworthy that the absence of a mother is common in animated female characters such as Lara. Mother characters tend to be dead, absent, or, at best, evil.
9. Lara's bio, available at http://www.geocities.com/trrepublic2/larabio.html.
10. The comment was posted by an anonymous fan on an unofficial website, avail-
    able at http://www.babyloveproducts.com/tomb/Gordon5.html.
11. *Whitney Biennial 2002: 2002 Biennial Exhibition*, ed. Lawrence R. Rinder,
    Debra Singer, and Chrissie Iles (New York: Harry N. Abrams, 2002), 18.
12. The original website featuring the interview no longer exists. A reference to
    Toby Gard's statement can be found online at http://www.vifu.de/students/gen-
    dering/ lara/LaraCompleteTextWOPics.html.
13. The brand names for which Lara's character was used include Sony Play
    Station, Seat, Lucozade, and Brigitte. See, *The Croft Times*, "Energy Drink,"
    May 1992, available at http://www.cubeit.com/ctimes/cover099.htm.
14. Birgit Pretsch, "A Postmodern Analysis of Lara Croft," August 2000, available
    at http://www.vifu.de/students/gendering/lara/LaraCompleteTextWOPics.hml.

15. Jens Schröter, "Lara Croft. Funktionen eines virtuellen Stars," 1999, available at http://www.theorie-der-medien.de/JS/texte/LARA_LETZTE/lara_letzte.html.
16. A patch often contains code to fix problems or "bugs" in a game. In this case, the patch alters the appearance of the game's main character. Patches and plugins, both official and unofficial, exist for many games.
17. John Belton, *American Cinema, American Culture* (New York: McGraw-Hill, 1994), 90.
18. Technological progress and literacy are intricately linked. Literate cultures, generally repressing the auditory sense, tend to favor vision. See, for example, Marshall McLuhan, *Understanding Media: The Extension of Man* (Cambridge, MA: MIT Press, 1994), 81–88.
19. Paul Virilio, "The Vision Machine," in *The Virilio Reader*, ed. James Der Derian (Malden: Blackwell Publishers, 1998), 134.
20. W. J. Perry, a former U.S. state under-secretary of defense, commenting on smart bombs and attack weapons. Quoted in Virilio, *The Virilio Reader*, 144.
21. According to a survey on gender and video games by the Oregon-based organization Children NOW, 38 percent of female game characters had "large" breasts and 46 percent had "unusually small" waists. In 54 percent of the games the female characters were fighting or "being violent." Available at http://www.childrennow.org/newsroom/news-00/pr-12-12-00.htm.
22. Laura Mulvey, "Visual Pleasure and Narrative Cinema," in *Art in Theory 1900–1990: An Anthology of Changing Ideas*, ed. Charles Harrison and Paul Wood (Cambridge: Blackwell Publishers, 1993), 967.
23. In my experience, companies producing three-dimensional gaming content of the nature discussed here are 90 percent to 95 percent male. This overwhelmingly male presence is no coincidence. For example, an advertisement recruiting new talent to a West Coast–based gaming company depicts a sunny poolside. The male employees of the company, all dressed in black and wearing black sunglasses, are seated around the pool. Standing behind them are a large number of tanned, blond women wearing tiny bikinis. The copy promises new employees will like working there. In another advertisement for a school offering computer graphics courses, the image of a sexualized virtual female body covers most of the page. The copy states that should prospective students not have a girlfriend they will learn how to create one.
24. Rosanne A. Stone, "Will the Real Body Please Stand Up?" in *Cyberspace: First Steps*, ed. Michael Benedikt (Cambridge, MA: MIT Press, 1992), 103–104.
25. Metro Active. Mary Spicuzza quoting Patti Miller in "Bad Heroines," March 2001, available at http://metroactive.com/papers/metro/03.15.01/cover/woman film-0111.html.
26 Mulvey, 967.
27. Jens Schröter, "Lara Croft. Funktionen eines virtuellen Stars," 1999, available at http://www.theorie-der-medien.de/JS/texte/LARA_LETZTE/lara_letzte.html.
28. An advertisement for the game *Duke Nukem*, for example, states, "The DOS (Den of Sin) rapidly becomes a pleasure palace filled with slave women and 'adult' entertainment. The station also becomes the central trading hub for one of the most hotly traded commodities in the universe, the human babe." Available at http://www.3drealms.com/babes/.
29. Jean Baudrillard, "The Hyper-realism of Simulation," in *Art in Theory 1900–1990: An Anthology of Changing Ideas*, ed. Charles Harrison and Paul Wood (Cambridge: Blackwell Publishers, 1993), 1049.

30. See, for example, David Gauntlett, *Media, Gender and Identity* (New York: Routledge, 2002); Justine Cassell and Henry Jenkins, eds., *From Barbie to Mortal Kombat* (Cambridge: MIT Press, 1998); and Sherrie A. Inness, *Tough Girls: Women, Warriors and Wonder Women in Popular Culture* (Philadelphia: University of Pennsylvania Press, 1999).

31. Michel Marriott, "Game Formula Is Adding Sex to the Mix," *New York Times,* November 7, 2002, sec. G1.

32. Examples of games with similar female characters are *Tekken III,* available from Namco; *No One Lives Forever,* available from Sierra and Fox Interactive; and *Resident Evil,* available from Capcom.

33 Valerie Steele, *Fashion and Eroticism: Ideals of Feminine Beauty from the Victorian Era to the Jazz Age* (New York: Oxford University Press, 1985), 176–177.

34. It should be noted that the pixelated nature of computer game imagery enhancing the "hard" look of the characters is not one of choice but one of technical limitation. In the near future this can be expected to change as the technology driving these games is becoming ever more powerful. It is questionable, however, if a smoother look of the characters will make them appear "softer" or will further contribute to the hard, fascist aesthetic.

35. Klaus Theleweit, *Male Bodies: Psychoanalyzing the White Terror,* vol. 2 of *Male Fantasies,* trans. Erica Carter and Chris Turner (Minneapolis: University of Minnesota Press, 1989), 206–207.

36. *The Croft Times.* "Lara Hit in the Face: Interview with Toby Gard," June 1997, available at http://www.cubeit.com/ctimes/news0007a.htm.

37. Theleweit, *Male Bodies,* 144.

38. Scott Bukatman, *Terminal Identity: The Virtual Subject in Postmodern Science Fiction* (Durham, NC: Duke University Press, 1993), 306.

39. Nancy C. M. Hartsock, "Masculinity, Heroism, and the Making of War," in *Rocking the Ship of State: Towards a Feminist Peace Politics,* ed. Adrienne Harris and Ynestra (Boulder, CO: Westview Press, 1989), 134.

40. Hartsock, 137.

41. Hartsock, 147.

42. Donna W. Cross, *Die Päpstin* (Berlin: Aufbau Taschenbuch Verlag, 2001), 565.

43. For a discussion on the interrelationship among gender, reproductive technologies, and representation, see chapter 3 in *The Gendered Cyborg,* ed. Gill Kirkup et al. (New York: Routledge, 2000).

44. Now Alias/Wavefront. The software in question is *3-D Paint Effects.* The advertisement was published in 1996.

45. Jacob Ward, "Crime Scene," *Wired* (May 2002) 80.

46. Mary Flanagan, "Hyperbodies, Hyperknowledge: Women in Games, Women in Cyberpunk, and Strategies of Resistance," in *Reload: Rethinking Women and Cyberculture,* ed. Mary Flanagan and Austin Booth (Cambridge, MA: MIT Press, 2002), 427.

47. Bataille, 42.

48. Klaus Theleweit, *Women, Floods, Bodies, History,* vol. 1 of *Male Fantasies,* trans. Erica Carter and Chris Turner (Minneapolis: University of Minnesota Press, 1987), 194–196.

49. For detailed reports on women and war, see, for example, Amnesty International online, http://web.amnesty.org.

50. Deborah Blum, *Sex on the Brain: The Biological Difference Between Men and Women* (New York: Penguin Books, 1997), 249.

51. For a discussion on the economic role of military technology, see Robert Reich, "High Technology, Defense, and International Trade," in *The Militarization of High Technology*, ed. John Tirman (Cambridge, MA: Ballinger Publishing Company, 1984).

52. Donna J. Haraway, *Modest-Witness, Second Millennium: Female Man Meets Oncomouse: Feminism and Technoscience* (New York: Routledge, 1996), 93.

53. *Parasite Eve* 1998, Available from Square.

54. *Bloodrayne* 2002, Available from Majesco, Inc.

55. An example of this is unmanned planes, called drones, used for surveillance and reconnaissance missions.

56. *The Croft Times*, March 1998, available at http://www.eidos.co.uk/lara/news.htm.

providing legitimate examples of female heroism. This tendency to read action heroines as figurative males is crystallized in the now-legendary figures of Lieutenant Ripley (Sigourney Weaver) from the *Alien* series and Sarah Connor (Linda Hamilton) from the *Terminator* series. Muscular, gun-toting, ass-kicking characters, these women are readily identified as performers of masculinity. Together these two figures have informed not just the portrayal of subsequent action heroines in films including *The Real McCoy* (1993), *Bad Girls* (1994), *Cutthroat Island* (1995), *Charlie's Angels* (2000), *Tomb Raider* (2001), and *Resident Evil* (2002), but also many of the scholarly discussions about gender and action cinema and the commercial press's quick identification of the new heroines as masculine proxies. A preoccupation of feminist film scholarship in recent years has dealt with the cultural implications of identification and the shifting landscape of gender roles when women cross over into the traditionally masculine terrain of toughness. That several of the first scholars to address these new roles for women identified them as "figurative males,"[3] "masculinized female bodies,"[4] and "Dirty Harriet[s]"[5] has led to a misconception that action heroines are *only* enacting masculinity.

The foundational work on women in tough roles, by writers Carol Clover and Cora Kaplan, effectively questions our cultural belief in gender absolutes by documenting the female characters' penchant for being just as tough as male characters. Their own work, and the subsequent wave of scholarship concerned with these new depictions of women, has approached these transgressive figures from a variety of perspectives. Film studies' ongoing fascination with Ripley from the *Alien* series is indicative of the range of interpretations that have been utilized. For example, Barbara Creed considers Ripley and the film in relation to concepts of the abject female body,[6] Paula Graham discusses the lesbian implications of Ripley's persona,[7] Janice Hocker Rushing interprets Ripley as a co-opted mythological archetype,[8] and Elizabeth Hills reads her as a "Post-Woman" able to function in the middle space between binaries.[9] The range of scholarly approaches applied to the figure of Ripley is indicative of the multiple ways strong female characters are being interpreted both within critical circles and presumably by audience members. But, as Hills points out, the fundamental appeal of these tough female characters for gender

Chapter 2

Gender, Sexuality, and Toughness: The Bad Girls of Action Film and Comic Books

Jeffrey A. Brown

Gear magazine's review of the film *The Transporter* (2002), opens with the declaration that "director, writer and producer Luc Besson knows better than most how to make a beautiful woman even more beautiful: arm her to the teeth."[1] This peculiar observation about a filmmaker best known for putting big guns in the hands of wide-eyed waifs in movies such as *La Femme Nikita* (1990), *The Professional* (1994), and *The Fifth Element* (1997) elucidates the problematic reception of tough women in action movies. When women are portrayed as tough in contemporary film, are they being allowed access to a position of empowerment, or are they merely being further fetishized as dangerous sex objects? Even within feminist film theory the modern action heroine has emerged as an extremely fruitful but difficult character to interpret. On the one hand, she represents a potentially transgressive figure capable of expanding the popular perception of women's roles and abilities; on the other, she runs the risk of reinscribing strict gender binaries and of being nothing more than sexist window-dressing for the predominantly male audience.[2]

A central concern for critics has been the common interpretation of the action heroine as simply enacting masculinity rather than studies is that they represent untypical female roles. Any critique that takes the unusualness of the female character as its starting point is likely to become mired in a language of "maleness" and "femaleness."

It is perhaps inevitable that discussions of shifting gender roles in film would be ensnared in the logic of either masculine *or* feminine, since this conceptual binary underscores our basic perception of the physical and behavioral differences between the genders. One of the problems is that the strict categorization of traits as male or female that has dominated film theory ever since Laura Mulvey's "Visual Pleasure and the Narrative Cinema" was first published in 1975,[10] means that any atypical portrayals tend to be interpreted as cinematic transvestism. This is a point I have argued elsewhere in relation to tough women in action films who enact gender roles in various forms and for differing purposes.[11] What I want to stress in this chapter is an alternative interpretation capable of accounting for both the toughness and the sexiness of action heroines that does not deny the engendered elements of these traits but incorporates them into a solitary figure that effectively critiques the very notion of stable gender identities. The action heroine does enact both masculinity and femininity. But rather than swapping a biological identity for a performative one, she personifies a unity of disparate traits in a single figure. She refutes any assumed belief in appropriate gender roles via an exaggerated use of those very roles.

Without doubt, the macho female action heroine continues to dominate attempts to integrate female characters (or, more importantly, the popular female stars who play them) into the narrative center of the profitable action genre. But the hard-as-nails action heroine is only one of the more visible variants of the tough-girl type. In fact, Yvonne Tasker, whose seminal *Spectacular Bodies: Gender, Genre and Action Cinema* (1993) set much of the interest in action heroines in motion, has devoted a great deal of discussion in her subsequent book, *Working Girls: Gender and Sexuality in Popular Cinema* (1998),[12] to variations such as the tomboy (*Speed*, 1994), the feisty heroine (*The Abyss*, 1989), the protective mother (*Fatal Beauty*, 1987), the official female partner (*Broken Arrow*, 1996), the wife/partner (*True Lies*, 1994), and the female partner as racial Other (*Strange Days*, 1995). But it is the variation, which Tasker spends the least amount of time discussing, the one she describes as "a fetishistic figure of fantasy derived from comic books and soft pornography involving an exaggerated statement of sexuality: performed quite precisely in the action/porn hybrid *Barb Wire* (1996) with Pamela Anderson," that I want to explore more fully in this chapter.[13]

The "fetishistic figure of fantasy" that Barb Wire and her ilk clearly represent is a difference in degree, not a difference in kind, from the other female characters who take center stage in the action genre. For all its faults, its campy performances, and its over-the-top presentation of Anderson's body, *Barb Wire* reveals the adolescent fear and desire of female sexuality that is exercised through the figure of all action heroines. Moreover, with *Barb Wire* and the film's comic book origins, we can discover, from a different angle, that the ascribed masculinity of the archetypal action heroines may have more to do with a controlled sexualization than a cross-gender performance. Rather than masculinized women, the action heroine often functions within the symbolic realm of the dominatrix by both breaking down and exploiting the boundaries between the sexes. It is because of *Barb Wire*'s exaggerated sexuality, not despite it, that the film can make explicit the fetishistic nature of the action heroine's real toughness. At a fundamental level every action heroine, not just those who are explicitly sexualized, mobilizes the specter of the dominatrix. It may be most apparent when the heroine is performed by a Pamela Anderson, Angelina Jolie, Jennifer Lopez, Lucy Liu, or any of the straight-to-video centerfold types, but it is also an important ingredient in what have been considered the more serious roles of Sigourney Weaver as Ripley and Linda Hamilton as Sarah Connor. My contention is that modern action heroines are transgressive characters not only because their toughness allows them to critique normative standards of femininity but because their coexistent sexuality (epitomized in *Barb Wire*) destabilizes the very concept of gender traits as mutually exclusive.

"Suck My Dick!"

The persistent interpretation of tough women in action films as figurative males is understandable given how clearly the role of action hero is defined as a masculine domain in contemporary

Hollywood films. But while the action genre has evolved in the 1990s to the point where the one-dimensional masculinity represented in the 1980s by the likes of Schwarzennegger and Stallone (and Willis, Van Damme, Lundgren, and Segal) is no longer bankable—their stoic, blue-collar, white masculinity being supplanted by such nonwhite and often comedic stars as Wesley Snipes, Will Smith, and Jackie Chan—their archetypes remain the standard against which all subsequent action heroes are read. Thus, an easy point of reference for newspaper reviews and magazine articles is to liken even the cartoonishly sexualized Pamela Anderson to Stallone (Pambo)[14] or Schwarzenegger (the "Lust Action Hero").[15]

Elizabeth Hills has complained, "Although these powerfully transgressive characters open up interesting questions about the fluidity of gendered identities and changing popular cinematic representations of women, action heroines are often described within feminist film theory as 'pseudo males' or as being not 'really' women."[16] Hills argues:

> one of the reasons why action heroines have been difficult to conceptualize as heroic *female* characters is the binaristic logic of the theoretical models on which a number of feminist theorists have relied. For example, feminists working within the dominant model of psychoanalysis have had extremely limited spaces within which to discuss the transformative and transgressive potential of the action heroine. This is because psychoanalytic accounts, which theorize sexual difference within the framework of linked binary oppositions (active male/passive female), necessarily position normative female subjectivity as passive or in terms of lack. From this perspective, active and aggressive women in the cinema can only be seen as phallic, unnatural or "figuratively male."

The alternative that Hills offers to the strict psychoanalytic gender binarism that codes active as exclusively male and passive as exclusively female is to interpret action heroines, particularly Ripley from the *Alien* series, according to Gilles Deleuze's notion of becoming. As the only character, male or female, who can transcend her original state of being and cognitively adapt to an external threat, Ripley becomes a form of post-woman operating in the productive spaces between strict cultural formations. In essence, Hills proposes that Ripley is best understood as moving beyond the restrictive gender dichotomy. She functions not in terms understood as male or female but as a transcendent and progressive character. The alternative that I wish to suggest here is that the tough action heroine is a transgressive character not because she operates outside of gender restrictions but because she straddles both sides of the psychoanalytic gender divide. She is both subject and object, looker and looked at, ass-kicker and sex object (see figure 2.1).

Like Hills, my concern stems from the now habitual interpretation of action heroines as men in drag, which limits the acceptability of toughness as a legitimate characteristic for women. But I do wish to stress that this concern does not mean I disagree with the interpretation of these heroines as enacting masculinity, merely that there are other factors that contribute to the appeal of the action heroine in her varied guises. In fact, the "figurative male" description of action heroines, which once seemed such a unique insight facilitated by film theory, now seems all too obvious in many movies. As the genre has become increasingly self-reflexive, the gender dilemma represented by the action heroine has become more overt. Where the masculinization of Lieutenant Ripley and Sarah Connor was in service of their respective films' plots, the gender transgression of more recent action heroines seems to *be* the plot. Both *The Long Kiss Goodnight* (1996) and *G.I. Jane* (1997) exemplify the self-conscious masculinization of their female protagonists. A brief review of these two films and their critical reception indicates the lengths the filmmakers go to in order to explore the rigidity of gendered roles and to position their heroines as intentionally transgressive, masculinized figures.

The Long Kiss Goodnight was the second attempt, after the notorious failure of *Cutthroat Island*, to establish Geena Davis as a major action star. The binary gender codes at work in *The Long Kiss Goodnight* are central to the film's plot. Davis plays Samantha Caine, a stereotypical Midwestern mother and schoolteacher who has been suffering from amnesia for eight years. With the assistance of down-at-his-heels private eye Mitch Henessey (Samuel L. Jackson), she discovers her old life as a cold war–era government assassin and, in the process, unwittingly becomes involved in

Figure 2.1. Pamela Anderson's Barb Wire combines a masculine and feminine iconocraphy

fighting her old enemies, who have allied with her former employer and are plotting to blow up the bridge to Canada at Niagara Falls in a fake terrorist attack in order to scare more anti-terrorist funding out of congress. As Samantha gradually learns about her previous lifestyle, her true persona, Charly, begins to reemerge. The transformation of sweet Samantha into ass-kicking Charly constitutes the central fantasy of the film and is clearly structured along traditional gender binaries. The self-discovery of *The Long Kiss Goodnight* is a literal stripping away of the feminine masquerade embodied by Samantha in favor of the underlying masculine character of Charly.

The film takes an obvious pleasure in juxtaposing Samantha's initial innocence and timidity with Charly's aggressive and violent personality. As Tasker notes, "if Samantha is determined by motherhood, Charly is (over)determined by an excess of phallic imagery."[17] Samantha is shown at the onset of the story as a loving mother to her daughter and as happily engaged to a sensitive man. But, this being an action film, audiences anticipate the demise of the sweet charade and revel in the increasingly violent abilities of the character. Though Samantha is initially surprised by her emerging skills, expertly handling a knife (which she humorously misinterprets as a sign that she was a chef) and instinctively assembling a high-powered rifle in mere seconds, the motherly disguise is soon abandoned all together. In a hyperbolically symbolic scene the final (re)masculinization of Samantha into Charly occurs during a torture scene. Submerged in freezing water, Samantha/Charly retrieves a gun from the crotch of a drowned corpse and proceeds to kill her torturer. From this point on the narrative revels in Charly's freed masculine behavior.

As Charly, she physically transforms herself by cutting her hair dramatically shorter and dyeing it blond, wearing harsher makeup, and giving up dresses and wooly sweaters for tight pants and a bullet-ridden black leather jacket. An awed Mitch watches the transformation as Charly begins to chain smoke and drink like a macho man, happily downing several shots of hard liquor and swearing like a trucker. As Mitch puts it: "You used to be all 'Phooey, I burned the cookies' now you walk into a bar and ten minutes later sailors come running out." She also becomes more sexually aggressive, asking an overwhelmed Mitch if he wants to fuck. And, most importantly, Charly is repeatedly shown as the master of phallic power, out-shooting, out-fighting, and out-thinking the villains at every encounter. The real plot of *The Long Kiss Goodnight* is not the anti-terrorist struggle, nor is it Samantha/Charly's efforts to save her daughter after the terrorists kidnap her. The real plot is the gender negotiation of feminine Samantha into masculine Charly and then the final attempt at a reconciliation between the two personas at film's end.

A year after the self-conscious gender exploration of *The Long Kiss Goodnight*, Ridley Scott, who had already directed the landmark tough-women film *Thelma & Louise*, also took the masculinization of a female hero as the main plot of his film *G.I. Jane*. Though more of a military basic training movie in the vein of *An Officer and a Gentleman* (1982) or *Heartbreak Ridge* (1986) than simply an action movie, *G.I. Jane* casts Demi Moore as Lieutenant Jordan O'Neil in the same masculinized mould as the quintessential action heroine. Capitalizing on real-life debates about women's expanding role in the military, *G.I. Jane* is the story of O'Neil's struggles to become the first female Navy SEAL. Like *The Long Kiss Goodnight*, the convoluted plot of *G.I. Jane* seems secondary to the film's main purpose, which is to document the transformation of Moore's character into a masculine proxy. The cover of *Sight and Sound* summed up the real importance of the film when it declared "Demi Moore Takes It Like a Man."[18] Though the overwrought surface message of the film is that women are perfectly capable of entering even the most masculine of military service, the implicit message is that she can only achieve success as a Navy SEAL by putting her femininity behind her and capitulating to the symbolic realm of what Lauren Tucker and Alan Fried in their analysis of the film refer to as "techno masculinity."[19] Her resolve to make the grade on the same terms as her male comrades is signaled by a *Rocky*esque montage of training and self-transformation. Tucker and Fried point out:

> O'Neil's transformation is initially signaled by the loss of specific physical indicators of her femaleness, one of the most overt of which is her long hair. In a dramatic scene, she slowly and carefully cuts off her hair without the aid of the briefly-absent barber. Her intense

personal training routine results in the loss of her period, and her body starts to take on a harder, more masculine look.[20]

Her more masculine appearance is matched by her mastery of masculine skills as she dominates such drill tests as the obstacle course and rifle assembly. Eventually she becomes the best and the most respected recruit in the class. Accepted by her peers as "one of them," O'Neil's masculine abilities are ultimately tested in a real combat situation where she manages to rescue first her commanding officer and then her whole platoon.

If their cumulative performances throughout the films do not make it clear enough that for these women to be tough they have to be masculinized, the triumphant moment for both Samantha/Charly in *The Long Kiss Goodnight* and for O'Neil in *G.I. Jane* is accompanied by the almost hysterically obvious, gender transgressive challenge to "suck my dick!" Charly shouts "Suck my dick, every last one of you bastards!" while driving an 18-wheel truck right at her enemies amidst the explosions of the film's climactic battle. Likewise, the utterance becomes a catch phrase in *G.I. Jane* when, after being beaten and thrown to the ground in front of her fellow recruits during a mock training mission, O'Neil defiantly tells the master chief to "Suck my dick!" Signaling that her resolve is still intact, O'Neil's utterance wins over her peers, who cheer her bravado and taunt their chief with a group chant of "Suck my dick!" In their essay about the gun as metaphorical masculinization in *G.I. Jane*, Tucker and Fried rightly observe that it is at this moment, as "she basks in the cheers and acceptance of her fellow recruits, [that] O'Neil's transformation into a rugged, individualistic techno-male is complete."[21]

Where the appropriation of the phallus performed by past action heroines has been detailed by their use of masculine characteristics and symbolic accoutrements like guns, swords, and muscles, the heroines of *The Long Kiss Goodnight* and *G.I. Jane* go a step further and verbally declare their appropriation. Moreover, in moving from wielding phallic symbols to declaring possession of a phallus, both of these characters not only further masculinize themselves but, more importantly, feminize their adversaries. They openly reveal their position of assuming power and strength through the rhetoric of gendered terms. "You do not have to be well versed in psychoanalysis to know that dick means power, the power towards which everyone, more or less unsuccessfully, aspires," wrote Linda Williams in her insightful discussion of Demi Moore's body upon the release of *G.I. Jane*. "To grasp the position from which 'dick' can be spoken and then to yell the word back at your assailant makes the speaker, whatever anatomy has destined them for, the better endowed."[22] The essence of the action heroine who enacts masculinity is crystallized in the open challenge to "suck my dick" extended by both Samantha/Charly and O'Neil. By assuming the traits of maleness, they gain access to a form of power (both physical and social) that has been systematically denied to women while simultaneously demonstrating that the association of "maleness" with "power" is not innate but culturally defined since anyone can mobilize even the most basic of male privileges: the privilege to assert phallic authority through reference to an actual phallus.

"Don't Call Me Babe!"

While the traditional binaristic approach to sexual difference that is grounded in the active male/passive female split is still undeniably essential to the reading of such films as *The Long Kiss Goodnight* and *G.I. Jane*, it is not the only way to explore the action heroine. "From this perspective [of binaristic logic]," Hills points out, "active and aggressive women in the cinema can only be seen as phallic, unnatural or figuratively male."[23] Hills own alternative approach is a consideration of Ripley from the *Alien* series as an adaptive, transformative, and alternative *feminine* figure. Yet even without rejecting the limitations of the "figurative male" thesis altogether, the array of types who fall under the category of action heroine bring the concept of gender transgression into question. Where the Rambo references to Sigourney Weaver's Ripley as "Fembo" and "Rambolina" seem warranted, the relatively tongue-in-cheek references to Pamela Anderson's Barb Wire as "Pambo" (made in both *The Toronto Star* and *The London Spectator*) underscore the absurdity of reading both Anderson and the character of Barb Wire through the lens of male action heroes.

Though Barb Wire does behave in ways that are coded as masculine (she fights, shoots, talks, and drinks like the toughest of screen characters), it would be ludicrous to think of her as a figurative male just because she enacts a cinematic style of toughness that has been predominantly engendered as masculine. Despite the presence of her gun and her bad attitude, it is nearly impossible to read *Barb Wire* as anything but a male fantasy when she is always dressed in revealing leather corsets with her hair perfectly coiffed and her make-up perfectly applied (see figure 2.2). The excessive presentation of Anderson's cartoonishly sexualized body seems on the surface to counter any transgressive potential that the film might hope for. But it is exactly this overfetishization of her sexuality and her violent abilities that facilitates an understanding of all modern action heroines as questioning the naturalness of gender roles by enacting both femininity and masculinity at the same time.

The film itself, as many critics observed, is an odd mix of softcore porn and action-movie clichés. Although it was the first big-budget feature starring a well-known celebrity to employ this formula so blatantly, it is a common foundation for a whole sub-genre of straight-to-video films. Anderson's role as Barb Wire is essentially a more action-filled version of Humphrey Bogart's Rick in this gender-reversed remake of *Casablanca* (1942). Set in a future where America has become a chaotic military state, Anderson's Barb Wire is, as the promotional materials put it, "the sexiest, toughest woman in Steel Harbor," who will "use any dangerous weapon, including her body, to take what she wants." Wire owns the most popular nightclub in town and moonlights as a bounty hunter. When her ex-lover shows up one night to ask for her help smuggling a renowned scientist out of the United States, she initially refuses. Repeatedly assaulted by the police and Nazi-like military, Wire finds herself morally obligated to help smuggle the scientist out of the country. The final scene has Wire and the corrupt chief of police, who has had a last-minute change of heart, standing on a rain-slicked runway repeating the famous ending of *Casablanca* with an appropriate updating of the dialogue: "I think I'm falling in love," says the chief, to which Wire snaps back "Get in line!" as the camera pans her leather-clad body one last time.

Figure 2.2. Male in drag or feminine masquerade?

Even with the plot's liberal borrowing from such a film classic, *Barb Wire* is a far cry from *Casablanca*. The extended opening sequence of *Barb Wire* is typical of a heavy-metal music-video fantasy and sets the tone of sexploitation for the rest of the movie. Wire, dressed in a skintight latex minidress, dances erotically while water is splashed over her body and numerous men hoot and holler their enthusiasm (she is, conveniently, undercover as a stripper). Shot entirely in fragmented, slow-motion close-ups of Anderson's famous body, the scene establishes Wire as a sexual icon for viewers. The message is clear: This body is in no way masculinized; it is a body to be looked at and desired. Even more importantly, the culmination of the scene establishes Wire's body as something not just to be desired but also to be feared. One audience member, grown increasingly obnoxious, shouts for her to "take it all off" and "show us what you've got, babe!" In response, Wire scans the crowd to find the offender and hurls her stiletto-heeled shoe at him, piercing him between the eyes. She leaves the stage angrily muttering, "If one more person calls me babe," which becomes a running joke in the film and sets up Wire's catch phrase: "Don't call me babe." The marketing of the film clearly tried to spin the phrase as a pseudofeminist tag line in the tradition of Dirty Harry's "Go ahead, make my day" and the Terminator's "I'll be back" and "Hasta la vista, baby." As the signature line of the film, "Don't call me babe" neatly crystallizes the fundamental conflict of Wire as action heroine. Despite the character's protest, the film is dependent on Anderson's status as the quintessential "babe" of the 1990s. Yet because she is supposed to be a tough action heroine, she quickly kills anyone who tries to position her as object rather than subject, who dares to call her "babe." Wire's body may be desirable, but as the promotional copy on the back of the video box emphasizes, it is also a dangerous weapon. Like nearly all of the action women who have come before and after *Barb Wire*, the film constantly struggles to find an appropriate way to sexualize and empower tough women.

Despite sharing some violent behavioral traits with previous action heroines, *Barb Wire* illustrates the impracticality of conceptualizing an action heroine as a figurative male. "Pambo" or not, her highly sexualized but also highly dangerous body is semiotically something altogether different. To grasp the full fetishistic appeal of the film, the comic book trend that gave birth to the character must be taken into account. The *Barb Wire* comic book series was published by Dark Horse Comics and was part of a larger industry trend known as the Bad Girl genre. The label of Bad Girls primarily refers to the highly sexualized nature of these female characters who dominated the struggling comics industry in the mid-nineties. In a blatant attempt to attract the attention of the predominantly male adolescent comics consumer, publishers flooded store shelves with new books featuring extremely leggy and buxom superheroines costumed in highly revealing, skintight outfits. In addition to *Barb Wire*, series such as *Lady Death*, *Lady Rawhide*, *Razor*, *Avengelyne*, *Witchblade*, *Double Impact*, *Vogue*, and *Fatale* quickly became hot commodities. The iconography was simple and central to their popularity. Each cover depicted a scantily clad babe striking a revealing pose and carrying a prominent weapon, usually a gun, sword, or whip. The cover of *Lady Rawhide* number 1 is a typical example of Bad Girl cover art, emphasizing the sex-kittenish body of the title heroine and her excessive weapons (see figure 2.3).

"For years," Roger Cadenhead wrote in the leading comics fanzine *Wizard*, "the conventional wisdom in comics has been that female characters can't succeed in their own books. After spirited efforts with protagonists like Wonder Woman and She-Hulk, companies resigned themselves to the fact that their largely male audience largely wants to read about large males."[24] The world of superhero comic books is still a bastion of adolescent power fantasies. Images of hypermasculine men continue to dominate the colorful worlds where every wimpy Clark Kent or Peter Parker can become a Superman or a Spiderman.

Ironically, it was the increased emphasis on "large males" as subject matter that resulted in the emergence of the Bad Girl trend in the first place. Through the 1990s, a shift within the comics industry to particularly stylistic artists as stars and the concomitant rise of several independent and creator-owned publishing companies resulted in an increasingly excessive representation of the male body. Hypermasculine characters are now routinely drawn with arms as big as couches and chests the size of minivans.[25] The Bad Girl subgenre emerged as an offshoot of the greater hypermasculine

Figure 2.3. Typical Bad Girl image combining sexual display and violent potential

shift in comics. Scott Bukatman's description of these new female characters captures the absurdity of their depiction:

The spectacle of the female body in these titles is so insistent, and the fetishism of breasts, thighs, and hair so complete, that the comics seem to dare you to say something about them that isn't just redundant. *Of course* the female form has absurdly exaggerated sexual characteristics; *of course* the costumes are skimpier than one could (or should) imagine; *of course* there's no visible way that these costumes could stay in place; *of course* these women represent simple adolescent masturbatory fantasies (with a healthy taste of the dominatrix). One might note that women participate more fully in battle than they once did. It's worth observing that they're now as powerful as their male counterparts. They no longer need protection; they are no longer victims or hostages or prizes.[26]

Many of the creators of these Bad Girl comics stress what Bukatman notes in his description; their creations are no longer damsels in distress waiting for men to save them. These female characters are typically as powerful, violent, skilled, smart, and self-assured as any of the male characters found in comic books. While this may indeed be a positive development, it is offset by the compensatory exaggerated feminine form, resulting in an odd combination of toughness and sexiness. At least at a symbolic level, the physical extremes that typify the Bad Girl (huge, gravity-defying breasts, mile-long legs, perpetually pouty lips, and perfectly coifed big hair) amount to an almost hysterical mask of femininity. That these female characters have exaggeratedly feminine bodies is not surprising given the superhero genre's preoccupation with ideal bodies. The interesting aspect is that in their sexualized hyperfeminine depiction they not only compensate for assuming traditionally masculine roles but also combine the symbolic "manliness" of toughness with the most basic symbols of "womanliness." Like Barb Wire in the film version, and to a lesser extent all the other heroines of action cinema, these characters embody and enact both genders, ridiculing the very notion of a stable gender position. The progressive impact of action heroines is not that they can enact masculinity (Ripley and Connor) or that they can be effectively masculinized (Samantha/Charly and O'Neil); it is that in every case they combine femininity and masculinity. The physical differences that mark these characters as male or female are ultimately revealed as nothing but symbols. These excessive gender images (long legs, large breasts, and sexy hair) exist only as a compensatory surface to the underlying theme that toughness does not need to be conceived as a gendered trait.

The complex combination of pouty fantasy woman and oversized weapons is part of a larger cultural system of fetishization within an iconography of pin-ups and soft pornography. The fact that the Bad Girls do so often seem to be merely posing in their skimpy costumes with their weapons held ready like so many frames of stylized S&M porn reveals a central paradox of the action woman: She is required to be both active and static at the same time. Building on Richard Dyer's observations of the muscular male pin-up,[27] Tasker notes the tension in film between "an image built, designed for contemplation in static poses and the situation of such images within the context of action. By extension it is possible to understand the difficulties involved in putting the eroticised female image from pin-up into 'action'; both she and the male bodybuilder are subject to display and to the need to 'pose.' "[28] Pamela Anderson is thus perfectly cast in *Barb Wire* since her star image is grounded in the popularity of her pin-up career, especially her famous pictorials in *Playboy* magazine. At the same time that this need to pose Anderson may hinder the narrative motion of the film, it does stress the important association between action women and photographic porn images. The Bad Girl comic-book heroine is the middle ground between the explicitly sexualized porn model and the ass-kicking Hollywood heroine. Not surprisingly, there are examples that reverse the *Barb Wire* trajectory, in which a popular television/pin-up/soft-porn star is chosen to embody an adolescent fantasy of comic-book womanhood. The link between the three different media forms (Hollywood action movies, Bad Girl comics, and pornographic images) used to express a certain type of female sexuality is so fluid that some real-life women have become fictional comic book characters, so to speak. For example, B-movie queen and former *Penthouse* "Pet of the Year" Julie Strain is now featured in *Heavy Metal* magazine as the cartoon heroine F.A.K.K. 2, and popular *Playboy* model Alley Baggett has become the subject of her own superhero comic book, *Alley Cat*.

The fetishization of these Bad Girls with guns, swords, and whips does not so much mark them as masculine as it marks them as dominatrixes. It is all part of a broader fetishizing of the female body. It is no coincidence that Pamela Anderson is clad in leather bondage wear throughout *Barb Wire*. Bukatman understates it a

little when he refers to the Bad Girls as "simple adolescent masturbatory fantasies (with a healthy taste of the dominatrix)."[29] There
is more than just a "healthy taste of the dominatrix" going on here.
These characters are first and foremost images of threatening
female sexuality. Their bodies may be alluring to the young male
readers, but they are also, like Barb Wire/Pamela Anderson's body,
"dangerous weapons." In a telling variation on the guns as phallic
symbol cliché, a mob boss asks about Barb Wire at the start of the
film by referring to her as the one with the "guns," meaning her
large breasts. The highly sexualized female body is as capable of
being coded as a weapon as it is as a passive plaything. Moreover,
this notion of the costumed heroine as a thinly veiled dominatrix is
not new. Even with Wonder Woman the analogy was obvious
shortly after her creation in the early 1940s. In her miniskirt,
armored bustier, and steel bracelets, she was the first in a long line
of moderately fetishized heroines. Clearly her famous golden lasso
has always been layered with implications of bondage: When men
are bound with it, they must submit to her will. And, tellingly, if a
man ever binds Wonder Woman with the lasso, she loses all of her
powers. Certainly the Jungle Janes and the Phantom Ladies who
appeared in the 1950s comics owed as much to the popular
bondage photos of Bettie Page as they did to their heroic male
counterparts such as Superman and Batman. The half-naked Bad
Girls who fill the comic book pages of today look and act less like
pin-up cheesecake and more like hardcore mistresses of pain. In
fact, while most of the publishers involved in the Bad Girl subgenre
publicly deny the fetishistic overtones of the characters by claiming
it is all just good, clean comic book fun, others have overtly recognized the dominatrix appeal of the characters.[30]

It is important to recognize that these Bad Girl bodies are presented as dangerous not just because they can fight or shoot but
because they are alluring. Being able to fight and shoot may make
them tough, but it is this toughness combined with overt sexuality
that makes them dangerous in a way that male characters can never
be. Given the age of many comic book readers, it is not surprising
that extremely attractive and aggressively sexual female characters,
who clearly embody a simplistic form of castration anxiety, find
some purchase. Like Delilah cutting Sampson's hair to steal his

legendary strength, many of today's Bad Girls are able to directly steal a man's power with just a touch or a kiss. Rogue, a hardbody Southern belle and one of Marvel Comics' X-Men, can steal a man's psyche by touching her flesh to his. Likewise, Broadway Comics's Fatale is described as a "powerful, good-looking woman born with the ability to absorb knowledge, skills and strength from other people, especially men, through physical contact." It is perhaps no small coincidence that for both Rogue and Fatale their preferred method for stealing a man's strength through physical contact is to kiss him. Where the superpowers of the comic-book Bad Girls are less than subtle metaphors for the ability of female sexuality to drain a man of his phallic powers, the same fetishistic themes exist in action movie heroines. In the comics, people of either gender can fly, throw cars around, or bounce bullets off of their chests. Likewise, in action movies people of either gender can fight, shoot, and blow things up. But in both genres only women can combine these tough skills with the threat of seduction. The Bad Girls of comics and the tough girls of action films combine threats that have been traditionally engendered as either masculine (toughness) or feminine (seduction).

The film version of *Barb Wire* is grounded in these fetishistic elements of the Bad Girl comic books and even builds upon them where it sees fit in order to both exploit the appeal of Anderson's body and to position itself as a quintessential action movie. Scene after scene in the film juxtaposes Barb Wire's sexual appearance with her penchant for violence directed at the men who ogle her. The opening striptease where she incapacitates a man with her high heel is one clear example of her violent response to males who presume her sexuality is on display merely for the pleasure of their gaze. In an extended scene that consolidates the fetishistic themes nicely, Wire, dressed as a dominatrix in thigh-high leather boots, fishnet stockings, a leather bustier, and a dog collar, poses as a prostitute who "likes to play rough" in order to gain access to a highly secured apartment building. Once inside the apartment of the fat, sweating, leering man she has picked up as her trick, she suggests he change into something more comfortable (so she can check out how to break into the apartment next door where her bail-jumping bounty is holed up). The trick asks if he can change into something less comfortable instead, and Wire plays along. When he returns in a leather body suit she tells him he has been a bad boy, takes a paddle, and cracks him across the back of the head so hard that he drops like a ton of bricks. Then in a flurry of action Barb Wire sets explosives and blows a hole in the wall, dashes through, beats up the bounty, and handcuffs him to the bed. When two bodyguards burst into the room with guns firing, she returns their fire from behind an overturned table (see figure 2.4). She defeats both in hand-to-hand combat after they run out of bullets, grinding her stiletto heel into the groin of one of them before killing him for calling her "babe."

Scenes like the one described above may seem ludicrous in a live-action movie, but it is true to the comic-book source material. *Barb Wire* is a perfect combination of comic-book Bad Girl and Hollywood action heroine thanks primarily to Pamela Anderson's famously extreme figure and some over-the-top action sequences. The film is a transparent representation of the fear and desire of women that is so consistently fetishized in the comics. While Anderson's performance of Barb Wire as a cartoonish dominatrix is indicative of modern Hollywood's ongoing practice of displaying

Figure 2.4. Action heroine as dominatrix

the film body as an erotic spectacle, it is not necessarily all that different than the more "respectable" instances of action heroines. The sexualized themes of fear and desire that are so obvious and visually apparent throughout *Barb Wire* may in fact be essential to the complex appeal of other action heroines as well. Even the most systematically masculinized of cinematic action heroines incorporate conventional feminine sexual attractiveness to some degree. The casting alone is indicative of the film industry's attempts to present established sex symbols as tough heroines in the hopes of creating a combination of sex and violence that might be irresistible to action film fans. My point is that every action heroine is a combination of conventional sexual attractiveness and violent abilities, symbols of fear and desire. The sex-symbol status of action heroine actresses is most obvious in the cases of Pamela Anderson, Demi Moore, Geena Davis, Angelina Jolie, and Mila Jovovich. But even Sigourney Weaver and Linda Hamilton have often been cast as sex objects in their roles outside of the *Alien* and *Terminator* series. While these characters may all enact masculinity, in their femininity/sexuality they are also enacting the principles of the dominatrix. The dominatrix-like qualities may be more apparent in *Barb Wire* than in more serious fare, but these qualities exist nonetheless.

I do not mean that all action heroines mobilize the dynamics of whip-wielding, leather-clad sexual sadists who punish men for pleasure (though even this extreme argument may be plausible). In fact, I think it is the overriding sexual implication of the term "dominatrix" that steered the discussion of action heroines in the exclusive direction of "figurative maleness" to begin with. Because the powerfully symbolic and marginalized sign of the dominatrix may superficially reduce these potentially groundbreaking characters to the level of mere sexual fetishes it has rarely been addressed in relation to tough women in film. The connotations of "dominatrix" may be an acceptable derision for a Pamela Anderson movie within film studies circles, but not for Ridley Scott or James Cameron–directed installments of the *Alien* series. But, I believe, the symbolic function of the dominatrix is at the root of all the images of tough women that populate action films, whether they are straight-to-video exploitation films or Academy

Award–winning feature films. I mean "dominatrix" here not as a kinky subcultural fetish but as a complex symbol that combines and exploits power (both physical and social) along the axis of gender (both masculine and feminine).

Beyond its distractingly symbolic surface, the figure of the dominatrix is an icon that, as Thais E. Morgan points out, "uses the signs of masculinity to mock masculinity."[31] The really transgressive potential of the action heroine may be that, as with the dominatrix, she mocks masculinity as she enacts it. Rather than crossing gender boundaries, the dominatrix combines them in a playful yet effective manner. While cross-dressing or performing the gender of the opposite sex is momentarily transgressive, it still reinscribes gendered traits as the norm, as gender specific, because they are presented as mutually exclusive. If the action heroine is a figurative male, the importance of signs such as muscles, self-reliance, competence, and control within the economy of masculinity is not really undermined but reinforced. But if the action heroine is read as a dominatrix the exclusivity of gendered traits is truly brought into question because one set of gendered signs does not replace the other; instead, the boundaries are confounded because they are combined.

Both the dominatrix and the action heroine combine disparate signs: male and female, subject and object, powerful and powerless, pleasurable and punishing. At their most rudimentary, these combinatory figures may represent castration anxiety for male viewers, but at their most progressive they also demonstrate the frailty of binary opposite cultural categories. When a curvaceous Pamela Anderson or a waif like Bridget Fonda (*Point of No Return*, *Kiss of the Dragon*) or Milla Jovovich (*The Fifth Element*, *Resident Evil*) or a school-girlish Drew Barrymore (*Bad Girls*, *Charlie's Angels*) pick up guns and proceed to kick ass, the playfulness of manipulating traditional signs is hard to miss. Like the dominatrix, the action heroine "refuses the terms of the social contract of sexual difference."[32] She does not just dress up as a male or simply enact masculinity. She dresses up as both male and female, enacting both masculinity and femininity. Thus she illustrates by example not only that gender is primarily a performance of culturally determined traits and conventions but also that these traits and conventions do not have to symbolize sexual difference. The signs of masculinity and femininity are not complete sets but individual pieces to be played with. "Suck my dick" and "don't call me babe" may seem antithetical, but, within the gender-reworking logic of dominatrix semiotics, both catch phrases are appropriate for the same female character.

Television V.I.P.s

Given the amount of critical attention devoted to the action heroine, it is important to note that most of these films were box-office failures. Despite the enormous popularity of *Aliens* and *Terminator 2*, none of the other action heroine films mentioned in this chapter was even a moderate success. Some of them, including *Barb Wire*, *Cutthroat Island*, and *V.I. Warshawski*, were infamous flops. While the larger-than-life male action hero continues to dominate movie theaters world wide, the figure of the action heroine struggles to gain a firmer foothold in feature films. Though the action heroine in her various guises is a progressive female character wrapped up in some obvious titillation for the predominately male audience of these genre films, perhaps the dominatrix overtones she embodies are still too unsettling for viewers within this realm of masculine fairy tales to accept en masse.

Yet, while the sexy action heroine has seldom found box-office success at the movie theater, she has become a hit on television. Contemporary television programs such as *Xena: Warrior Princess*, *Buffy the Vampire Slayer*, *La Femme Nikita*, *Dark Angel*, *Witchblade*, *Alias*, and *V.I.P.* have all built upon their initial cult appeal to become mainstream ratings giants. Taking their cue from the popularity of sexy but tough female characters, *Star Trek: Voyager* replaced the likes of Captains Kirk and Picard with the strong female Captain Janeway and the sexy but unemotional Borg engineer Seven of Nine.[33] Moreover, the current *Star Trek: Enterprise* has replaced Spock with a sexy Vulcan science officer in order to ensure their ratings competitiveness. These television tough women have received a great deal of attention from gender studies scholars in their own right.[34] Though the appeal of television heroines raises a variety of different issues, it is clear that the television shows are just as dependent on the sex appeal of the lead actresses as feature films are. Lucy Lawless (Xena), Sarah Michelle Gellar (Buffy), Peta Wilson (Nikita), and, of course, Pamela Anderson, who created and stars in *V.I.P.*, all represent modern ideals of female beauty and are routinely costumed in skimpy and skintight outfits. The dominatrix overtones of these living-room action heroines may be toned down a little bit from their big screen counterparts, but they still exist. Clad in a leather and armor bustier, Xena may be the most easily identifiable as a dominatrix-influenced fantasy, but the sight of an adolescent Buffy dressed in club wear and high heels as she kicks and stabs numerous ghouls to death is not that far off the mark, either. Nor does Pamela Anderson venture very far from the terrain of Barb Wire each week on *V.I.P.* as her bodyguard character runs around Los Angeles in various bikinis and latex minidresses with a gleaming revolver in hand.

Despite the surface similarities between the sexy and tough action heroines of the big screen and the small screen, there are two key differences that facilitate a widespread popularity for the television characters. First, the serial format of television makes it easier to grasp the heroines as more than mere fetish objects for male viewers. They may be sex symbols, but they are sex symbols that we come to know over time as fully rounded characters. This all-important character development is due to the serial format of television and is a component that is rarely achieved within the roughly two-hour time limit of feature films. Second, the content restrictions of prime time television necessitate a certain degree of campiness, which softens the sexism and often gives the narratives a tongue-in-cheek quality, signaling that audiences should have fun with the fantasy. A prime example of audiences embracing the campy aspects of the programs are the well-known legions of lesbian *Xena* fans who celebrate the close and potentially sexual relationship of Xena and her companion Gabrielle. Together, these two key elements distinguish television action heroines from film action heroines in a manner that allows women to embrace the characters without alienating male viewers. Nor is this an entirely new phenomenon. Women have always been able to identify with tough and sexy female characters on television even if the characters were intended by network executives as eye-candy for male viewers. Whether it was the leather catsuit–wearing Emma Peel of *The Avengers*,[35] or "TV's Private Eyeful" Honey West,[36] or even those queens of jiggle TV, Charlie's Angels,[37] female viewers are capable of latching onto the strength at the core of characters rather than just focusing on their outer beauty. If television is any indication, perhaps the real liberating and stereotype-breaking potential of female characters in action roles is that they can assume positions of power while also being sex symbols. This has subversive potential because it mocks masculine presumptions and undeniably illustrates that even the most cartoonishly feminine of heroines can also be tough, self-reliant, and powerful.

Notes

1. Luke Dawson, "Armed and Dangerous: Hong Kong's Shu Qi Keeps Cool Under Fire," *Gear 5*, no. 1 (September 2002): 27.
2. In addition to the essays collected in this volume and those cited in this chapter, recent studies of the action heroine include Sherrie A. Inness, *Tough Girls: Women Warriors and Wonder Women in Popular Culture* (Philadelphia: University of Pennsylvania Press, 1999); Jacinda Read, *The New Avengers: Feminism, Femininity and the Rape-Revenge Cycle* (New York: Manchester University Press, 2000); and Martha McCaughey and Neal King, eds., *Reel Knockouts: Violent Women in the Movies* (Austin: University of Texas Press, 2001).
3. Carol Clover, *Men, Women and Chainsaws: Gender in the Modern Horror Film* (Princeton: Princeton University Press, 1992).
4. Yvonne Tasker, *Spectacular Bodies: Gender, Genre and Action Cinema* (New York: Routledge, 1993).
5. Cora Kaplan, "Dirty Harriet/*Blue Steel*: Feminist Theory Goes to Hollywood," *Discourse* 16, no. 1 (1993): 50–70.
6. Barbara Creed, *The Monstrous-Feminine: Film, Feminism, Psychoanalysis* (New York: Routledge, 1993).
7. Paula Graham, "Looking Lesbian: Amazons and Aliens in Science Fiction Cinema," in *The Good, The Bad and The Gorgeous: Popular Culture's Romance with Lesbianism*, ed. Diane Hammer and Belinda Budge (San Francisco: Pandora, 1994): 196–217.
8. Janice Hocker Rushing, "Evolution of 'The New Frontier' in *Alien* and *Aliens*: Patriarchal Co-optation of the Feminine Archetype," in *Screening the Sacred: Religion, Myth, and Ideology in Popular American Film*, ed. Joel W. Martin and Conrad E. Ostwalt Jr. (San Francisco: Westview Press, 1995): 94–118.
9. Elizabeth Hills, "From 'Figurative Males' to Action Heroines: Further Thoughts on Active Women in the Cinema," *Screen* 40, no. 1 (1999): 38–50.
10. Laura Mulvey, "Visual Pleasure and Narrative Cinema," *Screen* 16, no. 3 (1975): 6–18.

11. Jeffrey A. Brown, "Gender and the Action Heroine: Hardbodies and the *Point of No Return*," *Cinema Journal* 35, no. 3 (1996): 52–71.

12. Yvonne Tasker, *Working Girls: Gender and Sexuality in Popular Culture* (New York: Routledge, 1998).

13. Tasker, 69.

14. Film review editor, "Pambo," *Toronto Star*, 9 May 1996, E1.

15. Kristen O'Neill, "Lust Action Hero," *Premiere Magazine* (May 1996): 70–75, 99.

16. Hills, 38.

17. Tasker, *Working Girls*, 87.

18. Linda Williams, "Demi Moore Takes It Like a Man: Body Talk," *Sight and Sound* 7, no. 11 (1996): 18–21.

19. Lauren Tucker and Alan Fried, "Do You Have a Permit for That?: The Gun as a Metaphor for the Transformation of G.I. Jane into G.I. Dick," in *Bang Bang, Shoot Shoot! Essays on Guns and Popular Culture*, ed. Murray Pomerance and John Sakeris (Toronto: Simon & Schuster Press, 1998): 165–174, quote pp. 170–171.

20. Tucker and Fried, 170.

21. Tucker and Fried, 172.

22. Williams, 20.

23. Hills, 39.

24. Roger Cadenhead, "Bad Girls: Who Says Female Characters Don't Sell? Don't Tell That to These Women or Their Creators," *Wizard: The Guide to Comics*, no. 38 (1994): 42–47, quote p. 42.

25. See Scott Bukatman, "X-Bodies (the Torment of the Mutant Superhero)," in *Uncontrollable Bodies: Testimonies of Identity and Culture*, ed. Rodney Sappington and Tyler Stallings (Seattle: Bay Press, 1994): 92–129, and Jeffrey A. Brown, "Comic Book Masculinity and the New Black Superhero," *The African American Review* 33, no. 1 (1999): 25–42.

26. Bukatman, 112.

27. Richard Dyer, "Don't Look Now," *Screen* 23, no. 3–4 (1982): 61–73, reprinted in *The Sexual Subject: A Screen Reader in Sexuality* (New York: Routledge, 1992).

28. Tasker, *Working Girls*, 70.

29. Bukatman, 112.

30. Gerard Jones and Will Jacobs, *The Comic Book Heroes: The First History of Modern Comic Books from the Silver Age to the Present* (New York: Prima Publishing, 1997).

31. Thais E. Morgan, "A Whip of One's Own: Dominatrix Pornography and the Construction of a Post-modern (Female) Subjectivity," *The American Journal of Semiotics* 6, no. 4 (1989): 125.

32. Morgan, 125.

33. For an analysis of the gendered roles of women in the Star Trek universe, see the anthologies by Ziaudin Sardar and Sean Cubitt, eds., *Aliens R Us: The Other in Science Fiction Cinema* (London: Pluto Press, 2002); and Marleen S. Barr, ed., *Future Females, The Next Generation: New Voices and Velocities in Feminist Science Fiction Criticism* (New York: Rowman & Littlefield, 2000).

34. See, for example, Rhonda V. Wilcox and David Lavery, eds., *Fighting the Forces: What's at Stake in Buffy the Vampire Slayer* (New York: Rowman & Littlefield, 2002); Bill Ogersby and Anna Gough-Yates, eds., *Action TV: Tough*

Guys, Smooth Operators and Foxy Chicks (New York: Routledge, 2002); and Elyce Rae Helford, ed., *Fantasy Girls: Gender in the New Universe of Science Fiction and Fantasy Television* (New York: Rowman & Littlefield, 2000).

35. Thomas Andrae, "Television's First Feminist: *The Avengers* and Female Spectatorship," *Discourse* 18, no. 3 (1996): 112–136.

36. Julie D'acci, "Nobody's Woman? *Honey West* and the New Sexuality," in *The Revolution Wasn't Televised: Sixties Television and Social Conflict*, ed. Lyn Spigel and Michael Curtin (New York: Routledge, 1997): 73–93.

37. John Fiske, *Television Culture* (London: Metheun, 1988).

Chapter 3

"It's a Girl Thing": Tough Female Action Figures in the Toy Store

Sherrie A. Inness

His pecs would make Arnold Schwarzenegger envious. Dressed in Army green fatigues, brandishing a machine gun, he snarls, "Make my day!" A group of muscled men, all clad in military outfits, stand ranked around him. Another figure stands confronting the males. She is dressed in leather and wields a spear that she holds in front of her, daring anyone to approach. Who is this woman, and what is she doing with these macho men? She represents a change that has occurred in the world of action figures.[1] Formerly dominated by men, this arena now includes a growing group of women.

We are all familiar with action figures, the over-muscled plastic figures that look as though they spent the last decade in the gym. Usually heavily armed and often members of the military (G.I. Joe) or a rogue team of steroid-pumped warriors, these action figures never hold desk jobs. Instead, they lead top-secret organizations of commandos, spies, soldiers, or vigilantes. These teams circle the globe, trying to make it safe for mere mortals. There are also "evil" action figures, intent on destroying the universe or plotting other nefarious deeds, who must inevitably be vanquished by the "good" guys. The bad guys do not hold desk jobs, either. When I visit any major toy store in the United States, hundreds of action figures confront me in the boys' section—rows of rows of little plastic male figures. Scores of different figures exist within a single product line. In the boys' section, action figures are just as common as are fashion dolls and baby dolls in the girls' section.

One trait that most action figures share is that they are male, which has been true for as long as they have existed. Whole teams of action figures in the 1960s, '70s, and '80s were composed solely of males. Females were scarce, sometimes nonexistent. Although males still largely outnumber females, in the last decade a greater number of women have begun to appear. Media commentators have noticed the popularity of these new figures. One 1995 article in *Brandweek* magazine notes, "It's a girl thing, or so it was in New York last week, as female superheroes . . . took top billing at Toy Fair after years of being upstaged by boys' action figures. . . . More feminine heroes haven't been on patrol since She-Ra left the scene in the late 1980s."[2] The article describes popular female newcomers, such as Bandai's Sailor Moon, and, for older girls, a Tank Girl action figure.[3] Another newspaper article in 2001 observes, "Action girls, [who] more [resemble] G.I. Joe than Barbie—have the licensing power today. 'There is a clear trend toward (tough) female characters,' says Russ Brown, the Marvel comic book company's head of consumer products, promotions, and media sales."[4] More toy lines now include at least one or— gasp!—two women, and these new additions are not relegated to the sidelines. They appear every bit as tough as their male comrades and every bit as ready to do battle. What does the increased prevalence of female action figures suggest about changing gender roles? How do these figures create new images for women of what it means to be powerful? Or do they only continue to perpetuate gender stereotypes?

Before turning to female action figures, we should define what constitutes an action figure. Action figures comprise a broad category of small figures (typically 3 3/4 to 12 inches) with plastic bodies that can be posed for action. They are often designed with movable joints so they can easily be posed in different ways, and sometimes even have hands that can grasp. This construction contrasts with the lack of flexibility of Barbie and other fashion dolls, stiff figures that do not lend themselves to the same sort of play as a flexible action figure. They sometimes have special abilities—for example, Steve Austin, the Six Million Dollar Man, was equipped with a bionic eye, which proved so popular that competitor Hasbro Toys came out with Mike Power, the Atomic Man, equipped with an "Atomic Flashing Eye" and transparent leg and arm to set him apart from hordes of rival toys.[5] Action figures are generally marketed with numerous accessories, whether laser blasters, spaceships, sports cars, or atomic airplanes, which may conveniently be purchased separately. (G.I. Joe has more than just a jeep, since that would be simple and too inexpensive for parents. He has an Army Ranger Attack Cycle, Mobile Assault Vehicle, Sky Sweeper Jet, Battle Blitz Tank, Assault Quad Vehicle, and many other vehicles of all varieties.) Children (and parents) are encouraged to purchase not only a single figure but a whole action figure universe, chock full of action figure booty. Sometimes it seems as though every television show and film from the last few decades has had its line of action figures, including female ones. *Beverly Hillbillies* had an Ellie Mae Clampett figure (Unique, 1960); *Family Affair* had Buffy (Mattel, 1967); *The Partridge Family* had Laurie (Remco, 1973); *Mork and Mindy* had a Mindy (Mattel, 1979); *The Simpsons* had Marge and Lisa Simpson (Mattel, 1990); *Batman: Legends of the Dark Knight* had Batgirl and Catwoman figures (Kenner, 1994); *Mulan* had Mulan (Mattel, 1998); and *Xena: Warrior Princess* had Xena, Gabrielle, and Callisto.[6] But it is difficult to compare an action figure of the Flying Nun to one of Rambo or one of Marge Simpson to He-Man, so a more limited definition is useful: Action figures are those that are depicted as physically and mentally tough heroes or anti-heroes. Thus, Rambo or Ripley qualify; the Flying Nun and Homer Simpson do not. This chapter focuses on female figures who have invaded the action-figure world, which has been traditionally predominantly male, and what these newcomers suggest about changing gender roles.

Action figures are intriguing to analyze because they are the quintessential boys' toys. Hasbro Toys invented the name "action figure" when it created G.I. Joe. Surmising that boys would not play with "dolls," the company wanted to create something a bit more "macho," something that would be more toy soldier than doll but that would be as big a seller with boys as Barbie was with girls.[7] In 1964, G.I. Joe was a huge hit. It seemed as though Hasbro's designers were right. Boys would not play with dolls, but they bought millions of G.I. Joe action figures. After the success of this first, many others followed, and they soon dominated the world of boys' play. Action figures are part of a much larger superhero universe composed of television shows, films, cartoon books, toys, and video games and filled with superheroes intent on saving the universe and super villains equally intent on destroying it. The world of superhero play is recognized as an important part of maturing for boys and girls. Jackie Marsh writes, "Children can feel relatively powerless in their daily lives, regularly confronting the rules and regulations placed on them by parents, schools, and society. . . . Children see superheroes as avenging this sense of powerlessness and serving as models for the kind of control they themselves want over a hostile environment."[8] Since children have little power in their lives, superheroes offer a chance to be powerful. Such play can offer children a reassuring sense of their ability to take on heroic roles, a feeling that can carry on into their lives as adults.

Despite the empowering aspects of this play, the superhero universe includes some disturbing messages about gender roles. The few female figures that exist (Wonder Woman is the most famous, but there are others, including Batgirl, Elektra, Catwoman, Black Canary, and Supergirl) are largely outnumbered by the hordes of males (Superman, Batman, Green Lantern, Captain America, Daredevil, Spiderman, Wolverine, Thor, Hawkman, Wolverine). When women do appear, they are frequently secondary to men; they are generally helpmeets to more important males or play clearly subordinate roles. For example, Superman obviously has a more dominant and important role than Supergirl, revealed in the fact that he is a "man" while she is only a "girl." This power imbalance is to be expected since, historically, males have been the primary users and creators of this universe. Marsh observes, "The superhero discourse is . . . produced by men, for men and boys."[9] Thus, males are usually the ones who play important roles as superheroes. This issue has ramifications beyond the playground. At stake is whether women can also be heroes in real life. Analyzing superhero action figures reveals a great deal, particularly about changing notions of the heroic. The increase in female action figures suggests that women are gaining a new access to heroic roles, which formerly have been predominantly the province of men.

Whether in the boys' or girls' aisle, toys help to create some of children's earliest experiences of the gender divide that separates males and females.[10] The impact of toys is something almost no child can avoid. What child does not own one toy or, more likely, dozens? Toys are an increasingly large market in the United States. Retail sales increased from \$4.2 billion in 1978 to \$17.5 billion in 1993.[11] By 2000, toys were a 23 billion market.[12] From early play, children learn that men and women have different duties in life. Barbie and her girlfriends are concerned about their next trip to the mall; G.I. Joe and his male teammates are concerned about how to prevent the next terrorist strike. Barbie, G.I. Joe, and other dolls and action figures create a gender-divided universe in which boys and girls learn about their differences, not their similarities.[13] This division, potentially, has a lasting impact as we mature, as Stephen Kline notes in his book, *Out of the Garden: Toys in the Age of Marketing* (1993): "Sex-typing of toys is an important source for separating the sexes in terms of the cognitive, emotional, and social skills that children acquire."[14] As he observes, gender stereotyping of toys is one way that boys and girls learn about the separate roles that are relegated to them as males and females, and the behaviors that they learn have an impact far past when the children grow too old to play.[15] From Barbie and other similar dolls, girls learn that they are supposed to be consumers, purchasing houses crammed as full of pink possessions as Barbie's Malibu beach house. Girls also learn about the importance of social relationships between men and women and of the significance of males. Barbie always seems to be preparing for a dream date or dream wedding. Through play, boys learn different roles. G.I. Joe and his comrades do not shop at the mall; they are too busy protecting the world, and if this requires violence, so be it. Boys learn that most problems can be solved by aggression.

One place where gender-typing is most vivid is the baby doll section, filled with baby dolls that drink bottles of formula, crawl, talk, wet their diapers, and cry until pacified. They are marketed and targeted at an audience of girls. None of the packages shows boys taking care of the dolls; the boxes display beaming, blissfully happy girls rocking their crying "babies" to sleep. In this realm, it is clear who is supposed to care for children. Despite the tremendous strides that women have made in society and the greater freedoms they now experience, this gender stereotyping of dolls has changed slowly in recent decades. Karen Klugman writes, "For all that some members of society advance notions of empowering women and making responsible caregivers of men, girls' collections of dolls reinforce the traditional female preoccupation with physical appearance and homemaking, while the boys' collections embody conflict and superhuman power."[16] She continues, our "childhood experience with fantasy play remains forever segregated into bride side and groom side."[17] Countless toys, including baby dolls and army soldiers, are resistant to change, perpetuating gender roles that seem to have changed little since the 1950s.

Toys' slowness to change stems from many reasons. When parents (or others) purchase toys, they bring their own memories about childhood. Adults feel nostalgic about their toys, one reason that they might purchase familiar ones like dolls or plastic soldiers. In addition, many adults believe that it is important to convey "correct" gender roles through toys and feel uneasy or hostile if toys are not "correctly" gendered. Manufacturers are aware that adults are nostalgic about their own childhoods and toys. Companies also recognize that numerous adults seek to preserve and perpetuate traditional gender roles, so many companies stick with designs that have sold well for generations. (Considering the traditional design of many toys, at least with reference to gender, it makes it interesting when toys, such as the female action figure, do change.)

The traditional gender roles that children are usually immersed in when young remain lurking in their psyches as they mature. Although a boy might not want to become a gun-toting G.I. Joe when he grows up or a girl a mall-hopping Barbie, those gender roles influence how children and adults construct their identities, even if they choose to question or reject such stereotyped roles. Also, this stereotyping proves remarkably durable in mainstream American society, where millions assume that females are responsible for child care and males for warfare. Myriad forces shape such stereotypes, but toys are one of the earliest and most influential for young children. Thus, action figures—and all toys from board games to baby dolls—deserve more scholarly scrutiny to tease out their gendered messages. If we are to understand how girls and boys mature into adults, we must explore this process through toys.[18]

Toys are particularly important for study because they, along with the mass media targeted at children, create what children's culture scholar Ellen Seiter refers to as a *lingua franca*.[19] At no other time in people's lives do they experience such a widely shared culture as during childhood. We share the same television shows, films, and toys, and this mass culture "provides a shared repository of images, characters, plots, and themes; it is through popular culture that children learn to communicate with their peers and with the world around them."[20] One aspect of this lingua franca is the role of superheroes; even as adults, we can rattle off facts about a variety of superheroes from Superman to Batman, from Catwoman to Wonder Woman. This superhero discourse, as mentioned earlier, shapes our sense of the heroic. It is also through this lingua franca that children learn about gender roles, as well as about a host of other ways that human society is structured. And even when we grow older and no longer participate actively in this lingua franca, it lurks in our subconscious, providing a common link to how we view the world. Thus, it is crucial to analyze the different strands, including the discourse about action figures, that make up this childhood language.

History of Female Action Figures

Before turning to contemporary female action figures, we should acknowledge their precursors.[21] The early female figures were never as fiscally successful as their male counterparts, lacking their brothers' marketing campaigns, so they soon vanished off toy stores' shelves. Despite their brief shelf lives, these figures challenged the notion that such toys had to be male and led the way for tougher female action figures.

The first female G.I. Joe action figure, the G.I. Joe nurse, appeared in 1967. Hasbro wished to discover if its success with the male action figures could be followed by success with a female counterpart, but the G.I. Joe nurse did not have much success with boys or girls and soon disappeared, leaving the G.I. Joe line an almost entirely male bastion for decades.[22] The Six Million Dollar Man—one of the most popular boys' toys of the mid-1970s—also spawned a female counterpart. Jaime Sommers, the companion to Steve Austin, first appeared in the television show *The Six Million Dollar Man* in 1976. She was a hit, so she was made a star of her own television show, *The Bionic Woman*. Like the Six Million Dollar Man figure, the Bionic Woman one proved popular, demonstrating that a market existed for female action figures as well as for male ones. Dressed in a jogging suit and running shoes, Jaime was ready to chase down the bad guys. She did carry a mission purse, complete with pretend cosmetics and a photograph of boyfriend Steve, which lessened her tough image. One commentator observed, "Kenner's Bionic Woman . . . was a super-person with 'Bath 'n' Shower' and 'Beauty Salon' accessories."[23] Jaime also owned a wardrobe of enough designer outfits to make Barbie turn green. The Bionic Woman had a floor-length peach gown complete "with pearl trimming and platform shoes," a red evening dress with "rhinestones and dress shoes," and a lilac dress with "butterfly ornament and matching shoes."[24] It is hard to run down the bad guys when wearing an evening gown and high heels, something that never concerned or worried the Six Million Dollar Man, who did not even own a tuxedo.

Wonder Woman was another action figure who was based on a successful television series, *The New Original Wonder Woman*, which first aired in 1975. Like the Bionic Woman, Wonder Woman proved popular as an action figure. A number of other female figures followed Jaime and Wonder Woman. She-Ra, the twin sister of He-Man, star of *He-Man and the Masters of the Universe*, was one of the most popular a decade later in 1985. She was featured in her own television show, *She-Ra: Princess of Power*. But her toughness was limited, since "magic, more than muscle, gave [her] the edge."[25] He-Man and She-Ra had different images: "He-Man [was] a muscle-studded medieval warrior. There [were] no clothing changes to accompany his transformation from Prince Adam. Indeed, it [was] hard to figure out how his identity remain[ed] a secret. She-Ra dolls, however, all [had] multiple clothes, long, flowing hair, and bathing-beauty looks."[26] The Bionic Woman, Wonder Woman, and She-Ra, plus a host of other lesser-known figures, proved to toy manufacturers that female action figures could sell.[27] With the limited success of the G.I. nurse, many companies had assumed that female figures were not marketable. These three demonstrated otherwise.

These figures embody an uneasy, unstable merger between the characters of G.I. Joe and Barbie—a role that current female action figures also have. They are still more likely than male ones to come equipped with "glamorous" accessories, such as designer gowns and cosmetics. Even today, the makers of female action figures struggle to balance beauty and sex appeal with toughness. This battle is a reflection of a larger cultural battle about tough women in the popular media. Although more images of tough women now appear, the women still, in many cases, must not appear too masculine and tough; in order to be marketable, they are frequently presented as feminine and heterosexually desirable.

In 1977 another female action figure appeared who was tougher and more independent than her earlier counterparts. Kenner produced Princess Leia, among other Star Wars toys, for the first time from 1977 to 1985. She was one sign in the world of toys that times were changing. In films, television shows, and books, tougher and more aggressive women were appearing, reflecting that women's real-life roles were also changing. Second-wave feminism caused many women to rethink their lives. In the workplace, women recognized that they could perform many of the jobs that men had dominated in the past, and millions of women were eager to adopt new responsibilities. In the home, women questioned gender stereotypes that made them responsible for cooking, cleaning, shopping for groceries, taking care of children, and a host of other chores that were considered "women's work." As women's roles altered in the workplace and home, so did their roles in the world of toys. Princess Leia represented a change in how female action figures were depicted. In the past, they had frequently been basically fashion dolls like Barbie. As mentioned earlier, both the Bionic Woman and She-Ra came equipped with large wardrobes of designer clothing, but Princess Leia wore relatively utilitarian outfits—one of the most common was a white robe over a full-length jumpsuit. Although she must have had astronomical dry cleaning bills, she was better prepared for action than Jaime in her floor-length peach gown and platform shoes. Princess Leia seemed more interested in saving the universe from Darth Vader than in shopping. Another change was that she did not serve as merely a man's sidekick or love interest; she had no picture of Han Solo in her purse. Although the Bionic Woman could kick down a steel door with her feet and rip apart a phonebook with her bare hands, she was still Steve's girlfriend. She-Ra was He-Man's twin sister and seemed secondary to her beefcake brother. Princess Leia was more independent.

The princess, however, had two males who could step in if the fighting grew too fierce. It took another female character, Ripley of *Alien* fame, to demonstrate just how tough women could be. As an action figure (Kenner, 1992), she revealed a new image of womanhood. Tough, muscular, heroic, she showed that women could handle the heroic roles long dominated by men.[28] She also was not merely a sidekick to a more muscular male. Instead, she played the central role, demonstrating that females could take on the heroic roles in action-adventure narratives that long had been dominated by males. Her success revealed that consumers were ready for tougher characters than Princess Leia or She-Ra. However, the acceptance of tougher female action figures was not always going to be an easy change in an area that had long been a predominantly male preserve.

G.I. Jane: Change in G.I. Joe Land

But what has happened to female action figures today? We've looked at some strong ones from the 1970s and eighties, but what about more recently? How have such figures changed, and what new roles do they offer for women? Do they allow them equal opportunities to play heroic roles or are those roles still relegated to men? I decided to try to answer these questions by visiting the G.I. Joe section of a near-by toy store. After all, even G.I. Joe has jumped into the female action figure fray. The new 12-inch female Joe, who first appeared in 1997, is much tougher than the 1967 G.I. nurse. A helicopter pilot—"one of the most dynamic roles available to female soldiers"—she is referred to only as "the U.S.

Army helicopter pilot."[29] Her accessories include "dog tags, a shoulder insignia, a Darth-Vaderesque flight helmet and a 9 mm Beretta pistol."[30] Surely, I assumed, this figure represented a change in gender roles that would be reflected in the entire Joe community, where women and men would be represented in equal numbers. But, once there, I discovered that was probably asking for too much; I thought that at least the females would make up a sizable, visible portion of the toys, and they would no longer be relegated to primarily stereotypically female roles, as was the early nurse.

It was eerie to discover how little had changed. Although millions of Joes have been sold over the decades (by 1993, 250 million figures and 115 million vehicles had sold), one would assume that none of the Joes was female when scrutinizing the shelves at Toys "R" Us.[31] There were scores of male Joes: the Desert Army Gunner, Army Desert Infantryman, Long-Range Sniper, Marine Raider, Basic Training Marine, and Vietnam Door Gunner. There was even a John F. Kennedy Joe. This was only the beginning; there were Jungle Recon, Ocean Assault, 26th Marine Expeditionary Unit, Basic Training Army, and Marine Light Mortar Joes. The shelves were packed with Joes of all descriptions. What was missing in this army was a female Joe, even just one. I searched the shelves, thinking that she might be lurking behind the Emergency Crash Rescue Joe or Korean War army Joe with recoilless rifle. Nothing. Where were the females? To discover whether females were better represented elsewhere, I visited the Batman section. It was not much better. There was one female figure, a Batgirl with Launcher and Projectile. As in the G.I. Joe section, the males were numerous, including Midnight Pursuit Batman, Night Assault Batman, Shadow Blast Batman, Attack Wing Batman, Shadow Copter Batman, Midnight Hunter Batman, and Night Shadow Batman. Robin was not as popular, represented by only Night Fury Robin. I was beginning to think that the role of females had not changed as much in the land of action figures, at least for G.I. Joe and Batman toys.

Since I did not discover many females in the solo G.I. Joe figures, I thought that I might do better if I went to the teams of Joes; they must include a few females. After all, for decades in the world of action hero toys, the team has been where women would be located. In a team of five, sometimes one female would lurk, demonstrating the manufacturer's belief in gender equality, as long as the females were a clear minority and never threatened the rule of the more prevalent males. Surely, I thought, the Joe teams would include a few females, but I was out of luck. A "four-man action squad" (an apt description) from the Corps Collector Edition included four men. There was not a single female team member, much less a "four-woman" action squad. Even the Emergency Rescue team of Joes contained no females; I had assumed that the sixties nurse might have found her modern home here. Women were as absent in the teams as they were in the solo action figures.

G.I. Joes are better at representing race than gender. Most teams included one or more figures of differing races. There were a number of solo male figures from different racial and ethnic groups. African Americans have been represented since 1966, when the "Negro Soldier" appeared. Hispanic representation is more limited. The first Hispanic G.I. Joe with a Hispanic surname was not marketed until 2001, although other earlier characters could have been interpreted as Hispanic due to their skin coloring.[32] Hasbro's G.I. Joe has been quicker to represent racial difference than gender difference, perhaps because racial difference seems to pose less of a threat to the machismo that has been the heart and soul of the line for so long.

I discovered later, however, that my trip to the local toy store did not reveal the true story about gender in G.I. Joe. Females are better represented—although not greatly—than the store's shelves led me to assume at first. Since the toys' re-introduction back in 1982, females have been included in the 3 3/4 inch figure line as both heroes and villains. The first female, Scarlett, appeared in 1982 and has been reissued in a number of other guises over the years. From 1982 to 1987, there was one female issued each year in this line of small figures.[33] In more recent years, a number of these figures have reappeared, and others have been introduced, including Scarlett, Cover Girl, Lady Jaye, the Baroness, and Zarana, but these figures did not appear on the toy store's shelves. Additional 12-inch female Joe figures have also appeared in recent years. In the Classic Collection figures, which included the female helicopter pilot, a second female appeared in 1998, a member of the 82nd Airborne Division. In 1999, a Vietnam nurse appeared. Female Joes do exist, and more are being produced, but, as I discovered, these figures still were not stocked on the Toys "R" Us shelves—or the shelves of many similar stores—next to the dozens of males. A two-tier system exists. On one hand, hundreds of male Joes are available at a major toy store. A few females might appear, but it is more common that they will not even be stocked. On the other hand, there is a highly select group of figures, including female ones, that are sold primarily to collectors, especially adults. These figures might or might not be available at a major toy store, leaving the average G.I. Joe aisle to be male dominated. Why? A major reason is that female action figures can be a hard sell to males. One newspaper commentator notes, "Despite the prevalence of female action heroes on movies and television, studio marketers say it's still tough . . . getting little boys to play with a girl doll—even one with two hip-clinging handguns."[34] For a toy line such as the G.I. Joe collection, which is marketed primarily to males and has been since its beginnings, including females risks that boys might not purchase the toys, so G.I. Joe remains a largely male bastion in order to retain its market share. A few females are sold today and have been sold since the 1980s, but those are always a minority to the males, not threatening the male universe of the Joes.

The lessons about heroism the G.I. Joe line conveys have not changed that greatly over the decades. A few females can enter this universe, if one can actually locate them, but most heroes are male, teaching young children the idea that the "acceptable" hero is male. In the land of the Joes, at least in Toys "R" Us, gender change seems glacial, but what about other action figure lines that are less aligned with masculinity than Joe and his crew?

Power Rangers: New Images of Women

There is hope in the toy store. Not all action figure lines are as male dominated as G.I. Joe and his buddies. Some lines give a more active role to women, and more of these lines have been appearing in recent years. One of the most important and successful to include females is the Mighty Morphin Power Rangers. They appeared in a Japanese television show that first aired in 1975. The show was subsequently adapted for a U.S. audience, appearing on Fox Television in 1993; it was an instant hit.[35] Power Ranger action figures were also enormously popular; over $300 million of figures and related paraphernalia sold in 1994.[36] This popularity shows no sign of flagging. Now, the show is aired in over 53 countries.[37] In October 2002, the Rangers celebrated their tenth anniversary in the United States. In that decade, Bandai America Inc., the toys' manufacturer, sold "148 million toys . . . including action figures, toysets, Megazords, [and] vehicles."[38] This means that a 5-inch Power Ranger can be found in one out of five U.S. houses.[39] What makes the Rangers particularly interesting for studying changing gender roles is that females have always had significant roles as both heroes and villains. Females have not been relegated to the status of sidekicks, but play as major roles as the males do. The large number of females marks an important shift in the action-figure aisle, especially when that shift results in one of the most successful, lucrative toy lines of the last decade—a toy line that clearly has become a significant part of childhood's lingua franca.

The television show's plot revolves around five average multiethnic teenagers who become Power Rangers.[40] Chosen by Zordon, commander of the forces of good, to protect the earth against evil, the teenagers have the power to morph into Rangers with superhuman powers. Each Ranger possesses a Zord, or fighting machine. Thus armed, the Rangers are prepared to battle the evil forces that threaten the world on a weekly basis. And audience members do not tire of watching the regular battles. One reason for this popularity is that the show's cast and storylines change every season. There are the Mighty Morphin Power Rangers, Power Rangers Turbo, Power Rangers Time Force, Power Rangers Wild Force, as well as others, and all of these Rangers confront new problems and face new foes. Such seasonal revision keeps children interested and results in more toys for eager purchasers to buy. Throughout these revisions, the Rangers have always included a large number of female characters, making it one of the most gender-diverse action-adventure teams and leading the way for other teams also to include a greater number of females.

One stride forward that the Rangers have made is that, since their introduction in the United States, women have been represented by more than the one token figure that many action teams have had for decades. The original Mighty Morphin Power Rangers included two females in a group of five heroes. Also, the lead villain, Rita Repulsa, was female. The two heroes challenged the notion that female heroism must be confined to a sole individual. They called into question a gender system in which it was assumed that men were the "typical" heroes. In previous decades, action-adventure teams might have included one female, but that balance was rarely questioned. The two Rangers questioned that gender balance. This shift suggested that females could no longer have the marginalized heroic roles that that they had held in earlier years. Having two of five Rangers be female suggested that female heroism was *almost* as common as male. However, the Rangers were careful not to tip the balance; female heroes were more common, but they still did not challenge men's dominance.

One way that the threat posed by the female Rangers is reduced is by having all the Rangers appear very similar in their superhero forms. Klugman notes, "The Power Rangers in their supernatural mode look identical, except for the colors of their outfits and the shapes of their masks."[41] It is difficult to determine the gender of Rangers as toys since the same mold is often used for males and females; the only difference is the color of the helmet. More recent lines of Rangers used a more feminine form for the females, but the differences are slight. Thus, the interchangeable forms make the addition of females less noticeable than they might have been otherwise.

Another way that the threat posed by the female Rangers to gender norms is mitigated is by having the female figures in the United States always be pink and yellow, while the male figures are black, blue, red, green, and white. Despite how many Rangers might come and go over the years, this color distinction does not vary, suggesting an essentialist separation between males and females. It comes as little surprise that the girls' colors are pastel, which suggests that females can be action heroes, but they must not stray too far from traditional femininity. The Power Ranger universe represents a change in traditional gender roles but not a change so broad that a male Ranger could be pink or a female Ranger blue.

Finally, the female Rangers also pose less of a threat to dominant gender norms because they exist in a fantasy world, very different from the realistic universe of the Joes. Fantasy and science fiction have had a long history of accepting tough, heroic women; they are only make believe, so they do not have to be taken too seriously, since they do not offer the same threat to stereotypical female gender roles that a female helicopter pilot does. It comes as little surprise that many female action figures, like the Rangers, exist in the realm of fantasy. For example, Xena, Buffy, and Lara Croft all were popular '90s action figures. They showed a more buff image of womanhood that was reminiscent of the Ripley action figure from the early '90s, but all three of these characters, like the Rangers, were part of an imaginary realm. In addition, the Rangers originated in Japan, and American culture has a greater acceptance for Asian females appearing as tough action-adventure figures. Americans are apt to label such figures as exotic and Other. This is one reason for the acceptance of females as action heroes in the Rangers and other action-adventure teams imported from Asian countries, including the Sailor Moon figures from Japan.

Although their tough image is reduced in a number of ways, the female Rangers still represent a step forward in the toy aisle in how women are portrayed. The female Rangers are every bit as important to the team as are the males. The women are not marginalized in the way that the female G.I. Joes are by being on the edge of the Joe universe. The Rangers demonstrate that females and males can both be heroes. This change, however, is limited by certain gender boundaries, which, even for the Rangers, prove durable.

Toys and Subversion

When we think about the gender-segregated universe of children's toys, including action figures, it is easy to assume the worst. We imagine girls growing up and desiring nothing more than their own pink abodes filled with pink possessions. We imagine boys growing up with the belief that violence is a good answer to any problem. There is no doubt that such stereotyped gender roles have a tremendous influence, but we also have to remember that children can be subversive, playing with toys in ways that do not support gender stereotypes. Cultural critic Susan Willis observes, "Barbie can slide down avalanches just as He-Man can become the inhabitant of a two-story Victorian doll's house."[42] Similarly, Dan Fleming discusses in *Powerplay: Toys as Popular Culture* (1996) how children interact with Barbie and Action Man (the British version of G.I. Joe): "The playing child . . . is not necessarily confined at first to the gendered positions we have identified—Action Man at center stage, Barbie looking on from the wings."[43] Children play with toys in ways that manufacturers never could have imagined. Boys and girls play with toys in subversive ways. Despite such play, it is also important to recognize toys' power to create a gender stereotyped world, one that influences millions of youth as they mature.

Although action figures have undergone tremendous changes in the last few decades, they still teach some conservative lessons about who the hero is. More women are taking up the hero role, but the majority of heroes remain men. The increasing number of women figures suggests that more heroic roles are opening to women, a shift that demonstrates changes in cultural conceptions of the heroic, but this is a slow change. Real women's roles are changing more rapidly than their roles in toys, reflecting the frequently conservative gender ideology conveyed by many mass-market toys.

The changing image of the female action figure has limits. A female figure (or two) is more apt to be included if she is surrounded by a team of male figures. She also might appear in a team of all females, as the Sailor Moon characters do or as a solo woman. These new figures, however, typically do not stray far from certain boundaries. They are typically feminine, attractive, slender, and white. Thus, such figures suggest that it is possible for females to be action heroes only if they fit a certain stereotype. We have to wonder whether this new image remains as difficult for women to obtain as earlier more stereotypically feminine roles in popular culture, since the majority of the world's women fail to meet these stereotypes, whether due to race, ethnicity, body size, or other factors.

Notes

1. For an article that discusses the popularity of action figures in recent years, see Peter Sucio, "Armed and Ready: After Drop in Sales, Action Figures Attempt Comeback at Retail," *Playthings*, September 1, 2001, 44.
2. Karen Benezra, "Toymakers and Animated Friends Take Heroic Steps Toward Girls," *Brandweek*, February 20, 1995, 9.
3. Benezra, 9.
4. Theresa Howard, "Ethnic Superheroes Power Way into Licensing," *USA Today*, June 14, 2001, available at http://www.usatoday.com/money/advertising/2001-06-14-license.htm.
5. John Michlig, *G.I. Joe: The Complete Story of America's Favorite Man of Action* (San Francisco: Chronicle Books, 1998), 182.
6. "Action Girl's Guide to Female Action Figures," April 13, 1999, August 15, 2003, available at http://members.aol.com/sarahdyer.
7. Michlig, 27–28.
8. Jackie Marsh, " 'But I want to fly too!' Girls Add Superhero Play in the Infant Classroom," *Gender and Education* 12, no. 2 (2000): 210.
9. Marsh, 211.
10. Articles that discuss the gender-stereotyped nature of contemporary children's toys and their marketing include Lisa Bannon, "Why Girls and Boys Get Different Toys—'Gender Neutral' Is Out," *Wall Street Journal*, 14 February 2000, B1, and David Volk, "A Pity in Pink," *Chicago Tribune*, June 29, 1997, 3.
11. Gary Cross, *Kids' Stuff: Toys and the Changing World of American Childhood* (Cambridge, MA: Harvard University Press, 1997), 7.
12. Toy Industry Association, Inc., Annual Sales 1996–2000, January 23, 2003, available at http://www.toy-tia.org/industry/statistics/sales.html.
13. Laura Berman agrees that a deep gap exists between boys and girls in the world of toys. She writes, "From a tender age, boys and girls are recognized as distinct species, each already embedded with its own culture, color preferences and play interests. . . . Neither would be caught dead playing with the other's color coded toys." See Laura Berman, "Toying Around with the Future of Gender: Girls Think Pink, and Boys Think Action," *Detroit News and Detroit Free Press*, February 16, 1991, C1.
14. Stephen Kline, *Out of the Garden: Toys, TV, and Children's Culture in the Age of Marketing* (London: Verso, 1993), 341.
15. Even toys' design conveys lessons about gender. Barbie and other fashion dolls have few joints, so such figures are best suited for display. They are poorly prepared for action. G.I. Joe and other similar action figures are specially designed with joints and flexible grips, so that they are ready for action at any time. Karen Klugman observes, "John Berger's observation about gender manifestation in visual arts, that 'men act and women appear' . . . applies to children's dolls as well. With guns, swords, . . . and sticks of dynamite, action figures for boys reinforce Berger's claim. . . . Jointed at the elbow as well as the shoulder and at the knees in addition to the hips, the dolls are capable of actually operating their weapons" Karen Klugman, "A Bad Hair Day for G.I. Joe," in *Girls, Boys, Books, Toys: Gender in Children's Literature and Culture*, ed. Beverly Lyon Clark and Margaret R. Higonnet (Baltimore, MD: Johns Hopkins University

Press, 1999), 171. Toy design carries important lessons about how boys and girls are supposed to perform their gender roles.

16. Klugman, 174.

17. Klugman, 182.

18. Other studies that focus on children's culture and gender issues include Catherine Driscoll, *Girls: Feminine Adolescence in Popular Culture and Cultural Theory* (New York: Columbia University Press, 2002); Sherrie A. Inness, *Delinquents and Debutantes: Twentieth-Century American Girls' Culture* (New York: New York University Press, 1998); Henry Jenkins, ed., *The Children's Culture Reader* (New York: New York University Press, 1998); Claudia Nelson and Lynne Vallone, eds., *The Girl's Own: Cultural Histories of the Anglo-American Girl, 1830–1915* (Athens: University of Georgia Press, 1994); Mary F. Rogers, *Barbie Culture* (London: Sage, 1999); Brian Sutton-Smith, *Toys as Culture* (New York: Gardner Press, 1986); and Valerie Walkerdine, *Daddy's Girl: Young Girls and Popular Culture* (Cambridge: Harvard University Press, 1997).

19. Ellen Seiter, *Sold Separately: Parents and Children in Consumer Culture* (New Brunswick: Rutgers University Press, 1993), 50.

20. Seiter, 50.

21. More information about the development of action figures can be found in Robert Young, *Action Figures* (New York: Dillon Press, 1992).

22. For additional information about G.I. Joe's history, see Michlig. For history about the development of the new female G.I. Joe, see Jeremy Derfner, "Plastic Girls with Guns?" *The Herald*, November 6, 1996, available at http://theherald.org/herald/issues/110696/derfner.f.html, and Michael Norris, "Move Over Barbie, Here Comes G.I. Joe," *Pentagram*, August 15, 1997, available at http://dcmilitary.com/army/pentagram/archives/aug15/pt_e08159/.html.

23. Cross, 215.

24. The Bionic Woman Toys Page, August 15, 2003, available at http://www.bionicwomantoys.com/links/home.htm.

25. Cross, 215.

26. Kline, 310.

27. In the late 1960s and early seventies, manufacturers produced a number of other female action figures: Batgirl, Supergirl, Isis, Wonder Woman, and Wondergirl figures from the television show *The Greatest Superheroes* (1972–78); a Police Woman figure from the show *Police Woman*; a Lt. Uhura figure from *Star Trek* (1974); and a Fembot figure from *The Bionic Woman*. This is a partial list. Comic books and cartoon shows were especially fertile breeding grounds for female action heroes in the 1960s, seventies, and eighties, but these females never threatened the dominance of male figures.

28. Ripley was accompanied by another equally tough female action figure, Vasquez (Kenner, 1997), a soldier tough and aggressive enough to take on any man.

29. Stephanie Gutmann, "Woman Helicopter Pilot Joins G.I. Joe's Army," *Plain Dealer*, August 9, 1997, 6F.

30. Gutmann, 6F.

31. "History of G.I. Joe," official G.I. Joe website, January 21, 2003, available at http://www.gijoe.com/authentic/pl/page.history/dn/default.cfm.

32. "Hispanic Joe Goes on Sale," BBC news, August 20, 2001, available at http://news.bbc.co.uk/1/hi/world/americas/1500891.stm.

33. Much of my information about the smaller 33/4-inch Joes came from an excellent website for those interested in the toys' development. See "Complete Guide to G.I. Joe: A Real American Hero," April 2, 2003, available at http://joes.propadeutic.com.
34. "Sexy 'Tomb Raider' Toys Seek Market," *USA Today*, June 21, 2001, available at http://usatoday.com/life/enter/movies/2001-06-21-tomb-raider-toys.htm.
35. "Power Rangers History," Character Products, 2000. October 21, 2002, available at http://www.characterproducts.com.
36. Kenneth R. Clark, "Kid Stuff: A $19 Billion Toy Market," *Chicago Tribune*, February 17, 1995, 1.
37. Power Rangers.
38. "Raving Toy Maniac," RTM News, February 4, 2003, available at http://toymania.com/news/message/24004.shtml.
39. "Raving Toy Maniac."
40. "Raving Toy Maniac."
41. Klugman, 175.
42. Susan Willis, *A Primer for Daily Life* (New York: Routledge, 1999), 31.
43. Dan Fleming, *Powerplay: Toys as Popular Culture* (Manchester: Manchester University Press, 1996), 202. Judy Attfield concurs: "Much could be learnt were we to study how children subvert the ready-made meanings inserted into toys by manufacturers" (86). The world that children create with toys is not always one that the companies could imagine.

Chapter 4

Embodying an Image: Gender, Race, and Sexuality in *La Femme Nikita*

Charlene Tung

"I was falsely accused of a hideous crime and sentenced to life in prison. One night, I was taken from my cell to a place called Section One—the most covert anti-terrorist group on the planet. Their ends are just, but their means are ruthless. If I don't play by their rules, . . . I die." So begins each episode of the television series *La Femme Nikita,* based on the Luc Besson film by the same name. In an unusual turn of events, a woman's voice, rather than a man's, invites us into Section One, a secretive high-tech world of espionage and covert anti-terrorist activities. It is Nikita herself who is the central figure in this dramatic, violent, and morally conflicted world. She is an embodiment of the increasingly visible television and cinema heroines: a physically powerful action figure in the form of a fashion diva. She is verbally and physically assertive, though selectively so. She can protect herself (and others) in hand-to-hand combat, as well as through precise control of handguns. Despite being forced to kill, she is one of the few within Section One who manages to retain her sense of humanity and compassion. She is depicted as a guardian of purity and innocence, the moral conscience of Section One.

That both women and men are drawn to this show is no surprise, especially given its combination of intriguing plot twists, sleek postmodern set designs, high-tech gadgetry, action scenes replete with explosions, and romance between the two leads played by Peta Wilson (Nikita) and Roy Dupuis (Michael).[1] Theirs is a hierarchical relationship; Nikita enters Section One as a recruit and is trained by Michael (a level 5 operative). True to gender stereotypes, she is the emotionally sensitive character who has qualms about killing in cold blood, while he is the contained man of few words who exhorts her to "just do the job." Throughout the series, the two are kept apart alternately by forces beyond their control and their own choice. While the show appeals to both men and women, I wish to focus on women in particular, as Nikita presents a heroine who is both remarkable and quite familiar.

This chapter draws upon a combination of texts, including my own viewing as a fan of the show, online fan discussion boards, classroom discussions at two state universities, and ten structured personal interviews, to address three questions: How might we understand the relationship between violence in *La Femme Nikita* and its possible empowerment for women viewers? In what ways does Nikita portray a kind of bodily transgression of the societal norms regarding women's bodies? In what ways do both the character and show fail to transgress boundaries of gender, race, and sexuality?[2] In short, how must a heroine be constructed in order for her to gain mainstream and popular appeal? And why is the construction so desirable?

Drawing from Martha McCaughey's book *Real Knockouts: The Physical Feminism of Women's Self-Defense* (1997), I suggest that *La Femme Nikita* and its female lead allow for the possibility of a different kind of female embodiment.[3] In McCaughey's study of women "self-defensers" (those women who both teach and participate in self-defense training), she finds that the physicality of self-defense enables women to embody a different code from the norm by encouraging them to replace the notion of women's weakness with the idea of female bodies as active and forceful. Applying this notion to spectatorship, I argue that viewing Nikita's physical strength in action (and the violence that is inherent within that) can be pleasurable and, through its fantasy, can embolden women.

This chapter will also address the complicated relationship between spectatorship pleasure and cultural critiques of gender, race-ethnicity, and sexuality. *Nikita* can be seen as part of what Kent Ono calls "neocolonialism" on television in which the "girl power discourse" is actually about white girl power. Further, as he points out in his article on *Buffy the Vampire Slayer*, "Recuperating white female angst and violent aggressiveness must be understood within the context of a racially gendered perspective . . . in relation to the social centrality of white people and the social marginality of people of color."[4] The surge of new physically powerful, fierce women warriors provides the possibility of an alternative embodiment for women, but they fail to truly transgress gendered boundaries, particularly with regard to race-ethnicity and heteronormativity. *Nikita* and its female star can be constructed as "feminist" and "empowering" for women, yet, at the same time, reinforce stereotypical notions of white womanhood and Western imperialism.

"New" Heroines

Television and mainstream film are increasingly sending images of physically powerful women into our homes and psyches.[5] Recent fare includes a string of "new" heroines in films such as *Tomb Raider*; *Crouching Tiger, Hidden Dragon*; *Charlie's Angels*, and *The Matrix*, as well as in television series such as *Dark Angel*, *Alias*, *Buffy the Vampire Slayer*, *Xena: Warrior Princess*, and, of course, *La Femme Nikita*. While the genre and storylines vary, these heroines all share in common portrayals as "kick-ass" women who can physically power their way out of dangerous situations using any combination of weaponry and martial arts, all the while maintaining traditional signs of femininity.

While tough women characters existed in past decades, the new heroines possess a slightly different combination of brawn and beauty. Similar to earlier heroines such as Emma Peel (Diana Rigg) in *The Avengers* and the stars of the original *Charlie's Angels* television series, these current heroines are fashion divas. For instance, *Nikita* costume designer Laurie Drew describes the aesthetic as "lean and mean."[6] She dressed Nikita (Peta Wilson) in day and evening wear from Prada, Dolce and Gabbana, Armani, Versace, and, for at least one of Nikita's suits, Gucci. In keeping with the sleek style of the sets, the look for Nikita was "spare, severe, and extremely Italian."[7] Shoes, depending on whether she was on a mission or in-house, ranged from stiletto pumps to (usually black leather) boots. Whether in sequined off-shoulder gowns for night-club scenes or all-black rock-climbing outfits for nighttime recon-naissance scenes, Nikita is draped in designer wear (see figure 4.1).

Yet unlike some of the earlier heroines, as in *Charlie's Angels*, heroines of recent years distinctly utilize their bodies as weapons, often shown physically fighting in hand-to-hand combat against *both* male and female characters. The new heroines are accomplished and successful fighters. They portray a self-assuredness and confident reliance on their physical strength to take out the bad guys. They often display "cut" physiques with "just enough" muscle definition. In doing so, they appear to be more in line with images of the 1980s and early 1990s, for example Ripley (Sigourney Weaver) in the *Alien* films and Sarah Conner (Linda

Figure 4.1. Nikita, in typical high fashion, awaits the mission profile

Hamilton) in the *Terminator* films.[8] However, while physically strong, few would ever mistake Ripley or Sarah Conner for fashion divas. And unlike Ripley and Sarah, current heroines aesthetically similar to Nikita are not closely associated with masculinity, either in their muscularity or aggression.[9] The new heroine does not follow previous cinema and television characterizations of tough women who are often portrayed as police officers or lesbians.[10] In short, she is constructed as masculine only in her ability to handle weapons and physically strike and fight back (see figure 4.2). She is depicted as both muscular and (hyper-)sexualized, while maintaining her emotional vulnerability. For better or worse, most of these new heroines are allowed to slightly push the envelope by exhibiting both superior physical strength (relative to earlier tough women characters and male characters they encounter), and traditional femininity or sex appeal. Xena is one of the recent nuanced examples of a heroine who crosses multiple boundaries. As Sherrie A. Inness points out, this heroine does not need male saviors, is physically tougher than the men surrounding her, maintains a connection to other women (Gabrielle), and does not focus

Figure 4.2. Nikita, expertly handling her weapon but maintaining elements of traditional femininity, protects herself and her team members

on gaining male approval or desire.[11] However, Xena remains more an exception than a rule for heroines.

The kick-ass heroines of the late 1990s and 2000s retain certain key characteristics that maintain their acceptability as female heroines and reaffirm male characters' masculinity (and that of male viewers).[12] For example, a tough woman, past and present might have a male father figure in her life who is physically stronger or more competent, or is her love interest. Or she may have "mothering" qualities, be emotionally sensitive, or be the moral conscience of the show. Any of these qualities, singly or in combination, suffices in an effort to retain her femininity in light of her ability to shoot weapons (e.g., Ripley and Sarah Conner in the 1980s), her stoicism and intellect (e.g., Dana Scully in *X-Files* in the 1990s), and her physical strength (e.g., Sydney in *Alias* in the 2000s). So while more recent heroines are surrounded by slick aesthetics and technological advancements in filming and illustrate a higher level of mastery over their bodies and weaponry, the mythical norms of female comportment are only partially called into question. As a scan of the popular media articles on *Nikita* illustrates, focus falls on Nikita's fashion styles and her "sexy" body.[13] Although some writers exhort her "girl power," they rarely attempt to address the character's attraction for women viewers, instead assuming a heterosexual male audience—focusing on Nikita's appeal as an *über*-babe (tall, thin, blond, blue-eyed, pouty lipped).[14] Nikita's construction as heterosexual object is a logical and necessary solution to the "problem" of her physical power. While she is portrayed as a highly capable operative, an expert shot, and physically strong, Michael is her superior in shooting and killing, as well as within the organizational structure of Section One. He is also her unrequited love interest for much of the series. Nevertheless, typical of many of the new heroines, she does challenge ideas of woman's proper comportment as demure, feminine, dainty, nonaggressive, and nonviolent.

One of the hallmarks of the new heroine is her ability to utilize her body to effectively kick, punch, maim, and kill others, particularly men. This kind of physicality inherently involves violence. To the extent that violence is considered integral to the construction of masculinity, and hence antithetical to femininity, the existence of (violent) heroines is in and of itself transgressive. Yet the outcry by many mainstream critics and viewers to *Thelma and Louise* illustrates how female characters who embody and enact violence are seen as stepping outside boundaries of acceptable femininity. Given this response, how do we understand the popularity among female viewers of the violence enacted by Nikita? A closer examination of *Nikita* illustrates, first, how a female protagonist can be accepted as the heroine within a violent world, and, second, how female viewers especially gain pleasure from viewing a particular kind of violent body.

Violence and *La Femme Nikita*

Violence is present in a variety of formations throughout Nikita (see figure 4.3). The premise of Section One as a covert anti-terrorist organization assures that this will be the case. One *Nikita* fan comments, "This show fits into the category of what television executives would probably call fantasy violence."[15] Her use of the term "fantasy violence" draws attention to how *Nikita* is filmed in ways that rarely show realistic human suffering or excessive gore.

Figure 4.3. "Fantasy violence"? Enemies of Section One torture Nikita

The common exceptions are scenes in Section One's torture chamber, where variations of drugs and shock treatment are used to extract intel (information) from captured enemies. There may be sweating and screams on the part of the prisoner, but more often than not, the camera cuts away as Section One torture operatives walk in. Further allowing fans to overlook Nikita's acts of violence is that she does not kill in cold blood, only in self-defense (that is, every mission). She is also not involved in the violent world that is Section One by choice but as one who was falsely accused of a crime and then recruited against her will. Finally, Section One as an anti-terrorist organization relies on a traditional caricature of evil, mostly non-Western Others as enemies. This allows viewers in the West to conveniently overlook or justify the violence.

Turning to female reception of *Nikita*, it is clear that the female star's violence is read as both intriguing and repulsive. Remarks by students in my classes reflect the array of conflicted responses to these new fierce women. After viewing compiled clips of some of these heroines, including *Nikita*, one student asserted, "I don't find images of women fighting empowering at all. Violence is violence. And I don't think it's appropriate or desirable." Another remarked, "I don't want to see women being violent, acting just like men!" As reflected here, the rise in physically assertive and aggressive women onscreen draws attention to the ambivalent relationship between feminism and female aggression.[16] These comments are understandable, particularly from a cultural feminist stance. While reclaiming power and anger has been a therapeutic approach forwarded by some feminists, cultural feminists have focused on honoring what they see as women's caring and nonviolent nature. Cultural feminists generally share the belief in women's natural relational capacity as caregivers, pacifists, and moral guardians.[17] Reinforcing this belief is a set of dominant assumptions (both social and sociobiological) about violence and bodies that indicate that it is more socially acceptable for the male body to enact violence than the female body.[18]

However, complete adherence to cultural feminist arguments against women's capacity for violence has a tendency to reinforce the still-dominant images of passive women. McCaughey writes, "Rejection of all violence leaves no room for women's self defensive violence," nor, I add, any viewing pleasure of women as physically and verbally aggressive.[19] It also tends to name as deviant Others any who do enjoy or experience female aggression. A womanhood wholly constructed as nonviolent, nurturing, and life-affirming disavows alternative embodiments of woman as physically powerful or violent. It does not acknowledge the power available to girls and women through viewing Nikita and other sexy, dangerous women.[20] As Judith Halberstam provocatively suggests, deploying imagery of female (and black or queer) retaliation and revenge may have the possibility of "shift[ing] the experience of fear from the marginalized body to the white male body."[21] She draws attention here to the possibilities that open up for women upon viewing violent heroines. For just as prevalent in the classroom were responses of excitement and approval for the images of fighting women. Typical of this stance, one student exclaimed, "I felt powerful watching those women. I want to learn to move like that!" Another chimed in, "I don't really see it as violence. . . . I would watch these even if they weren't [protecting] themselves. I like their . . . power." What is striking in these and similar expressions is that the violence is overlooked and accepted in favor of the image of the fighting female heroine.

To examine this further, I focus on the question of women's "embodiment," or how women understand, use, and experience their bodies through movement. In paying attention to alternative images, such as Nikita, we can gain insight into "how the social gets lodged inside the body."[22] Nikita and other similarly physically powerful female characters bring with them very real possibilities for how women carry and protect themselves. Fantasy allows women viewers to integrate the violent imagery and female embodiment in a positive fashion.

Fantasy, Embodiment, and Nikita

In multiple ways, fantasy is a central organizing principle for not only *Nikita* but much of the film and television heroines we have seen in recent years. For example, Sydney in *Alias* is a graduate student who is secretly a double agent for the CIA and its enemy operation, SD-6. She jets off to glamorous locales around the world in between school assignments and work obligations. Max of *Dark Angel* is part of a futuristic post-apocalyptic world. Lara Croft in *Tomb Raider* originates from a virtual existence as video-game personae. *La Femme Nikita* also relies on a fantastic realm in numerous ways. Incredible elements abound in each episode—from surreal leaps in real time and place (with no signs of jet lag); to high-tech gadgetry and surveillance techniques; to storylines and events (for example, Michael and Nikita somehow inconspicuously driving through war-torn Croatia in a brand new white Land Rover, he sporting a bright blue ski jacket, she in a stylish fur-lined hood, both surrounded by refugees on foot, dressed in gray and brown rags), to the preponderance of English speakers in every foreign country. Many of this genre's kick-ass female heroines exist only in otherworldly realms. Yet, while the possibility of entering those worlds is highly unlikely, the fantasy of the female fighting body can be transformed into the real (see figure 4.4).

Figure 4.4. Ready to defend herself, Nikita's stance suggests an alternate embodiment for female viewers

It is this fantasy that carries with it the possibility of destabilizing notions of women's victimization, powerlessness, and physical vulnerability, and in doing so, it is an overwhelmingly tempting proposition. The presence of fantasy elements is central to understanding viewer acceptability of violence. Halberstam, calling on Benedict Anderson's notion of "imagined communities," suggests that "imagined violence" is crucial in understanding the transgressive possibilities of disruptive images. She defines this as "the fantasy of unsanctioned eruptions of aggression from the wrong people, of the wrong skin, the wrong sexuality, the wrong gender."[23] The potential for violent response, as illustrated by Nikita, not only empowers women but also provides the possibility of an imagined fear on the part of the would-be attacker. This begins to break down the dominant idea that a woman cannot or will not fight back to save herself and others.

Within *Nikita*'s fantasy and its subsequent impact on women's desires and understandings of themselves, we can begin to unravel the strands of contradictory impulses. It is not simply the fantasy of having Nikita's hyperfit body (a "killer body" in more ways than one) that is alluring. It is the fantasy of a female fully embodying and utilizing her physical strength that speaks to many women who view Nikita as "her own arsenal: a breathing, organic weapon of kicks and karate blows."[24] While it is true that what Nikita does is pure fantasy on one level, on another, she (or a stunt double) is very much moving her body in such a way as to successfully physically defend and assert herself.[25] One female fan explained to me, "Just seeing [Nikita] run, take cover, shoot, and protect herself . . . to see her moving with so much strength and assurance, is exciting!" Another remarked, "I like to imagine I am Nikita—that I can move like Nikita—have her body of course, but also that physical power to hold and shoot guns and knock someone out."[26] Viewing Nikita move in a physically assertive manner enforces imagined possibilities at the bodily level that can then be acted out in the real world. Against the reality of women as victims of violent crimes, such fantastical images are significant.

Moving images of physically powerful women are part of the "discourse that challenges traditional views and creates a new female body."[27] One female fan online explained, "[After watching

Nikita], I'm also trying to be more assertive in life in general. I'm not going to literally twist someone's arm or threaten them when I want things done my way, but there's nothing wrong with standing up for yourself when it's necessary."[28] She illustrates how Nikita enables women to imagine alternative bodily schemas. Imagined violence does not advocate female aggression per se, but it does, as Halberstam suggests, disrupt the "assumed relationship between women and passivity or feminism and pacifism."[29] Through Nikita, women are given the possibility for a new embodiment, one that speaks against the dominant media imagery of women as inherently physically weak, as objects of male desire and in need of male protection. This can indeed contribute toward women living lives in ways other than the social script assumes.[30]

However, despite the transgressive possibilities described above, the depictions remain contained within boundaries of certain gendered and racialized discourses. Just as female-enacted violence may be more acceptable given certain storylines (protecting one's self, fighting evil, or saving the world), the female body's acceptability as a heroine is similarly bounded. The fantasy of the physically powerful female body is desirable and acceptable precisely because it is a particular kind of female body, one that is not only gendered but also raced and sexed as well.

Constructing the Acceptable Fighting Female

The acceptable fighting female must fit into pre-existing tropes. By taking into account race, sexuality, and nation, it is clear that *Nikita* reinscribes notions of Western and white heteronormative superiority. That "West-is-Best" is communicated on multiple levels. For example, Nikita's work for a Western-based anti-terrorist organization feeds "naturally" into "blasé killing of 'the Other.'"[31] Section One is constructed, through language, dress, physical location, and storylines, as representing the West. Terrorists never emerge from within the United States or allied nations but from "rogue" splinter groups from unstable regimes in Eastern Europe, Africa, Asia, and the Middle East. As a covert anti-terrorist organization that even the CIA turns to for assistance, Section One is portrayed as the most effective, wide-reaching organization, with its operatives constantly being sent to locations around the world. While Nikita may continuously question the killing Section One engages in, the viewers do not. We are to see that Section One is the only thing between us (the West) and worldwide chaos. Taken from this perspective, the show is anything but transgressive, relying as it does on Western imperialist discourses.

Further, Nikita is constructed as the embodiment of Western heterosexual fantasy while not surprisingly, the narrative reinforces a compulsory heterosexuality.[32] *Nikita*'s almost exclusively male writers follow a standard formula that builds romantic tension between male and female leads and, in particular, incorporates an outside force that keeps them apart.[33] As the series premise requires, Michael and Nikita cannot have a "normal" relationship because they do not live in a normal world where free will exists. The writers want viewers to want the consummation of Nikita and Michael's relationship. True to form, the central figures and their relationship-that-can-never-be was continually cited by female fans as a major appeal of the show.[34]

With few exceptions throughout their relationship, Michael remains in control literally and figuratively, not only as her superior on missions but as her sexual partner. In the beginning of season two, the two consummate their relationship for the first time. However, they must keep their relationship hidden from Section One. In numerous episodes, he literally has to hold her off of him as she leans forward with yearning. He exudes control not only of himself but also of her. In "Approaching Zero," when she says, "I can't wait to be with you anymore," he bluntly tells her to "Get over it." He is the quintessential Rational Man, in control of both his body and emotions. He is more cognizant of the risks, deciding when, where, and under what conditions the two can act on their desires. Nikita remains overly emotional and, reflecting the heterosexual male fantasy, unable to control her desires.

Yet at the end of season four, and into the final season, the institutional power in Nikita and Michael's relationship experiences a major shift. Nikita triumphs over all of Section One when she is revealed as a spy who has been secretly collecting information for the past three years in order to destroy Section One.

Arguably, this is one of the few moments when she seems fully in control of her own destiny, let alone her relationship with Michael. In this somewhat tantalizing turn of events, she rises to power and orders the cancellation (death) of Michael through a suicide mission. She eventually helps him to escape, but not without coldly asserting, "I never loved you."

In this, Nikita's possibly crowning moment, many *Nikita* fans breathed a collective gasp of outrage and betrayal, a blow to the love fantasy of Michael and Nikita together forever. Judging from online fan sites and the letters to Warner Brothers and the USA Network, many fans were furious with the ending. In large part due to tremendous fan support and organizing, *Nikita* was brought back for a final eight episodes and a new ending was rewritten to culminate in a more "acceptable" conclusion in which Michael and Nikita both profess their love for each other.[35] This was a testament to the success of the heteronormative narrative throughout the series.

In the final season, while no wedding actually takes place, marriage as the ideal romantic ending remains. This is insinuated in the final season's reunion scene between Michael and Nikita, which takes place at a church. She is clothed in a long black leather coat, fitted at the bodice, draping down much like a wedding gown. It sweeps the ground as she proceeds down the aisle. He, as symbolic groom, is dressed in black and silently enters from the side of the altar. She asks, "You want to do this [return to Section]?" He replies, "I do." The entire scene is written and performed to conjure up images of a wedding for him and her, once again speaking to the normative heterosexual romance that "naturally" concludes with marriage.

Finally, the compulsory heterosexuality inherent in the Michael–Nikita storyline makes recognition of a queer desire difficult. Marilyn Farwell, author of *Heterosexual Plots and Lesbian Narratives*, points out that the traditional narrative structure, with a hierarchical relationship between male and female as the foundation (similar to Michael and Nikita), makes a storyline featuring primary bonding between two women a logical impossibility.[36] With the exception of Madeline, who is Nikita's female superior and was originally portrayed through a mother–daughter dynamic, all other main characters in *Nikita* are male. Most female guest characters with substantial parts are written, to some extent, as Nikita's competition for Michael's attention.

Race and Sexuality in *La Femme Nikita*

Similar to other fierce female heroines, Nikita is acceptable as a heroine precisely because she does not challenge gender norms too much. Further, it is important to note that the casting of blond, blue-eyed Australian actress Peta Wilson also fails to transgress racial and ethnic constructions of who best typifies a heroine. Nikita then, serves to function as part of an ideological apparatus that favors and maintains a particular kind of white Western heroine. Viewership within a Western context ensures that pre-existing stereotypes of race and ethnicity are what images of fighting heroines play against and through. For example, contributing to her ability to be seen as a heroine in the context of the Western imperialist discourse forwarded in *Nikita* is the fact that Wilson is not marked as "foreign" either through skin tone or (non-Western) accent. Further, she can be seen as transgressive in her violence and assertiveness only against the background assumption that "woman" is normally and naturally nonviolent. Yet if we take into consideration racialized stereotypes, it becomes clear this assumption is held primarily with regard to middle- or upper-class white women. This section of the chapter expands on the racialized heroine, arguing that this new womanhood typified through Nikita and other popular kick-ass heroines is constrained by race, ethnicity, and sexuality. The mass and popular acceptance of the new heroine is predicated in many ways not only on her heterosexuality and her maintenance of femininity but also on her whiteness. In particular, I draw attention to two categories of racial difference, Asianness and blackness, as they intersect with *Nikita*.

Depictions of women of color exist in relation to stereotypes that concurrently implicate both race and sexuality. Historically and to this day, women of color have been framed outside of American society's boundaries of acceptable womanhood and hence constructed as presumably failed women.[37] Through the experience of slavery in the United States and elsewhere, black women have been constructed in opposition to white women. For example, Kimberly Springer writes, "African Americans are thought to be always already violent due to their 'savage' ancestry. . . . When it comes to women, race, and violence, white North American women are assumed to have been provoked to violence; they are not permitted violent impulses."[38] Already configured as oppositional to white womanhood, black women's physically powerful and violent bodies onscreen are not read identically to white women's bodies. So what appears transgressive for the white female heroine may not be so for the black female heroine. Further, not only does violence mark black female bodies as unfeminine, but it renders their sexuality suspect as well. Black women have traditionally been typified through sexual deviance and excess, wantonness, and bestial desire, as the "Jezebel." Other dominant filmic representations of African American women reflect European American views of black women as the "Mammy" (loyal motherly slave to master's children) and, more recently, the "Sapphire" (or emasculating matriarch).[39]

Against such a backdrop, the physically powerful black woman resonates differently than her white counterpart within the collective imagination. In addition to referencing violence, images of physically strong black women recall a history of enslaved black women's work, disrupting notions of female physical weakness and dependence on men. In her controversial 1851 speech at one of the earliest women's rights conventions, Sojourner Truth remarked, "I have plowed and gathered into barns and no man could heed me—and ain't I a woman?"[40] Her words draw attention to the reality that poor and working-class women of all colors have always engaged in hard manual labor. She reflects back the absurdity and contradiction inherent within society's racialized ideology regarding women's proper space (in the literal and figurative home) and comportment (prim, proper, protected). The notion of a physically weak and vulnerable woman in need of male protection is not readily assumed about black, poor, or working-class women. Hence, images of the physically powerful black female body resonate against a different cultural setting than the physically "fierce" white body of Nikita.

Furthermore, television and movies have long provided imagery of what could be termed tough and violent black women. Television and movies rely on depictions of tough black women as prostitutes, "tough-talking" addicts, criminals, or single mothers fighting the system.[41] Unlike depictions of tough white women, little attention is paid to maintaining the emotional vulnerability of the woman. There is ostensibly no need to uphold or tread lightly so as not to overwhelm white middle-class norms of womanhood, since black women are perceived to already be outside of this construction.

Violence and black womanhood have been constructed in tandem. Marguerite Rippy, in her analysis of black film star Dorothy Dandridge points out that many African American women in film have been positioned as objects that provoke not only male desire but, moreover, destructive violence.[42] Media images of black women as tough are read against the backdrop of violence against black women's bodies both cinematically and in real life. Standing up for herself, fighting back, is not in the name of the same virtuosity, domesticity, purity, and innocence portrayed by the white kick-ass woman. Given this, a fierce kick-ass black woman is more likely read as hyperaggressive, wild, untamable, and vicious rather than as an admirable warrior woman breaking down age-old stereotypes that white women invoke. Unlike the characterization of Nikita and other white heroines, who are read as expanding conceptions of femininity, a physically fit and strong black woman furthers the characterization of the failed nonwoman.

Moreover, black female bodies have stood for both sexual and racial difference in comparison with normative white heterosexual women. In this way, popular characterizations of tough women as lesbians converge with racial stereotypes. Race, criminality, and lesbianism have often been associated in the popular and biological scientific imagination. Beginning in the early nineteenth century, both criminologists and popular culture depicted lesbian inmates as physically menacing and, early on, as primarily black.[43] To the extent that both lesbians and black women's sexuality are already characterized as deviant and voracious, the black lesbian body becomes, ironically, acceptable to viewers.[44] She is also already linked to masculinity (physical strength) and toughness in a way that white fierce women are not.

Shifting to the construction of women of color within *Nikita*, we find that there are only a handful cast as supporting characters in the five seasons (96 episodes). Examining a few of those portrayals provides some insight into how race, gender, and sexuality intersect in the show. Reflecting stereotypes of race and sexuality, two of the few episodes that incorporate black women as substantial supporting characters have lesbian sexual overtones. While Nikita is constructed as heterosexual through her relationship with Michael, the only scenes that hint at bisexuality or lesbianism involve black women. Illustrating this portrayal of black (lesbian) women are scenes from the episode "Soul Sacrifice," in which the character Terry is played by a black actress. In one scene, Nikita and Terry, undercover, enter a nightclub as a pseudoqueer couple. Nikita's arm is draped nonchalantly yet possessively over Terry's shoulders as they saunter in. Nikita's costume can be read as "drag" with her cowboy hat, boots, and spurs, while Terry is a typically hypersexualized "Jezebel" in a tight push-up bustier. Similarly, in the episode "Open Heart," the sexually deviant (lesbian) angry-black-woman script is played out. Taking cues from the lesbian women-in-prison genre, when Nikita goes undercover in an all-women prison, we are introduced to Jenna, a black woman who is clearly the "lead bitch" in the prison. She is cast as the aggressor, acting upon her desire through caresses and kisses after Nikita takes the fall for her in a nighttime reconnaissance assignment within the prison. Nikita is the innocent who is seduced, the ill-fated Section operative who must play along for the sake of the mission. In this way, the sexual purity of Nikita (and white womanhood) remains intact. The episode parallels Freedman's analysis of early 1900s writings on prison lesbians: "These accounts usually represented African-American women prisoners as masculine or aggressive and their white lovers as 'normal' feminine women who would return to heterosexual relations upon release from prison."[45] In short, in "Open Heart" the casting serves to put off the white woman's lesbian possibility.[46] By the end, we learn that Jenna has used Nikita (sexually and emotionally) as a ploy in order to be taken back to Section headquarters in order to blow up the building. Not only is Jenna portrayed as a cold and callous lesbian, but also she turns out to be a literal human time bomb. She becomes the epitome of the "explosive" black woman, furthering not only racialized stereotypes of black women and violence but also recent cinematic trends depicting the lesbian as killer.[47]

"Open Heart" has been read by some as signaling a free play of sexuality on the part of Nikita. Seen through a heterosexual male gaze, she can be viewed as "a fashion plate with a runway walk who sexually swings both ways." This writer points to how the camera focuses in on a "close-up tongue-twining kiss" between Nikita and Jenna.[48] While this scene could be taken as suggestive of Nikita's queerness, in the context of the rest of the show, it reflects the heterosexual male voyeuristic fantasy of lesbian lovers in action. Nikita's acceptability as bisexual/lesbian/queer is not only fed by heterosexual male fantasy, which assumes a traditionally feminine "lipstick" lesbian, but by the believability of the sexually voracious and aggressive black lesbian who seduces her. Overlooking their raced bodies is the only way that Nikita's lesbian possibility can be celebrated or relished. Without those preconditions, viewers heavily invested in the Michael–Nikita romance would be outraged indeed.

Both black and Asian/Asian American women's portrayals occupy a cultural space not held by white women.[49] Much like the aggressive and tough black female, the Asian female body finds a ready niche in the Western imagination. Independent films notwithstanding, little has changed since 1989, when filmmaker Renee Tajima-Peña described images of Asian/Asian American women as coming in two forms: the lotus blossom baby and the dragon lady. The lotus blossom baby (also known as china doll or geisha girl) refers to the stereotypical representations of Asian women as shy, passive, and/or sexually exotic beauties. The dragon lady is ruthless, cold, and unforgiving—often she is a madame or an evil seductress. Cultural stereotypes, informed by United States militarism, already figure the Asian female body as both masculine (female Fu Manchu) and hyperfeminine (the Suzy Wong prostitute).[50]

Portrayals of tough Asian women, such as Jen (Zhang Ziyi) and Shu-Lien (Michelle Yeoh) of *Crouching Tiger, Hidden Dragon* or any number of Hong Kong kung-fu films, counter dominant ideas about passive Asian female bodies.[51] As Lynn Lu writes, "Viewing

Asian women as active subjects within the finite constraints of on-screen fantasy can offer valuable clues for resistance to the rigid constraints of real life."[52] Against a cultural milieu in which Asian/Asian American women are portrayed as passive, obedient, and nonthreatening to both white men and women, the Asian woman as martial arts expert renders the Asian woman's body a site through which women can view and desire an alternative embodiment. However, what does it mean that our heroines, outside the martial arts genre, do not in fact have Asian or Asian American bodies?[53]

The Asian/Asian American heroine cannot help but be read differently than the white heroine. While Asian heroines within the kung fu genre provide alternative embodiments on one level, on another, they reinscribe notions of the "natural" connection between martial arts and Asian bodies. And although ninjas are commonly associated with Asian males, the popular imagery of Asian males as emasculated and feminized vis a vis white male characters, allows the dragon lady/lotus blossom (Asian female) to shift seamlessly into the ninja (Asian male) stereotypes.[54] The kick-ass Asian/Asian American woman is not so transgressive in this light because she fits neatly into a preexisting cultural stereotype. Western viewers fully accept and expect to see an Asian/Asian American woman capable of martial arts.

The fact that we see physically powerful Asian/Asian American women's bodies primarily in martial arts films indicates the limits upon which an Asian heroine is accepted. Screened in a Western context, these women (and the films themselves) are often exoticized. Take, for example, Crouching Tiger, Hidden Dragon. While media critics focused on the women's "martial arts" finesse, they drew attention not to the force of it but rather to its "dance-like" or "balletic" nature.[55] Rather than being judged for her physical strength, Zhang Ziyi was described as "porcelain," while she and Michelle Yeoh were interchangeably "lithe."[56] Even Western critics who called the film "feminist" couched their judgment within Western imperialist language. Lisa Schwarzbaum, writing for Entertainment Weekly, stated that Crouching Tiger, Hidden Dragon, "advances a revolutionary agenda of female equality, in a country that traditionally—officially—undervalues females."[57] Another movie critic wrote, "In some respects, Crouching Tiger,

Hidden Dragon could be considered a feminist film, since it depicts powerful female characters at a time in history when society looked upon women as little more than property."[58] Without engaging here in a close reading or critique of the film's feminism, what is striking about such commentary is that the film is dubbed "feminist" not by virtue of the women's physical strength but on the basis of a perspective of Chinese society as backward and steeped in patriarchal values and institutions (and an assumption that the United States and other countries are not).[59] The women's physical fierceness is not the focus largely because, through a Western gaze, martial artistry tends to map smoothly onto Asian/Asian American women's bodies. Hence, their transgression becomes defined through their perceived foreignness compared to the "liberated" white Western female, rather than through their physical power and strength.

A closer examination of Hong Kong kung fu film genre illustrates that even in this limited field of representations for Asian/Asian American female fighters, there exists an inability to reconcile femininity with the "masculine" martial arts. Wendy Arons writes, "For even as [kung fu] films depict women as strong, independent, and capable fighters, they continue to embed such images of women within a context that defines femininity in terms of physical beauty and sexual attractiveness to men."[60] In this way, depictions of female Asian heroines mirror the constraints on white female heroines. The Asian heroine then is acceptable and enticing as a fighter for the very reason that she fails to truly transgress bodily borders. As long as she maintains her femininity, and her foreignness (her connection to martial arts), Western viewers can accept her as heroine.

The other popular understanding of Asian/Asian American women's physical prowess and power is in relation to sexuality. The exotic woman schooled in sexual pleasures commonly emerges in media depictions. One example is the character Ling (Lucy Liu) in the television show *Ally McBeal*. Ling combines the dragon lady with geisha girl in her portrayal of a manipulative girlfriend who uses her long black hair and dripping candle wax to seduce her boyfriend. Actress Peta Wilson's established imagery does not play against dragon lady/ninja stereotypes, which threaten to undermine her character's transgressive possibility. If Asian/Asian American women were cast as Nikita-like characters, their imagery would have to contend with additional notions of femininity not read onto white female bodies.

Turning to the casting of Asian or Asian American actresses in *Nikita*, I find that, unlike the few roles utilizing black women, the roles for Asian/Asian American actors tend not to rely on or draw upon ethnic stereotypes for the most part. However, Asian-cast female characters do portray weak hapless women in general, in juxtaposition to Nikita's physical and emotional fortitude. The acceptable configuration for the Asian female in *Nikita* appears to be as either enemy or Michael's love interest. Regarding the former, in three episodes, Asian/Asian American women were minor characters who were connected to terrorist groups or were criminals. As for the latter, in a season one episode, Michael's wife Simone was played by an actress of Asian ethnicity. Yet, having been held captive for three years, she did little more than moan and groan in a cell, eventually killing herself. In another example, an Asian Indian actress was cast for three episodes as Michael's second wife, Elena, and mother of his biracial child. Elena's storyline had her duped, unaware that Michael had been on a deep-cover assignment to marry her in order to get to her terrorist father. Both examples were welcome changes to the show's nearly all-white cast. But while we can catch glimpses of Asian/Asian American actresses every so often as extras, they are generally Section One operatives seated (silently) in the background—rarely physically active on a mission. They are not actors so much as bystanders. These women are not heroines.[61] This absence further enables the fantasy of Nikita's strength and physicality. Her higher status is defined against their silence, invisibility, and inactivity. The absence of such heroines of color reinforces the idea that the heroine must be white.

She's Still My Heroine

Despite awareness of *Nikita*'s shortcomings, I continue to be drawn to it. In the end, can I say that Nikita and the show transgress gender boundaries? It seems clear that we have an image of a powerful woman trained in martial arts and schooled in the effective use of weapons. But, despite having a strong action-oriented and physically fierce central female character, *Nikita* employs a largely heteronormative script in terms of race, gender, and sexuality. The narratives mostly maintain dominant notions of love, romance, and sex, as well as of Western imperialism. Further, the narrative plot lines do not center on Nikita. She is the one who is most in the dark (as are the viewers) as to the real reasons for Michael's behaviors. And a traditional narrative structure focusing on a hierarchical relationship between a dominant male and subordinate female protagonist, as well as heterosexual male fantasies and the romantic ideal of love and marriage, keeps the status quo intact as well. Nevertheless, Nikita and similar female characters have the ability to disrupt gender ideologies at the bodily level. This is true to the extent that women have a visceral response and want to embody that image of her fighting and defending herself.

While I may be critical of the white embodiment of female fierceness, I cannot help but be drawn to it, in lieu of other representations. In light of the limited construction of women of color in media representations, it is difficult to avoid contradictions between spectatorship of popular cultural representations such as *Nikita* and political/cultural critiques. bell hooks points out in an article on black female spectatorship, "The extent to which black women feel devalued, objectified and dehumanized in this society determines the scope and texture of their looking relations."[62] Here she emphasizes that viewing pleasures are rarely uncomplicated. To the extent that I live in a world in which reality and media indicate that women are victims of violent crimes, where Asian American women are largely exoticized, and where female physical weakness is assumed, I am captivated by Nikita's power. This is true despite questions about how race and ethnicity impact the construction of that image and its desirability. The dominant construction of the heroine still fails to speak either to the absence of or the disturbing representations of women of color. For while we increasingly see women portrayed as physically and emotionally strong characters, when we look for more nuanced understandings and representations of women at the intersections of race, class, sexuality, and ethnicity from the television and movie industry, we are often left wanting.

The relative absence of physically strong heroines as central characters in film and television results in a situation in which reception of physically powerful onscreen women may be welcomed over any other internal objections (be it violence, heterosexism, racism, or Western imperialism). In return for withholding the above critiques, viewers can watch Nikita's feats of adventure and courage and receive messages of invincibility, capability, and physical strength. It is a trade-off. Images such as those of Nikita provide women viewers with a model for an intense female physicality rarely seen on screen and, importantly, the possibility of embodying that image.

Notes

1. *Nikita* aired on cable USA Network (formerly known for its coverage of World Wrestling Federation matches) from 1996–2001. *Nikita* reruns found a new home on cable Oxygen Network in fall 2002.
2. These findings are not meant to be representative of all women fans of female heroines or even of *Nikita* but rather to illustrate one mechanism of receiving the images and the factors within the images that may impact audience reception. Thank you to students' in-class discussions from spring 2001 and fall 2002, interviewees, on-line fans, and Frances Early, Kathleen Kennedy, Kris Montgomery, and Sherrie A. Inness for comments on previous drafts.
3. Martha McCaughey, *Real Knockouts: The Physical Feminism of Women's Self-Defense* (New York, NY: New York University Press, 1997).
4. Kent Ono, "To Be a Vampire on Buffy the Vampire Slayer: Race and ('Other') Socially Marginalizing Positions on Horror TV," in *Fantasy Girls: Gender in the New Universe of Science Fiction and Fantasy Television*, ed. Elyce Rae Helford (Lanham, MD: Rowman and Littlefield, 2000), 166.
5. See, for example, John Dempsey, "Femme Leads Earn Piece of the Action: Action Heroines Earn Bigger Ratings," *Variety* (July 14, 1997): 25–27; Michael Ventura, "Warrior Women," *Psychology Today* 31, no. 6 (November–December 1998): 58–62.
6. Betty Goodwin, "Screen Style: La Femme Nikita," *Ultimate TV* (October 1997), available online at http://lfnforever.tripod.com/id11.htm.
7. Ibid.
8. Joel Surnow, *LFN*'s executive story editor/consultant likened Nikita to the women in *Aliens* and the *Terminator* movies. "Oui, Nikita," *Los Angeles Times*, 3 August 1997, available at http://lfnforever.tripod.com/id10.htm.
9. This, despite a storyline illustrating Ripley's mothering "instinct" in *Aliens*.
10. See Yvonne Tasker, *Working Girls: Gender and Sexuality in Popular Cinema* (New York: Routledge, 1998).

11. Sherrie A. Inness, *Tough Girls: Women Warriors and Wonder Women in Popular Culture* (Philadelphia: University of Pennsylvania Press, 1999), 166–168. For more on Xena see Joanne Morreale, "Xena: Warrior Princess as Feminist Camp," *Journal of Popular Culture* 32, no. 2 (1998): 79–87; on the possibility of Xena's lesbianism, see Robin Silverman, "What Xena Giveth, Xena Taketh Away," *The Gay and Lesbian Review Worldwide* 8, no. 15 (2001): 32; Michele Kort, "Xena: Cyberprincess" *The Advocate (The National Gay & Lesbian Newsmagazine)* (March 2, 1999): 24.

12. Inness, 30–49.

13. For example, Alysia Bennett, "Remote Origins of a High-Style Heroine," *The Record Online* (January 2, 1999); Julia Shih, "Sexy Nikita Makes Waves for USA," *Michigan Daily News Online*, available at http://www.pub.umich.edu/daily/1997/apr/04-07-97/arts/arts4.html; see also an online archive of newsarticles at http://lfnforever.tripod.com/id9.htm.

14. For example, Susan Kittenplan, "TV's Girl Power," *Harper's Bazaar* (September 1998): 510–516.

15. Personal interview, June 15, 2001. San Francisco, California.

16. Martha McCaughey, *Real Knockouts: The Physical Feminism of Women's Self-Defense* (New York: New York University Press, 1997), 12.

17. For example, Carol Gilligan, *In a Different Voice: Psychological Theory and Women's Development* (Cambridge: Harvard University Press, 1982); Rosemary Tong, *Feminist Thought* (Boulder: Westview Press, 1998), 45–93.

18. McCaughey, 25.

19. McCaughey, 147.

20. See Debbie Stoller, "Brave New Girls: These TV Heroines Know What Girl Power Really Means," *On The Issues: The Progressive Woman's Quarterly* (fall 1998): 42–45.

21. Judith Halberstam, "Imagined Violence/Queer Violence: Representations of Rage and Resistance" in *Reel Knockouts: Violent Women in the Movies*, ed. Martha McCaughey and Neal King (Austin: University of Texas Press, 2001), 245.

22. McCaughey, 40.

23. Halberstam, 263.

24. Steven Erickson, "The Woman Warrior," *Los Angeles Magazine* (January 2001): 1.

25. Actresses who play these heroines often comment exuberantly on the physicality necessary for the roles. See Robert Abele, "Angelina's Big Adventure: Star of 'Lara Croft: Tomb Raider' Comes Out With Both Guns Blazing," *San Francisco Chronicle*, 10 June 2001, 37.

26. Personal interviews, June 20, 2001. Berkeley, California.

27. McCaughey, xv.

28. Accessed from the message boards at http://www.ljconstantine.com/nikita on July 15, 2001.

29. Halberstam, 263.

30. There are indications that female fans actually are moved to become more physically strong. One online fan wrote, "The main influence of the show, or rather the Nikita character, on me is that it finally gave me the push I needed to start martial arts." Accessed at http://www.ljconstantine.com/nikita on July 15, 2001.

31. Personal interview with fan, June 15, 2001. San Francisco, California.
32. See Adrienne Rich, "Compulsory Heterosexuality and Lesbian Existence," *Signs: Journal of Women in Culture and Society* 5, no. 4 (1980), 631–660.
33. Out of a total of 96 episodes, only 5 episodes were written and/or directed by a woman.
34. See the message boards at http://www.petawilson-online.com, and http://lfnforever.tripod.com.
35. USA Network's offices received more than 25,000 letters and e-mails from 40 countries after the fourth season of *LFN* concluded. Fans also bought a full-page advertisement in the *Hollywood Reporter* protesting the end and calling for another season. The network responded with a truncated eight-episode season. Porter Anderson, "Career that Won't Quit: La Femme Again." CNN, January 1, 2001, available online at http://www.petawilson.com/articles/.
36. Marilyn Farwell, *Heterosexual Plots and Lesbian Narratives* (New York: New York University Press, 1996), 15–16.
37. See Carrol Smith-Rosenberg, *Disorderly Conduct: Visions of Gender in Victorian America* (New York: Oxford University Press, 1986), 265.
38. Kimberly Springer, "Waiting to Set It Off: African-American Women and the Sapphire Fixation," in *Reel Knockouts: Violent Women in the Movies*, ed. Martha McCaughey and Neal King (Austin: University of Texas Press, 2001), 174.
39. Robyn Weigman, "Black Bodies/American Commodities: Gender, Race, and the Bourgeois Ideal in Contemporary Film," in *Unspeakable Images: Ethnicity and the American Cinema*, ed. Lester Friedman (Urbana: University of Illinois Press, 1991), 313; Leith Mullings, "Images, Ideology, and Women of Color," in *Women of Color in U.S. Society*, ed. Maxine Baca Zinn and Bonnie Thornton Dill (Philadelphia: Temple University Press, 1995), 258.
40. Sojourner Truth, "Sojourner Truth Speaks, 1851," in *Early American Women: A Documentary History, 1600–1900*, 2d. ed., ed. Nancy Woloch (New York: McGraw-Hill, 2001), 274–277.
41. Examples include Pam Grier as Foxy Brown and the four women of *Set It Off*, especially Queen Latifah's Cleo. For discussion of Cleo, see Springer, 178–181.
42. Marguerite Rippy, "Commodity, Tragedy, and Desire: Female Sexuality and Blackness in the Iconography of Dorothy Dandridge," in *Classic Hollywood, Classic Whiteness*, ed. Daniel Bernardi (Minneapolis: University of Minnesota, 2001), 178–209.
43. Estelle Freedman, "The Prison Lesbian: Race, Class and the Construction of the Aggressive Female Homosexual, 1915–1965," *Feminist Studies* 22, no. 2 (1996): 397–424.
44. For more on representations of black lesbians in film, see Laura Sullivan, "Chasing Fae: *The Watermelon Woman* and the Black Lesbian Possibility," *Callaloo* 23, no. 1 (2000): 448–460.
45. Freedman, 400.
46. See Judith Mayne, *Framed: Lesbians, Feminists, and Media Culture* (Minneapolis: University of Minnesota Press, 2000), 115–145.
47. Mayne, 23.
48. Ventura, 58–59.
49. I use "Asian/Asian American" to be inclusive of and cognizant of the conflation between the two terms.

50. See Yen Espiritu, *Asian American Women and Men: Race, Love and Labor* (Philadelphia: Temple University Press, 1995), 86–107; and Deborah Gee's film *Slaying the Dragon*, 1988.

51. *The Heroic Trio* (1992) and *Wing Chun* (1994) are two of the more notable Hong Kong kung-fu films with female heroines.

52. Lynn Lu, "Critical Visions: The Representation and Resistance of Asian Women," in *Dragon Ladies: Asian American Feminists Breathe Fire*, ed. Sonia Shah (Boston: Beacon Press, 1997), 26.

53. One recent exception is actress Lucy Liu as Sever in *Ecks vs. Sever* (2002).

54. For more on Asian male imagery in films see Gina Marchetti, *Romance and the "Yellow Peril": Race, Sex, and Discursive Strategy in Hollywood Fiction* (Berkeley: UC Press, 1993).

55. See movie critic Roger Ebert's review, for example. "Crouching Tiger, Hidden Dragon," *Chicago Sun-Times*, December 22, 2000, available online at http://www.Suntimes.com/ebert/ebert_reviews/2000/12/122211.html. For a sampling of similar commentary, see the Sony Pictures website for the film at http://www.sonypictures.com/cthv/crouchingtiger/sony_rev_quot.htm.

56. See, for example Gina Carbone, "Crouching Tiger, a Triumphant Leap Forward," *The Portsmouth Herald*, January 18, 2001, available online at http://www. seacoastonline.com/calendar/1_18c_ent.htm; and Lisa Schwarzbaum, "Crouching Tiger, Hidden Dragon," *Entertainment Weekly*, November 29, 2000, available online at http://www.ew.com/ew/article/review/movie/0,6115,89945~1|13483||0~00.html

57. Schwarzbaum, "Crouching Tiger."

58. Online review for The Cinema Laser website, available at http://www.thecinemalaser.com/dvd2/reviews/crouching-tiger-hidden-dragon-dvd.htm.

59. For critiques of the Western media's celebration of the film's "feminism," see Oliver Wang, "Women Warriors," popmatters.com, available at http://www.popmatters.com/film/reviews/c/crouching-tiger.html; and Jerome Yuan, "Where's the Tiger? Where's the Dragon?," Asian American Movement eZine, available at http://www.aamovement.net/art_culture/filmreviews/tigerdragon2.html. Both sites accessed December 18, 2002.

60. Wendy Arons, "If Her Stunning Beauty Doesn't Bring You To Your Knees, Her Deadly Drop Kick Will," in *Reel Knockouts: Violent Women in the Movies*, ed. Martha McCaughey and Neal King (Austin: University of Texas Press, 2001), 27–51.

61. One exception is the Asian/Asian American actress playing Jasmine (whose name recalls the lotus blossom, incidentally), part of a group of teenage Section recruits, a twice-recurring role in seasons four and five.

62. bell hooks, "The Oppositional Gaze: Black Female Spectators," *Reel to Real: Race, Sex and Class at the Movies* (New York: Routledge, 1996), 209.

Chapter 5

Throwing Down the Gauntlet: Defiant Women, Decadent Men, Objects of Power, and *Witchblade*

David Greven

The TNT network sci-fi/fantasy series *Witchblade* constructs a great tough woman—a woman who defies masculinist power while wielding it—in its action heroine Sarah Pezzini (Yancy Butler), a tough New York City homicide detective. Lynda Carter's 1970s Wonder Woman may have had her bullet-deflecting bracelets, but Sarah Pezzini has something even more inventive and powerful: the titular Witchblade, a bracelet with a stone center that seethes to liquid-fire life when it grants her premonitory glimpses into the murders she investigates with the help of her partner, Danny, and the rookie cop they are training, Jake. When Sarah is in danger, the bracelet transforms into an ancient gauntlet, an arm-length metal sheath that deflects enemy fire as its protruding blade punctures foes. In addition to its many other skills, the Blade is a great choreographer, allowing her to leap and hurtle through the air with strobe-lit glamour as bullets ricochet off the gleaming, lustrous metal. When the Witchblade is activated, she throws down a metaphorical and a literal gauntlet against her enemies, who are usually but not always male. Rather, Sarah *threw* down the gauntlet: Like *Dark Angel*, *Witchblade* was abruptly cancelled in 2002 after two seemingly successful seasons; *Birds of Prey* lasted only a few weeks before it, too, was cancelled. These surprising and multiple cancellations of action heroine television shows suggests that, though action heroines dominate genre TV, their fierce vitality masks a justifiable uncertainty about their futures.

As if in response to her increasing vulnerability in the rapidly transforming field of genre-TV programming, the action heroine, so recently elected as a popular culture fixture, has been undergoing some radical changes. While Dana Scully and Captain Kathryn Janeway, part of an earlier wave of tough-women heroines, were irreducibly human despite their respectively occult and sci-fi trappings, the TV action heroine is increasingly removed from the category of the merely human. If the trends of action heroine shows are any indication, the action heroine is rapidly losing her hold on the category of the human, growing more prevalently *meta*human. The term "metahuman" is introduced on *Birds of Prey* by crime-fighting wheelchair-bound cyber-genius Oracle (formerly known as Batgirl) to describe the more-than-human genetic traits of her young ward, the Huntress; the term aptly and collectively describes the new race of women warriors.

Perhaps the action heroine who instigated this trend toward metahumanity is the cloned Ellen Ripley of *Alien: Resurrection* (1997), in whom both human and acid alien blood commingle. The Huntress of *Birds of Prey* is the daughter of Batman and Catwoman; she possesses feline traits, eyes that narrow into panther's slits as jaguar cries suffuse the soundtrack. *Dark Angel*'s Max has in her genetic mix feline DNA, which manifests itself as the periodic sexual heat that overwhelms her. Buffy is a born slayer, the sympathetic doppelganger to the nightshade demons she harvests and reaps. *Alias*'s Sydney Bristow (Jennifer Garner), deserves inclusion in this weird family of hybrid women because, while Sydney, the undercover CIA agent working to topple the evil pseudo-CIA organization SD6, is ostensibly human, she has been linked to uncanny intrigue, as the seeming realization of a fictional Renaissance prophet/inventor's prediction that a particular woman will "render the greatest power unto utter desolation." And the blood of an ancient line of warrior women flows through Sarah Pezzini's metahuman veins.

One way of understanding the tough woman of action heroine shows is that she exposes with especially vivid clarity the complex uncertainties—the blurry instability—of current cultural understandings of gender and sexuality. In this regard, the tough woman, especially in her metahuman defiance of even categorization by species, serves as a helpful example of the fluidity of sexual and gendered roles in our "posthuman" moment. Neither quite male nor female, hero nor heroine, animal nor human, immortal nor mortal, the tough woman of the action heroine genre boldly resists a network of categorizing programs, remaining intransigently unclassifiable. In this manner, she resembles the witches who cause such consternation in *Macbeth*: Bearded, they "should be women" but resemble men, while wielding a power Macbeth foolishly believes he can control (1.3.45).[1] (We will return to *Witchblade*'s associations with *Macbeth*.) Though the increasing tendency toward metahumanity in the TV tough woman suggests a desire to transcend those problematic old categories of gender and sexuality, in this chapter I will be chiefly exploring the ways in which the tough woman-witch of *Witchblade* complicates gendered and sexual categorizations.

My own identification as a gay male with action heroines, my ardor for Jaime Sommers, Captain Janeway, Sarah Pezzini, and many other similarly marvellous women of wonder, leads me to hope that tough women *do* represent a positively radical force in our culture.[2] On a personal level, I have always felt a special kinship with and ecstatic revelry in the figure of the action heroine. One could argue, as well, that the action heroine genre *itself* represents a transgressive assault on the misogynistic and homophobic codes of our heteronormative, racist, misogynistic culture.[3] In part, my chapter demonstrates that identification with a genre, such as the action heroine show, itself a battleground for ideological impulses, produces an irresolvably conflicted response in the viewer.[4] As a result, my treatment of *Witchblade* is simultaneously celebratory and condemnatory. My investigation of *Witchblade*, especially in its comparison of the show's two seasons, each very distinct in tone and agenda, explores both the exhilarating and the excruciating possibilities inherent within the construction of the tough woman-action heroine. This essay begins with a consideration of both the potential radicalism in and reactionary implications of *Witchblade*'s newfangled construction of the tough woman as both ancient warrior and modern woman, a collapse of "recovered" historical heroism and postfeminist womanhood. In this regard, this chapter focuses on certain key themes. *Witchblade* makes innovative uses of the historical and pop-cultural figure of the witch. This essay considers the ways in which the series reimagines the witch, the embodiment of male castration anxieties, as a tough woman. *Witchblade* ultimately casts Sarah in the role of scourge of nonnormative (in other words, queer) men. This chapter considers, then, the tough woman's relationship to manhood generally. Does the tough woman exist not only to challenge men but also to shame them for their inadequately realized manhood? Adding further complications, we have to consider the matter of Sarah's highly legible queerness on the show: If, as I do, you see her as a queer heroine, how does her disciplinary disdain for and retaliation against "decadent" men inform her status as a tough and potentially queer woman? As I will also argue, Sarah is deployed as a disciplinary weapon against deviant women, as well. How can she be a queer character if her chief function is, eventually, the annihilation of her fellow queers?

The Witchblade is an unwieldy if sexy extrusion of warring gendered anxieties, symbols, and powers; both masculine and feminine in form and affect, it refuses one gendered identity. Does the Witchblade grant Sarah toughness, or does her toughness manifest itself as the Witchblade (see figure 5.1)? Does the Witchblade, drawn to Sarah precisely because, in terms set by the series, she embodies the "stronger" sex, merely fulfill her innate womanly toughness—or does it instead imbue her with the fleeting *illusion* of toughness? Does it symbolize her tough-woman power, or does it only temporarily grant such power to her? Does the Witchblade make Sarah feel like a natural woman, or is it a part of her because she *is* one? The complexities of her weapon match the gendered complexities of Sarah's construction as tough woman and action heroine: Is the tough woman "really" a male hero in tough-woman drag? This question informs the central concerns of this chapter.

Figure 5.1. Sarah Pezzini (Yancy Butler), wielder of the Witchblade. Does the Witchblade grant Sarah toughness, or does her toughness manifest itself as the Witchblade?

Essentialist Toughness: The Witchblade and the Line of Mythic Warrior Women

Witchblade rewrites women's history as a secret narrative of ongoing female heroism. Sarah embodies centuries of tough-woman defiance. The series rewrites essentialist theories about women (for example, childbearing women are the embodiment of nature) as indications of Sarah's superior toughness, wherein lies her appeal for the woman-favoring Witchblade. *Witchblade* constructs a tough woman action heroine who has existed throughout history: Sarah Pezzini is only the latest incarnation of the warrior-woman wielder of the Witchblade.

A long line of warrior women have wielded the Witchblade, a mixture of historical and fictional women warriors: Mirene, a Gorgon Amazonian queen; Cleopatra; Boudicca, the Celtic warrior of ancient London; the Celtic warrior/goddess Cathain (an amal-gam of traditional Irish mythological figures); Joan of Arc; and the fictional Elizabeth Brontë, a British state department linguist sent to infiltrate Hitler's government in Mata Hari fashion. Played also by Butler, many of these women—Sarah's past selves—appear in visions provided by the Blade; the episode "Periculum," in which the Blade infuses itself with Sarah's DNA as it puts her through near-death initiation rites, testing her suitability to be a wielder, heavily features Sarah's ancestors/past selves. The series seems driven by and to accept wholeheartedly the Devil's philosophy as expressed in Martin Scorsese's film version of *The Last Temptation of Christ* (1988): "There is only one woman, different faces." Sarah has existed throughout time; she is only the latest incarnation of an essential woman warrior.

Since the Blade can only be worn by women, it is a gender-pure warrior line. The blade is the Key to all Mythologies. Able to link to and synthesize all the great women warriors throughout time, the Blade is a controlling metaphor for the intermittent outbursts of formidable, militaristic female fury throughout history. (Along these lines, the Witchblade's contempt for men is a defining aspect of the series.) As Elizabeth Brontë describes the Blade to Sarah in "Periculum," "It is a branch ripped from the Tree of the Knowledge of Good and Evil." In other words, it is directly linked to sexual knowledge—the power to recognize nakedness, shame, and sexual difference. The Blade contains ancient secrets about sexual power, albeit essentialist and female sexual power. Though the Blade in bracelet form is a yonic,[5] as opposed to phallic, symbol—it is horizontal and circular rather than vertical and upright—there is never an indication that it is itself, in one way or another, gendered—only that it craves/worships/dominates female wielders. Sarah's Witchblade transformation is a collage of gendered symbols. In moments of danger, she raises her arm to her face in a militaristic gesture of defiance. The bracelet then transforms into the forearm-length gauntlet. In so doing, it becomes a metal maw that devours Sarah's arm. In opposition to the idea of gauntlet as maw, when the weapon morphs into its fullest form, as a sheath, and sprouts its signature Blade (much longer in the more heteronormative season two), it is much more clearly a phallic weapon. Noncoherent in gendered terms, the Witchblade, in either bracelet or sheath-sword form, could be described, in Thomas Doherty's words about the art direction in the *Alien* films, as "abstract genital," simultaneously "penile and uterine."[6]

Ian Nottingham, the supersoldier assigned to monitor and protect Sarah, tells her in "Conundrum": "Women wear the Witchblade because they can stand pain. The same reason you bear the children. Life is born of pain." In other words, the Blade is directly linked to the anguish of childbirth that only women can endure, and hence favors women specifically for their reproductive powers. Witchblade's emphasis on reproductive powers as emblematic of women's strength—child bearing makes her the tougher sex and hence the favored one for the Witchblade—rigidly demar cates reproduction as women's chief distinction. This series bias interestingly conflicts, however, with Sarah's own childlessness and indifference to conventional "womanly" behavior.

Considering the essentialist bases upon which the Witchblade favors women, it is interesting that the Witchblade enables Sarah to embody essential female sexual power *while* wielding phallic male strength. In strobe-lit Witchblade transformations, she stereoscopically appears as a chainmailed warrior, sword in hand, who takes off her helmet to release flowing springs of lush, loose Pre-Raphaelite raven hair. Armored and sensual, phallic and feminine, the Witchblade-wielding Sarah is an ingenious compromise between the normatively reproductive woman tied to Nature and the Western, phallic masculine hero. The emphasis the series places on the essentialist, ancient mystery of woman mitigates the threat of deviance represented by the virilized, phallic woman Sarah becomes once she "amps up," in her young friend and sidekick Gabriel's words ("Transcendence"), the Witchblade. In other words, we are continuously reassured that even though she wields the phallic Witchblade, Sarah is still a normal woman, since the Blade only responds favorably to *women*, whose strength is manifested by their reproductive capabilities, their essential mysteries. Ultimately, the series suggests that women can wield the phallic strength of the Witchblade because of their essential womanly toughness. While not uninteresting, this idea emblematizes the series' determination to have it both ways—to construct a postmodern tough woman who nevertheless symbolizes archetypal femininity.

The Witchblade allows Sarah to be both ancient/eternal, in that it is a retro, medieval weapon, and hypermodern, in that it is an emblem of postfeminist strength. In the ways that it collapses, unites, and creates a chasm between ancient and modern modes of femininity, the Witchblade is the perfect emblem for Sarah Pezzini, who, as one of the few witches (the Witchblade, once worn, turns her into a witch) ever to be the center of a dramatic series, realizes the competing histories and symbolic meanings of the figure of the witch. Behind every great Blade is a greater witch.

Seasons of the Witch: The Witch as Perverse Tough Woman

Despite its insistence on the natural powers of the woman, *Witchblade* nevertheless constructs an action heroine out of a figure always associated with the decidedly unnatural: the witch. Fascinatingly, the series puts the figure of the witch at the center of the action. The witch creates interesting problems in the construction of the tough heroine. Especially relevant in light of *Witchblade*'s focus on the importance of women's reproductive powers is Diane Purkiss's discussion of the simultaneously hard and boundless fantasy body of the witch:

> The formlessness of the witch's body is also attested by her ability to transform herself into other bodies, to shift shape [a pronounced Witchblade trope]. . . . The witch could unfix the limits of her body by shifting shape. . . . This Protean fluidity was frightening because it meant that there was perpetual uncertainty about the witch's "true" identity, and because the witch's boundlessness recalls the fantasy mother, engulfing. . . . [But] the witch could also be understood as unnaturally hard and dry. . . . If the formless body of the witch . . . was a source of terror, the hard witch also frightened. Her resistance to the violence of her assailants . . . makes her a problem in terms of gender: she is not supposed to be as hard as a hero.[7]

Considering the ideological associations of the witch's boundlessness and hardness, Sarah Pezzini is an ideally realized witch, in that she is both historically liquid and phallically hard. During her Witchblade transformations, in which she oscillates between visual metaphors of hard masculinity and soft femininity, she perfectly embodies the historical, hard/soft witch. Through Yancy Butler's extraordinary performance, Sarah fluidly alternates between affective modes, from a steely, hoarse-voiced toughness to a soft, tender vulnerability. Sarah-as-witch is emblematic of the tough/tender dichotomy in the action heroine, who is almost always depicted as a "feeling" woman beneath her tough-woman surface.

Sharon Russell discusses the competing folkloric and religious myths of the witch: "On one side, the witch is a person, usually female, who is responsible for maleficium, evil acts. . . . On the other side, the witch is the participant in Satanic rites, inversions of orthodox Christian practice."[8] The independence of the witch is an important feature of her representations in folklore and literature. But pop-cultural myths of the witch hold at their core a male deity who sexually controls women; furthermore, the myth itself manifests deep male fears about the castrating threat of women's sexuality, making the witch, like film noir's femme fatale, problematic as a potentially feminist icon.

Though Russell finds that the witch in film, "where male control enters as a central theme," must give up the independence she enjoys in folklore and literature, I would argue that it is on television and not in Hollywood film that the witch most pervasively loses her self-dominion.[9] In Hollywood movies, witches do not usually have to give up their independence: They generally work alone. Witches have usually been cast as the decadent enemy of domestic normality—as in Disney villains such as Maleficent of *Sleeping Beauty* (1959) and Ursula, the tentacled terror of *The Little Mermaid* (1989)—or as evil sexual predators, femme fatales who cast spells on clueless hunks. The witch always retains her independence in Hollywood at the cost of being portrayed as an "unnatural monster," as Jason calls his witchy wife in *The Medea* of Euripides. A fairly good index of Hollywood movies' treatment of the witch is the wonderful/terrible Arnold Schwarzenegger extravaganza, *Conan the Barbarian* (1982). Conan engages in raucous sex with a dark, wild-eyed woman, a witch who appears to be his savior. But the proceedings grow too raucous, and the woman morphs into a clawing animal. Conan manfully wrests the witch off of his violated form and casts her to broil in a fiery pit, where she seemingly belongs.

Wes Craven's television movie version of Lois Duncan's young adult novel *Summer of Fear* (1978; the film is also known as *Stranger in Our House*) routinely and uncritically positions the witch not as a threat to bland suburban conformity but as the usurper of the domestic mother/wife's position.[10] In contrast, *Sleeping Beauty*'s Maleficent—who has grandeur, wit, and imperious power and dons dragon-drag to annihilate fairy-tale kingdoms—appears wholly indifferent to male companionship. She also does not crave the heterosexual bliss she threatens; instead, she strives only to thwart and ultimately destroy it. The innate tough-mindedness of the witch's indifference to normative desire and her destructive attack on normality has usually been softened on television by laugh tracks and goofiness. In the words of two critics writing about *Sabrina, the Teenage Witch*: "despite providing many potential moments for particular kinds of prime-time feminist pleasure, the series' affirmation of traditional patriarchal feminine concerns with physical beauty, acquisition of heterosexual male attention, and responsibility for others undermines Sabrina's access to independence and contains her feminist potential as a role model."[11]

Sitcom witches are the farthest thing from independent women, even if their husbands and boyfriends are not exactly Satanic lords, either. It is noteworthy that most TV witches live in sitcomland: *Bewitched* (which was driven by Elizabeth Montgomery's antic pluckiness and lesbian diva Agnes Moorehead's superbly sour wit, and was not without its pleasures), *I Dream of Jeannie* (if the *djinn* can be even viewed as a witch), *Tabitha* (*Bewitched*'s short-lived sequel), *Sabrina, the Teenage Witch*, and others like them. *Charmed* is a compromise between the sitcom and the angsty teen-girl drama. Another show that straddles genres, the funny-scary *Buffy the Vampire Slayer*, features a witch, Willow, but she is conceived as a bumbling, geeky girl-witch sidekick, never as the main character (though Willow received a spectacular, if regrettably short-lived, make-over as an evil, world-annihilating terror in the show's sixth-season finale). Sarah Pezzini's cop-drama witchiness allows her to eschew some of the conventional trappings of the sitcom witch. Though often dressed in sexily youthful outfits, we never see Sarah worrying about her beauty (though her perpetual exposure of her belly button defies cop-drama credibility and, wittingly or not, ties her to Jeannie, who was pointedly not allowed to show hers). Though involved in heterosexual relationships, Sarah only begins to fret openly about her lack of them in the more reactionary season two.

As noted, Sarah is, then, one of the few witches at the center of a television drama. "Perhaps one of the reasons why the witch has never gained extended popularity as a horror figure," writes Russell, "is that she embodies fears that men would rather forget. Because witches are believed to have the power to cause impotence, they are the ultimate expressions of male fears of castration. . . . [Even though the witch-myth is a male creation,] the only valid reversal of it would be to have it . . . turn on its creator."[12] In this regard, *Witchblade* is a deeply radical show, in that its witch rebels against the satanic lord who offers to be her master and defies his minions.

Kenneth Irons, mysterious billionaire head of Vorschlag Industries, is the satanic lord of this witchy show. He once wore the Witchblade, which of course rejected him; his hand still bears the wound-scar the Blade burnt into it. He obsessively tracks the progress of the Blade and its wielders; the Witchblade has partially granted him a longer life span, but he must keep nourishing himself with wielders' blood to sustain it, hence his obsessive fixation with Sarah. His genetically engineered supersoldier henchman, Ian Nottingham, does Irons's bidding—assassinations, stealth missions, stalking Sarah—but in conflicted ways: He appears to love Sarah (see figure 5.2).

Irons is an old money satanic lord. Debonair, mordant, fiendishly wealthy, with an indeterminate British-Nazi accent and icy hair, he is obsessed with the Blade and tests out Sarah's fitness to wield it. Irons could be seen as representing the male center of a witch cult, and thus perpetuating the pop-cultural myth of the witch as a moaning, idolatrous worshipper of Satan who is controlled by a satanic priest, which denies the witch her folkloric/ literary independence. However, Sarah's battle-to-the-death

Figure 5.2. Brother, lover, rival, or assassin? Genetically engineered super soldier and Black Dragon Ian Nottingham (Eric Etebari)

antagonism toward him satisfies Russell's castration dictates in that Sarah actively attempts to thwart, "reverse," Irons's male domination. Her defiant—and lonely—stance toward Irons in season one is by far the most radical aspect of the series.

A commentator in *Bitch* magazine notes, unhappily, that Sarah does not have any good female friends.[13] Actually, this is not quite true—she does seem to maintain a friendship with the coroner, Vicky Po. But Vicky is not a regular character, and we never see the two women socializing; they exchange humorously barbed comments over cadavers. Nor do we see Sarah hanging out much with male friends, either, although her relationship with her police partners is clearly meaningful to her. *Witchblade* makes Sarah (especially in season one) a starkly isolated figure; at the same time, it emphasizes a cultic male bonding that sharply contrasts with her lone-witch isolation. In season one, she is caught within and between twinned and linked male homosocial worlds. The captain of her precinct, Bruno Dante, is a scuzzy, corrupt misogynist eager to eliminate Pezzini. Like some honcho from a bad military film, he views her as a pernicious disruption to his cozy and covertly criminal male police world. Dante begins wooing Jake, the blond, ex-surfer rookie Sarah trains, to become a member of his secret vigilante organization, the White Bulls, who "sign" their kills with long gold bullets with a titular bull insignia. Dante's crew of cronies meet for clandestine meetings that are filmed as if they are Satanic rituals. And, it turns out, Dante really does work for Satan: He is an employee of Kenneth Irons.

The mythological references deepen the homosocial theme. The episode "Diplopia" uses the Welsh myth of the Huntsmen of Annuvin, super-powerful brothers who gain the strength of their slain brethren, to symbolize the episode's murderous cloned brothers. The White Bulls can be interpreted as a variation of the Cult of Mithras. Originally a Persian religion and later a Roman one (as Roman culture cross-fertilized with those it colonized), this cult focused on the great warrior Mithras, slayer of the Primeval Bull; much like the White Bulls, the Cult of Mithras only accepted male members. In both "Parallax" and "Consectatio,"[14] we learn that Ian is a member of an elite special forces unit called the Black Dragons, a secret, experimental military unit that Irons's Vorschlag Industries funded. Not only do Irons and Ian form a secret male society, but also Ian is part of another secret male society Irons underwrites.

Sarah is juxtaposed against not only the homosocial but also the potentially homosexual. Intriguing instabilities characterize Irons's relationship with Ian—or at least with the latest cloned version of the "Ian" model (the genetics angle is a science-fiction addition to this fantasy series). Irons is Ian's "father" and treats Ian like his dutiful, loyal son; Ian responds in appropriately filial fashion. But their relationship is also figured in classic S&M fashion as a perfect sub/dom set-up. Irons looms above the nearly equally tall Ian, who does not make eye contact and keeps his head slavishly, submissively lowered. Irons always seems on the verge of physically punishing subservient Ian for any outbursts, pushing his head down, even slapping him on occasion. But then Irons also occasionally treats Ian with deferential, cooing affection. The relationship between them is almost deliriously homoerotic.

In his book *The Explanation for Everything*, Paul Morrison questions why homosexuality is always used as the "explanation" for Nazism.[15] In light of this question, it is fascinating that the series makes sure to link homoerotically inclined Irons to the Nazis, with whom he was cozy. (We see "stills" of him hanging out with Hitler and other SS members.) Just as Elizabeth Brontë pitted herself against the homosocial/homosexual order of the Nazis in her work as a spy (and role as a wielder), Sarah pits herself against the sexually suspect, decadent male worlds presided over by Irons, who infuses his homoerotic homosocial cults with a Nazi "decadence." As Luchino Visconti's 1968 film *The Damned*, with its climactic homosexual Nazi orgy, demonstrates, the Nazis have often been tied to homosexuality in the popular culture imaginary. By linking Irons to Nazism, the series not so subtly reinforces the idea that the male cults of the series are homosexual in practice. If Irons is the symbol for the homoerotic decadence potentially present within the homosocial, is Sarah, in her fierce opposition to Irons, the sworn enemy of the homoerotic-homosocial? What exactly is her relationship to the homosocial? The homosexual?

The Tough/Phallic Woman as Scourge

Like the 1992 film *Alien³*, *Witchblade* places a strong, tough woman within a homosocial setting, where her very femininity makes her alien and troublesome. But is there also a way in which Sarah is irrelevant to her own series?

Like the witch, Kundry, in Wagner's opera *Parsifal*, Sarah is the only major female figure in a ruthlessly homosocialized world. The series emphasizes her stark singularity by foregrounding the group male mentality organized around her. Gay critic Richard Mohr's provocative and troubling work on the homosocial is helpful in this regard—is Sarah used the way Kundry, in Mohr's view, is used in *Parsifal*: as the device for the confirmation of the superior purity of all-male worlds?[16]

Kundry is a "sempiternal witch," "a mocking witness to the Crucifixion." As the only distinct woman in this opera about the knights of the Holy Grail, Kundry is "excluded": "[S]he dies because the opera calls out for masculine closure. . . . Kundry's absence is required so that the values of masculine worlds are realized." The only two males able to withstand her sexual enchantment are the vengeful sorcerer, Klingsor, and the chaste, heterosexually disinclined Parsifal. Mohr is right to view as deliriously homoerotic this opera in which "knights, young men, and boys" all obsessively pursue a looming phallic totem, the Spear of the Crucifixion, and its beneficent symbolic value. It is Mohr's uncritical endorsement of Wagner's misogynistic erasure of Kundry that is disquieting. Mohr forces one to endorse a misogynistic program in order to celebrate homoerotic homosociality—a deeply unfair position in which to place a reader.

We might understand *Witchblade* as a variation on Wagnerian themes in *Parsifal*. Ian Nottingham could be a grail knight in a fallen, unbelieving world, while Irons could be the vengeful, occult Klingsor. The extraordinary gallery of pretty-boy types in the entire cast—Gabriel, procurer and vendor of exotic objects, who eerily resembles Sarah with his dramatic dark eyebrows, huge gamine eyes, and sensual lips; Jake, with his surfer sexiness and dreamy blondness; Danny, Sarah's partner, whose put-on machismo seems like a protective cover for a wounded softness; darkly, broodingly handsome Ian, like a Latino Rochester—could represent the varieties of male beauty. It should be noted that numerous websites extol the beauties of Kenneth Irons. Where does lone Sarah fit into this obsessively masculinist world? Is she, like Kundry, the "mocking witness" to the spectacle of homosociality?

Strangely, Sarah would appear to exist as agent of moral hygiene—to cleanse the queer potentialities of these masculinist worlds. Both Irons and Dante lead intensely homosocial worlds underpinned by the view of women as dangerous infectious agents. Irons constantly directs Ian to eliminate Sarah; Dante constantly directs Jake (and his Bulls) to eliminate Sarah. Woman becomes the obstruction to male–male relations. If she were eliminated, these male worlds could operate without her distracting resistance. But the series implies that Woman needs to be present lest the desire that undergirds these male worlds continue to intensify. In this way, even within a series saturated with queer imagery and themes, Sarah is used both as a force to illuminate homoerotic desires (by being in such stark juxtaposition against them, on the one hand, and by being herself legibly queer, on the other) and as a force to vanquish them. The series suggests, then, that Sarah's toughness—her intermittent, Witchblade-facilitated access to phallic male power—not only isolates her from both other women and from the men whose power she has usurped but also displaces and threatens male dominance and bonding, which is always, on this series, homoerotically charged. Ultimately, Sarah's Witchblade slices through layers of homoerotic intrigue. Is she unwittingly a basher? There is a suggestion here that this tough woman has been hired to rid the world of pansy men.

Season two especially reinforces this point, all but announcing its near-total erasure of the previous season's highly suggestive queer themes. Season two kills off the Irons character, though his unmoored spirit continues to roam. Season two keeps Ian largely in isolation, his highly suggestive relationship to Irons—who, being mostly dead, makes only cameo, ghostly appearances—now nearly eliminated. Season two removes the homoerotic threats that saturated season one; the tough woman has successfully cleaned up this decadent town.

In season two's second episode, "Destiny," Irons wields the Longinus Lance, the tool used to ascertain if crucified Christ was dead—an almost explicit *Parsifal* allusion. Irons and the Lance versus Sarah and the Witchblade: This is a battle to the death between queer and heteronormative forces. In "Destiny," Irons's Longinus Lance, like the Spear of the Crucifixion in *Parsifal*, represents the disturbing queer sensibility of the first season; it is a symbol for Irons, who represents decadent all-male worlds, and, as wielded by him, the Lance becomes a queer phallus, pitted against the yonic Witchblade. The new general homophobia of season two cheapens Sarah's eventual victory over Irons; the Witchblade's ultimate victory over the Longinus Lance could be viewed as Kundry's triumph over the Grail Knights, the witch's triumph over male domination. Instead, it plays like a homophobic agenda's exploitation of the woman warrior as annihilating scourge of deviance.

The mesmeric homoerotic tableaux of season one keeps its ideological leanings unfixed, its queer potentialities liquid. Season one leaves Sarah unconstrained by the usual sexual and gendered limitations of television female heroism. Her own sexuality and gender are almost as elusive as that of Irons, Ian, and the others. But by season two, she, no less than the others, is locked into conventional gendered and sexual place. Season two seems obsessed with turning Sarah into a "normal" woman and the Witchblade into a denatured super-weapon, a mere improvement over the phallic gun—a custom-made lady-weapon, truly strong enough for a man but made for a woman, as that old deodorant commercial so memorably put it.

The most disappointing aspect of season two is Sarah herself. A vital, loudmouthed, gutsy, unremittingly tough presence in the first season—but, through the complexity of Butler's superb performance, a vulnerable one, too—Sarah becomes in season two muted, wan, forlorn. Having lunch with Danny and his wife in "Lagrimas" (an episode in which Sarah falls in love with Cartaphilus, the still-living man behind the myth of the Wandering Jew), Sarah uncharacteristically complains about not having a boyfriend. (Insensitively, "sensitive" Danny and his wife begin extravagantly making out at the table!) In "Parabola," Danny has to lecture Sarah about the difficulties of not being "white and heterosexual," whereas she is the one who nearly pummeled Jake for being homophobic in the previous season's "Diplopia." The pugnacious vitality of her toughness in season one transmutes into a dangerous drippiness in season two, as if to suggest that, without the homoeroticism to contend with, her toughness goes slack. The really perplexing element of this aspect of the show is that it positions her as deeply opposed to homoerotic homosociality while being heroically pro-gay ("Diplopia"), pro-women, and readably queer herself. These incoherent elements in her persona need to be more closely explored.

Tough Enough to Be Queer

If Sarah gains energy from opposing decadent homoerotic male cults, her obsession with the fate of young women facilitates an interpretation of her as a lesbian heroine. She dons the ultimate tough-guy guise: that of the cowboy. In fact, she closely resembles

James Fenimore Cooper's stoic, chaste cowboy Natty Bumppo. She is as interpretably queer as Natty Bumppo and for many of the same reasons: Both Sarah and Natty maintain a chaste purity that almost precludes sustained commitment to heterosexual relationships. In the pilot film (from which the series was derived), she obsessively hunts down the evil mobster Gallo, who murdered a wayward childhood friend of Sarah's, a young woman who had become a prostitute. Much like the Russell Crowe character in *L.A. Confidential*, Sarah is brutishly prone to martial combat with men yet tenderly respectful of women and touched enough by their plight to protect them from male harm—to be their guardian/ avenging angel. Like Crowe's character, Sarah beats up men who beat up women. (In this regard, she is also a variation on John Wayne's character in the famous John Ford Western *The Searchers* (1956). Wayne is obsessed with the purity of his young niece, who has been captured by Indians.) Like Clarice Starling in *The Silence of the Lambs* (1991), Sarah is obsessed with saving young women. In "Conundrum," she must rescue a young blonde woman, a model, from death. The shot of black-clad Sarah holding the blonde woman she has rescued at the climax of the episode visually reads like a queer version of a John Waterhouse painting of knight and maiden: The tough dark Sarah holding the soft, femme, fair girl she has saved is a powerful visual metaphor for a new lesbian reimagining of the conventional hero. It also represents a reimagining of the archetypal Dark Lady and Fair Lady of Western literature as two halves of a lesbian pair (similar, and explicitly lesbian, Dark-/Fair-Lady pairings exist in David Lynch's *Mulholland Drive* (2001) and Brian De Palma's *Femme Fatale* (2002); in the lesbian noir *Bound* (1996), we have, instead, an interesting Dark-Lady/Dark-Lady pairing).

As if to confirm the radicalism of this tableau, the next episode, "Diplopia," explicitly raises the question of Sarah's sexuality; in fact, she raises it her*self*. One of the cloned-brother killers, who has a taste for same-sex eros, kills a gay couple. Investigating the crime with Sarah, rookie Jake makes disparaging comments about gays, who obviously freak him out. "Jake, you're a *raging* homophobe!" chastizes Sarah. Later, she confronts him more aggressively: "Good looking guy like you, Jake—wonder why I never made a move on you?" When bewildered Jake says that you can tell who is a homo by looking at them, she challenges, "Could you tell by looking at me?" He looks much more bewildered at this point.

In the queer club where one of the cloned murderers hunts, Jake (newly reformed and sporting an undercover "gay" look) asks Sarah (in drag) if she is really . . . *you know*. She gives no answer but does kiss him, ostensibly to attract one of the cloned brothers. From afar, to the killer's eyes, it looks like two men kissing. Admirably, she never tells Jake she is *not* gay—but in the very next episode, the aptly named "Sacrifice," Sarah, channeling Cathain, falls in love with Conchobar, her long-lost soul mate—lest we have any doubts about Sarah's sexuality. In "Diplopia," the antihomophobic angle is not fully radical—given its gay serial killer, the episode's antihomophobic rhetoric may be an example of what Roland Barthes called "inoculation," a gesture toward tolerance that masks a larger strain toward bigotry. Still, when Sarah calls Jake on his antigay prejudice, she is thrillingly unflinching and forthright. That's why it is so disappointing when she has to be lectured on tolerance in season two, which, obviously freaked out by Sarah's unflinching season one toughness, takes great pains to make her softer and more "womanly."

Though the series gives Sarah the odd lover—sometimes really odd, like Conchobar and Cartaphilus, the' "Wandering Jew" of myth ("Lagrimas")—each of these romances ends unhappily, with shattered Sarah weeping over their dead forms. Cursed by her inexorable solitude, she is both an archetypal pure-quest hero, devoid of distracting and corrupting sexual entanglements, however threatened by them (like the medieval figure Gawain), and the classic loveless single woman throughout the history of Hollywood film and television. This allows her to be an object of heterogeneously erotic contemplation: Ostensibly heterosexual, as her romances evince, yet never in a relationship for very long, Sarah is readily conceivable as a coded queer heroine, fighting the forces of male evil to protect vulnerable young women, a striking fusion of butch and femme.

In season two, the series takes greater and more consistent pains to mitigate lesbian readings. Danny reminds Sarah that she is "heterosexual" in one episode ("Parabolic"), and she complains about her sad single-lady lovelessness in "Lagrimas." Yet another version of the Fair-/Dark-Lady pairing is offered in the season two finale, "Ubique," but this one almost self-consciously refuses lesbian interpretability: Sarah must battle a "false wielder," the "time-walking" Lucrezia Borgia, a towering figure of female evil, here realized as a blonde supermodel with a taste for tawdry, murderous sex and a palpable relish for power. "Dark clouds are upon us," she informs Sarah as she wields the strength of the purloined Witchblade before Sarah's astonished eyes. The Dark Lady pitted against the Fair in a battle to the death, the Lucrezia-vs.-Sarah showdown challenges the series' own lesbian reimagining of dark/fair female archetypes. While there is a delicious frisson in their face-off—Kate Levering's Lucrezia is like a female Lestat, Anne Rice's vampire angel as candy-perfume girl—it is also a sim-plistically conventional "bitch fight." Falsely wielding the Witchblade, Lucrezia stabs Sarah with it. The now super-long blade goes through Sarah's body as she moans and cries. Tender woman–woman love in season one transmutes into sadomasochistic woman–woman violence in season two.[17]

Unsex Me Here?: The Witch as Double and the Tough Woman as Pure Hero

The series finale "Ubique" seems, finally, baffled by Sarah's sexuality. Is she a coded queer heroine—or is she more properly seen as a male hero in drag? For that matter, is the tough woman always already the male hero in drag? A further analysis of the series' saturation in mythological themes allows us to synthesize some of the issues already discussed in this chapter: tough women, action heroines, the witch, and the construction of the queer hero-ine. Analyzing Sarah's relationship with the character of Dominique Boucher yields interesting insights into these questions.

One of the most arresting figures of the series, Dominique, intro-duced in "Conundrum," craves the Witchblade, even though it has rejected her. The head of a high-fashion modeling-agency, she is a "false wielder." Revealed as such, she morphs into Medusa, swarming snakes simulating hair. Later, she becomes a croaking old-woman guide for Sarah in her battle against Irons: in other words, a modern variant of the Cumaean sibyl who guides Aeneas through the underworld in *The Aeneid*. Once incarcerated, Dominique begins to age rapidly, and the sound-effects people make her voice *basso profundo*. She mocks Sarah when she seeks help and guidance about using the Witchblade. "Look it up on the Internet, under Talismans," sneers the now cronelike but ever-demonic Dominique, "charms . . . *fairy* tales." Ingeniously, Sarah coaxes this sibyl-sphinx into giving her some helpful if cryptic answers—"*Brood-mare!*" Dominique hisses typically. In relation to Dominique, Sarah is alternately Perseus, who decapitates Medusa, and Aeneas, the hero in need of a guide.

In this manner, it is intriguing that the idea of the false wielder, the "bad witch," is so integral to Witchblade. A built-in feature of the action-heroine genre is the double, the foil, the "bad witch" to the action heroine's good one. Why is this a stalwart, unvarying feature of action-heroine shows?

If the action heroine/tough woman is a male hero in disguise, her annihilation of the double/foil allows her to vanquish femininity and womanhood while ostensibly retaining these innate qualities (see figure 5.3). In this manner, the tough woman as a construct is

Figure 5.3. Is the action heroine/tough woman a male hero in disguise?

a fantasy for a kind of new and improved womanhood—ostensibly female yet evacuated of "womanly" qualities. The campaign to eradicate the double is purgative, designed to rid the tough woman of the taint of archetypal female weakness, deviousness, avarice, evil. In this manner, the tough woman is woman in name and form only, since her chief function is to eradicate the female.

Dominique is the clear foil to Sarah, her demonic doppelganger in her avarice for the Blade and in her unsuitability to wield it. In the season one episode "Maelstrom," Conchobar is abducted by Irish militants who plan to trade him for his IRA terrorist brother. One of these militants, the especially crazed Fiona, eventually gains possession of the Witchblade and kills Conchobar (Fiona's expression as she marvels in evil glee at her newfound powers is one of the more unsettling sights in the series; she looks like a child not horrified but elated by witnessing the primal scene); Sarah executes her. Kenneth Irons, his hand scarred by contact with the Witchblade, can also be read as a gender-disguised male witch and Sarah-double, with his hocus-pocus machinations. In "Static," a psychologist and secret murderer, Anna Granger, tries to foil Sarah in her own bid for the Blade. Intriguingly, the villain of *Birds of Prey* is Harley Quinn, psychiatrist to the Huntress and the Joker's secret girlfriend; Quinn is clearly the "shrink"-wrapped foil to good witch Oracle, the new identity of now–wheel chair-bound Batgirl.

On *Bewitched* the wholesome Samantha had to contend with her foil, the devious Serena. Jaime Sommers in *The Bionic Woman* had to wrest away her purloined identity from the psychotic clutches of her double, Lisa Galloway ("Mirror Image," "Deadly Ringer"), as well as battle Dr. Franklin's robot women with human face masks, the Fembots, the terrifying realization of Jaime's intermittent fears of becoming more robot than human. Max faced off her would-be assassin twin on an episode of *Dark Angel*. *Star Trek: Voyager*'s Captain Janeway memorably confronted her evil pseudo-double (a woman who pretended to be her) with the line: "Nice hair!" ("Live Fast and Prosper"); the monstrously cruel, seductive, and witty Borg Queen is the Terrible Mother to Janeway's Good Mother. And in the series' last episode, "Endgame," Captain Janeway confronted a diabolical future version of her*self*, Admiral Janeway. Considering the sheer number of Hollywood gothics with twinned females—*The Dark Mirror* (1946), *A Stolen Life* (1946), *Dead Ringer* (1964), *Sisters* (1973), the classic TV chiller *Trilogy of Terror* (1975), and others—twinned females would appear to be a compulsory, innate generic trope, the Madonna always counterbalanced by the Whore. No surprises, then, when Aras, Sarah's evil twin, appears in season two's aptly named "Palindrome."

Madonna/Whore, Fair Lady/Dark Lady, Good Twin/Evil Twin, Good Witch/Bad Witch: The split halves of iconic, archetypal female identity are always visually and symbolically reinforced through representation. It is almost as if the creation of the heroine always produces an evil by-product, or as if the good heroine must always be counterbalanced by a bad, or as if good witches' virtues could only be confirmed through bad witches' vices. The Bad Witch attempts to replace normativity with perversity and decadence. Dominique, Fiona, Anna Granger, Aras, Lucrezia Borgia: All threaten to seize possession of the Witchblade from the noble Sarah—and their deviance is only an intensified and distorted form of Sarah's own, in that the Witchblade allows her access to properly masculinist, phallic power. Conquering and even annihilating the false wielders/bad witches allows Sarah to exorcise her own gendered perversities.

Is Sarah, then, Heroic Virtue, come to annihilate the Hags' reign, as he does in Ben Jonson's 1609 *Masque of Queens* (this masque features noble women, the titular queens, and their demonic, hag, antimasque counterparts)? Is she Perseus, come to decapitate Medusa, the foully ugly threat to male power? Following Freud's lead, if we view the Medusa's head as symbolic of the primal scene, the writhing dark serpents representing pubic hair and the terror of adult sexuality, what does it mean for the heroine—a woman Perseus—both to see and decapitate (symbolically, by killing her) Medusa?[18]

In this manner, Sarah can be both a radical and a deeply reactionary figure. Sarah's annihilation of Medusa can be seen as a thrilling feminist appropriation of an androcentric (male-dominated) myth. But it can also be setting a thief to catch a thief—using a woman to expunge womanly deviance in a way that mirrors Sarah's tough-woman deployment as antihomosexual scourge.

Just as she apes Perseus, Aeneas, and Heroic Virtue, Sarah emulates another classic form of the male hero, the cowboy, specifically the mysterious gunslinger. As has been noted, she resembles James Fenimore Cooper's isolated and sexually inviolate cowboy Natty Bumppo. Her relationship with her partner Danny Woo eerily simulates that between Natty and Chingachgook in Cooper's famous Western, *The Last of the Mohicans*. Natty roams the woods like a forest king, only obeying his own primitive laws; the Mohican Chingachgook is his constant companion.[19] Much like Natty, Sarah, associated with cowboy justice (vigilantism, a penchant for killing criminals), follows her own moral code, often opposed to the "law and order" she ostensibly upholds. Danny becomes her Chingachgook. In season one, Danny is murdered by Gallo, the gangster; he then becomes Sarah's spirit guide. As an Asian American, Danny fulfils many roles at once. He functions as the uncanny Other who provides Sarah with insights, heightened perception, and so on; he also allows her to maintain a passionate, intimate relationship that does not involve—that, in fact, precludes—sexual experiences, much like the friendship Natty Bumppo maintains with Chingachgook. An isolated cowboy in the guise of a modern woman, whose law-and-order–defying Witchblade antics (much like Natty's forest wildness) ensure her status as renegade, Sarah enjoys a pure marriage of minds with Danny, who provides her with the uncanny edge of his exotic expertise.[20]

Considering her vigilant opposition to other witches and to homosocial cults, and her tough-woman appropriation of the role of the heroic male warrior, Sarah becomes an unusual figure: the witch as rebel loner and outlaw (since many season one episodes explicitly depict her as outside the law). As Neal King and Martha McCaughey note, "Some fear that Hollywood films like *The Silence of the Lambs* undercut tough women by imbuing them with strong emotions, such as fear, maternal protectiveness, or ambivalence about killing."[21] Whatever fears are aroused by Sarah's overly protective feelings toward young Gabriel are cancelled out by Sarah's ruthless penchant for exterminating deviant threats to her pristine rebel-loner heroism.

The series suggests that having subsumed the role of male hero, Sarah is estranged from the world of men. By being a witch at war with her evil doppelgangers, she also eschews the female homosocial realm of fellow witches. Ultimately, her tough womanliness ensures her isolation, her remove from social ties of any kind. "A man who don't go his own way is nothing," Robert E. Lee Prewitt says in the Pearl Harbor classic *From Here to Eternity* (1953). A tough woman goes her own way because she has nothing: no friends, no lovers, save the metal that sheathes her desires within its own designs. The tough woman of *Witchblade*, then, represents a very strange sort of hero in that she seems representative, in the end, of no group or identity or problem or impulse in particular. As Marjorie Garber writes, "Power in *Macbeth* is the function of neither the male nor the female but of the suspicion of the undecidable. The phallus as floating signifier is more powerful than when definitely assigned to either gender."[22] Sarah Pezzini as tough woman is the floating signifier of *Witchblade*—a figure of power with no clear tie to either gender, visibly potent but finally ungraspable, unattainable: not of this world. It would appear that we are meant to see her as a zone of undecidability, from whence she draws her peculiar power.

Lady Macbeth's Problem and the Tough Woman Solution

If any work anticipates the peculiar problems of gender and sexuality both posed by and emblematic of *Witchblade*, it is Shakespeare's *Macbeth*. A character obsessed with gaining and sustaining power, Macbeth desperately attempts to outmaneuver the witches who reveal his fate and destiny; his obsession with them informs the attempts made by various males in *Witchblade* to control modern-witch Sarah. The witches remain ungraspable, unaffected by Macbeth's increasingly violent demands. Bearded and spectral, they represent the play's construction of a gendered uncanny, a gender-identity twilight zone.

Like the witches, Lady Macbeth, with her desire to be "unsexed," her ruthless renunciation of any trace of conventional womanhood, especially the maternal, blurs gendered categories (1.5.40–54). She equates phallic power with the ability to kill those in her way; in *Macbeth*, inflicting violence without fear makes you

Figure 5.4. Is Sarah a new-styled Lady Macbeth, equating phallic power with the ability to kill those in her way?

properly a man (2.2.52–5) (see figure 5.4). If Lady Macbeth's problem is that she is the wrong gender—in that being a woman in a patriarchal culture always already prohibits her from accessing the phallic power she so feverishly desires (it remains equally elusive for Macbeth, who cannot grasp the "dagger I see before me")—the tough woman as represented in *Witchblade* comes to seem an ingenious solution to Lady Macbeth's problem. Rather than being unsexed, Sarah Pezzini manages to retain her status and identity as a woman while wielding a weapon that grants her phallic power. The construct of the tough woman, then, allows Sarah to achieve what Lady Macbeth cannot: to wield murderous phallic power without having to be unsexed. Neither quite male nor female, opposed to both males and other females, a new sex and gender complete within themselves, tough women are a parthenogenetic feat of self-created heroism.

What ultimately precludes a liberating radicalism in this *Witchblade* model of the tough woman is that it replaces Lady Macbeth's problem with a new one. If the heroine intransigently opposes, as I have argued, the homophobic and misogynistic codes of patriarchy, *Witchblade*'s tough woman is not a heroine. How can you be a female hero when your principle task is to annihilate deviant women and men? Instead, the tough woman as embodied by Sarah Pezzini is a female Terminator, designed to look and act like a patriarchy-defying heroine but programmed to destroy patriarchy's deviant enemies, queer men and power-seeking women.

As the initially bracing but ultimately bruising development of *Witchblade* makes painfully clear, the tough woman too easily and readily falls into enemy hands, where she is reprogrammed into a retaliatory weapon against the very radical forces she seemingly and potentially mobilizes and embodies. The tough woman, increasingly figured as nonhuman, as metahuman, comes to seem like the Medea or the Lady Macbeth of our era, the terrible threat of the virilized woman, an unnatural monster, unsexed and inaccessible, forever the pawn of and the impasse between radical and reactionary forces.

Notes

1. William Shakespeare, *Macbeth*, ed. Kenneth Muir (London: Arden, 2001). All subsequent references will be from this edition.
2. In speaking about my own gay-male identification with the action heroine, I am inspired by Tiina Vares's work on female audience response to action heroines. She writes: " 'pleasures,' and the lack thereof, in action heroines cannot be 'read' off film texts, but are the product of a contextual intersection between viewers and films in a particular social and historical context." See Tiina Vares, "Action Heroines and Female Viewers: What Women Have to Say," *Reel Knockouts: Violent Women in the Movies*, ed. Martha McCaughey and Neal King (Austin: Texas University Press, 2001), 240.
3. In her terrific book *Recreational Terror*, Isabel Cristina Pinedo discusses the inherent difficulties of being a feminist critic who loves the horror genre: "[I]t matters what representations of women abound in culture, [but] the tendency to see the horror film as monolithically destructive of female subjectivity overlooks the contradictory dynamics within the genre as well as the complexity with which audiences respond to it." The horror film, Pinedo argues, must be appreciated in all of its complexity; I would argue similarly on behalf of the action-heroine (and also horror) genre. See Isabel Cristina Pinedo, *Recreational Terror: Women and the Pleasures of Horror Film Viewing* (Albany: SUNY University Press, 1997), 71.
4. Philip Green warns us against making too much of the "postmodern standpoint from which the cultural field is seen as (among other things) a realm of plurality,

150   David Greven

play, and multiple meanings, where members of different subcultures are seen as appropriating cultural commodities for their own subcultural—sometimes even subversive—purposes." Make too much of this and we risk ignoring "that there is an enduring material structure of cultural power to which those of us who merely consume cultural commodities are subject." See Green, *Cracks in the Pedestal: Ideology and Gender in Hollywood* (Amherst: Massachusetts University Press, 1980), 6.

5. "Yonic" is a term derived from stylized representations of female genitalia in Hindu symbolism.
6. Thomas Doherty, "Genre, Gender, and the *Aliens* Trilogy," in *The Dread of Difference: Gender and the Horror Film*, ed. Barry Keith Grant (Austin: Texas University Press, 1996), 196.
7. Diane Purkiss, *The Witch in History: Early Modern and Twentieth Century Representations* (New York: Routledge, 1996), pp. 125–127. This is an invaluably comprehensive study.
8. Sharon Russell, "The Witch in Film: Myth and Reality," in *Planks of Reason: Essays on the Horror Film*, ed. Barry Keith Grant (Lanham: Scarecrow Press, 1996), 113.
9. Russell, 118.
10. For a good discussion of *Summer of Fear*'s presentation of the witch as domestic threat, see Gregory A. Waller's essay "Made-for-Television Horror Films," in *American Horrors: Essays on the Modern American Horror Film*, ed. Gregory A. Waller (Urbana: Chicago University Press, 1987), 156–157. I disagree, however, with this essay's overly generalized critique of TV horror, often a more radical genre than Waller allows.
11. Sarah Projansky and Leah R. Vande Berg, "Sabrina, the Teenage . . . ?: Girls, Witches, Mortals, and the Limitations of Prime-Time Feminism," in *Fantasy Girls: Gender in the New Universe of Science Fiction and Fantasy Television*, ed. Elyce Rae Helford (Lanham: Rowman and Littlefield, 2000), 27.
12. Russell, 121.
13. Kate Epstein, "Where the Girls Aren't," *Bitch: Feminist Response to Pop Culture* no. 15 (winter 2002): 16.
14. The "Consectatio" is a pastiche of *Gilgamesh*, an epic that foregrounds bonds between men; Gilgamesh and the wild man Enkidu are united in their opposition to the goddess Ishtar, a dynamic mirrored by *Witchblade*.
15. Paul Morrison, *The Explanation for Everything: Essays on Sexual Subjectivity* (New York: New York University Press, 2001), 140–172.
16. Richard D. Mohr, *Gay Ideas: Outing and Other Controversies* (Boston: Beacon Press, 1992), 135–139.
17. Elyce Rae Helford does a very helpful job of unpacking subtextual primetime lesbian themes in her essay "Feminism, Queer Studies, and the Sexual Politics of *Xena, Warrior Princess*," in the collection edited by her, *Fantasy Girls*. See in particular "Lesbian Text and Subtext," 139–142 and "Butch/Femme Identities," 146–152.
18. See Sigmund Freud, *Writings on Art and Literature*, ed. James Strachey (Stanford: Meridian, 1997), 264–265.
19. Natty and Chingachgook's friendship represents, in Leslie Fiedler's famous words, "the pure marriage of males, sexless and holy, a kind of counter-matrimony, in which the white refugee from society and the dark-skinned

primitive are joined till death do them part." Leslie Fiedler, *Love and Death in the American Novel* (1960; New York: Dell, 1966), 211.
20. Renee L. Bergland's recent study *The National Uncanny: Indian Ghosts and American Subjects* (Hanover: Dartmouth University Press, 2000) examines the ways in which Indians in fictions like Cooper's are depicted as ghostly figures on their way to becoming actual ghosts. Bergland analyzes the discursive implications of this stylized treatment. Danny Woo's ghostliness is especially interesting in this regard.
21. Neal King and Martha McCaughey, "What's a Mean Woman Like You Doing in a Movie Like This?" *Reel Knockouts: Violent Women in the Movies*, ed. King and McCaughey (Austin: Texas University Press, 2001), 17–18.
22. Marjorie Garber, *Shakespeare's Ghost Writers: Literature as Uncanny Causality* (New York: Methuen, 1987), 111.

Chapter 6

The Cruelest Season: Female Heroes Snapped into Sacrificial Heroines

Sara Crosby

On May 22, 2001, Max ends Fox's first season of *Dark Angel* strapped to a gurney, her heart shredded by a self-inflicted gunshot wound. On May 22, Buffy concludes her vampire slaying with a suicidal leap. On June 18, the creators of *Xena: Warrior Princess* realize the "full circle" logic of the feminist icon's six seasons by arranging for the warrior princess to commit suicide—twice.[1] In one brief, bloody spring, American television orchestrated the suicides of almost its entire cast of tough, heroic female leads. Why did these women kill themselves? What cultural logic demanded this carnage? One compelling strand of criticism tends to theorize the deaths of tough females as a patriarchal reaction to political threat: Patriarchy criminalizes and then violently eradicates the "monstrous-feminine" or metes out the ultimate punishment to women who have become just "too tough or too strong."[2] More optimistic interpretations read their suicides as resistance to patriarchy's incorporation or a transcendence of its reality, an imaginative feminist move forward "dedicated to mythic if not immediately realizable alternatives."[3] The tough women of 2001 died heroically, even admirably, and often with mystic trappings that would seem to support this second explanation. They did not simply fall victim to a misogyny that interprets women's aggressiveness as criminality to be punished.

The motivation for their suicides, however, swings toward the first explanation: Their guilt, abject self-hatred, and regressive sacrifice to the needs of a patriarchal community undercut the rhetorical posture of feminist transcendence. This chapter attempts to unravel this impasse by situating the tough female heroes' sacrifices within an ideology that has proven historically capable of accommodating both the tough, heroic feminine and its necessary sacrifice.

The most plausible candidate for this expansive ideology is republicanism. From Jefferson's yeoman farmer to the Western's hardy frontiersman, American republicanism links muscular self-assertion and individualism to heroism and political power. Its historians and critics clash over if and how republicanism applies to women.[4] Is republicanism liberating and protofeminist or oppressive and neopatriarchal? Does it justify individual desire, regardless of gender, and protect the right to pursue heroic self-identity and political empowerment? Or does it create a sexist binary between the passive, feminized represented and the active, masculine representative? The answer is "yes" to both questions. Republicanism enacts a compromise through the bodies of tough female heroes. Its muscular, self-actualizing ethic creates them, and then patriarchy reclaims them by transforming them into sacrificial heroines.

Republican individualism has long accommodated American women's desires for tough, heroic identities and continues to push tough female heroes into mainstream culture. For over 200 years, popular American literature has stretched to produce women who race miles across country, sneak through enemy lines, plow 60 acres with a babe on each hip, and tomahawk "savages" with ease.[5] But, in spite of their accomplishments, their narratives end by denying them the male hero's ultimate goal: political authority wielded to reform and empower his own community. The patriarchal community cannot afford to let tough female heroes take this step; for, unlike even the most radical republican male heroes, tough female heroes "pose the deepest threat to patriarchy's authority."[6] By asserting their authority and heroic personhood as women, they destroy the notion that they enjoy being and must be either criminals or self-sacrificing victims. They deconstruct gendered hierarchy, the bedrock upon which patriarchy rests, and open the way for a democratic feminist community.

In order to maintain the patriarchal community in the face of this challenge, without undermining its individualist ethic, republicanism institutes a "rubber band effect" for tough female heroes. They may engage in tough heroics until they encounter a "snapping point," where the narrative asks, "For whom? For which community?" When tough female heroes reach either the end of their stories or a crucial place in their character arcs, when the question of final purpose logically comes to the fore, the narrative snaps them into sacrificial heroines.[7] The end asserts the moral of the story and cannot be allowed to remain open-ended. The further the female hero has gone, the more independent and powerful she has become, the more punishing and drastic the snap.

The most draconian snap is suicide, the final and complete erasure of female agency in sacrifice that tough female heroes suffered in 2001. But before they reach that ultimate snapping point, they must assume three fundamental "truths" about themselves and about their communities. First, like Eve, they bear a burden of guilt. While male heroes often experience guilt, they do so because they have failed to be heroes. They commit crimes of passivity. For instance, Spider-Man fails to stop the thief who later murders his uncle. His guilt subsequently motivates his heroism. Tough female heroes feel guilt *because of* their heroism. Their agency, their toughness, is their sin. Second, the patriarchal community averts a collision with republican individualism by making women want to alienate their power. Because of their guilty criminality and because of their passive "nature," female heroes do not want their transgressive toughness. They want to give it up and be "just normal girls," to let the men do the heroics. The cult of sacrificial heroinism makes tough female heroes' guilty alienation into something heroic that they want. They want redemption; they want to relinquish their power and physical agency. Third, the only stable or pragmatic possible community is the patriarchal community. Its hierarchical structure requires that some (masculine) people have more "personhood" and importance than other (feminized) people. If feminist communities have begun to form around female heroes, the narrative must discount this incipient social order as dystopian or unimportant in comparison with the real community.

Tough female heroes must then make a clear choice that prioritizes the patriarchal and dismembers the feminist society.

On their way to suicide, Max, Buffy, and Xena struggle through these stages of guilt, denial, and final community choice. This essay follows them as the republican rubber band snaps these tough female heroes into sacrificial heroines and transforms feminist narratives into patriarchal affirmations.

Guevara's Patriarchal Revolution

Of the three heroes, *Dark Angel*'s Max Guevara races with the greatest alacrity through these assumptions. She grapples perfunctorily with guilt about her genetically induced aggressive sexuality and youthful violence, and she occasionally dreams about being "a regular girl." But she dodges most of the criminalized tough female hero's guilt and denial because she never threatens a feminist transcendence of patriarchy. She always and inevitably chooses the patriarchal community, and that "choice" appears so natural and necessary, so genetically predetermined even, that she often seems to have no agency at all. Unlike Buffy or Xena, Max totally inhabits the role of chimera, "the perfect female" completely fabricated by and for a patriarchal agenda.[8] Although *Dark Angel* clothes its narrative in a rhetoric of liberal tolerance and individualism and gestures toward feminist egalitarianism, the series assumes these liberating poses in order to smuggle in a deeply reactionary argument. It sells itself as being all about choice, but the choices it gives Max are between patriarchy A or patriarchy B. Her heroic journey thus consists of flights from one male authority to another. Her suicide at the end of season one deepens these commitments and establishes the female and feminist identifications from which she must fly.

Both intra- and extranarrative elements construct Max for male interests and shape her narrative destiny from beginning to end. She starts life as a super-soldier, genetically engineered by and for that quintessentially masculine institution, the American military, and we later discover that an elusive figure, known as "Father," crafted every single gene in her body to fulfill his messianic destiny. The series also visually built her for the delectation of the male

gaze. Everything from costuming to camera work strives to sexualize the barely legal Max. The mainstream media responded with
reviews that sighed over Jessica Alba's "scx kitten appeal" and
"down-pillow lips" or repeatedly ogled the teenager's "pillowy
lips" and cat-suited buns.[9] *Dark Angel* palliates Max's toughness
with Alba's youth, cat suit, and Twiggy physique but also has her
spend the first season subject to uncontrollable tremors that
incapacitate her and allow the male heroes to save the day.[10]

Despite this functionalization and incapacitation, the tough
female hero could still work toward the empowerment of a feminist
community. Her bare existence undermines patriarchy, and the
series appears as if it could promote feminist and democratic goals
more radically and on more levels than any previous superhero
show. *Dark Angel* vests itself in all the trappings of feminist social
justice, poised to challenge class, racial, sexual, and gender hierar-
chies. Unlike most American heroes, Max scrapes by at the bottom
of the social scale as a minimum-wage bike messenger (with a little
cat burglary on the side). Her work community consists of one of
the most diverse casts ever assembled on television: from a cosmic
Jamaican to Max's black lesbian roommate to the transgenically
multiracial Max herself. She also rejects Manticore, her hierarchical military "home," and, at first, devotes her heroic energy to
recovering an egalitarian vision of the domestic. She searches for
her fellow escapees, a "family" made up of a horizontal grouping
of "brothers and sisters," rather than the vertical relations between
parent and child. But this quest, these feminist-democratic poses,
and Max herself are only set up to be snapped up by a patriarchal
community and its regressive goals.

The key to this appropriation and the male protagonist that
saves Max most of the time is Logan Calc, a.k.a. the panoptical
"Eyes Only." He is an idealistic muckraker who, in his own words,
uses his wealth and Max's brawn to combat the corrupt "law of the
jungle" that reigns over a post-apocalyptic Seattle. *Dark Angel*
wastes no time in shifting its hero between masters, and the first
episode starts with Max fleeing the military and ends by partnering
her with this older love interest. He, not Max, is the series' focus,
and we see her through his eyes only. The first episode sets the
tone when Logan faces her into a mirror. Thinking that he wanted

to show her the antique, she prices it, but he corrects her and instead fawns over the more perfect object, "the most singularly beautiful face I've ever seen." His gaze defines her and impels her to follow her (his) heroic agenda. He writes the poem that figures her in the stereotypically feminine sacrificial role of a "dark angel," and she takes on this heroic identity only after she subordinates her physical power to his political goals and literally starts to work for him. Associating her with feline imagery, the premiere suggests that, without his influence, she would have continued using her prowess for thievery under the "law of the jungle."

Logan gives Max the choice to be "an active participant" in either an animalistic and predatory society or in his human and civilized alternative. He refers to an America that supposedly offers republican individualism to its citizens, that is, the opportunity to fulfill their desires. He, however, imagines these self-actualizing citizens as an extremely limited population. When Max questions his wish to return to "the good old days" of huge disparities in wealth, when the poor died unnecessarily from disease and the rich wasted "obscene amounts of money" on trivial pleasures, he responds, "Even if they took it for granted, they still had a choice. Now they don't." The "they" he refers to is not the poor, who certainly did not choose to die of disease, but the wasteful rich. In contrast to the gauche nouveau riche, Logan identifies with the slightly more responsible and culturally sophisticated old wealth robbed by the feline (and feminized) "law of the jungle": "We got screwed out of living in a time when *we* could hang out for the afternoon in a café someplace, wearing $2,000 watches" (emphasis added). Logan's use of the pronoun "we" works to incorporate Max into this elite group with him. She ends the episode by accepting Logan's moral judgment, believing that in order "to go do the right thing," she must "help" Logan in his crusade for a renewal of patriarchal privilege. The onset of her heroism begins by "snapping" her into supporting the moral good of an absurdly elitist patriarchal community.

The most profound snap occurs at the end of the first season, when the series erases all possible identifications for our hero except patriarchal ones, redefines her "family," and thrusts her in the role of sacrificial heroine for this now patriarchal community. Max teams up with the father figure who had trained and then pursued her, Colonel Lydecker, to take down Manticore and, more importantly, "the bitch" who usurped Lydecker's position and began murdering Max's "brothers and sisters." Logan, Lydecker, and her remaining siblings then stage the final showdown and "bring the war home." Max successfully blows up the lab, but on her way out, she encounters her most dangerous foe: herself. She and a younger clone face each other across a clearing in the woods; Max the elder hesitates, Max the younger shoots (see figure 6.1). Although *Dark Angel*'s creator, James Cameron, originally intended to leave her a corpse, "a lot of people got upset," and the writers came up with the next best thing: killing her "brother," Zack.[11] Back at the lab with her body, Zack breaks free from his captors and shoots himself in the head so that the government doctors can replace her butchered heart with his. The last scene leaves Max strapped to a hospital bed helpless while "the bitch" who heads up the lab leers over her and welcomes her "home to us . . . [t]o me." Our lens, Logan, ends the season sitting on top of the ruined Space Needle and wondering "if she's still out there."

Figure 6.1. Max's first death scene with her two Daddies, Colonel Lydecker (left) and Logan (right)

Although Max's decision to turn and fight appears empowering, the details problematize this feminist interpretation. First, we discover that the true villain is not Daddy Lydecker but an irrationally murderous Mommy Bitch who wants to entrap Max in her sadistic female-led "home." Throughout the first season, "the bitch," as Lydecker calls her, remained the nameless embodiment of the monstrous-feminine, the powerful and thus cruel woman. Lydecker deserves redemption, but "the bitch" will only receive poetic justice, when at the beginning of season two one of her own guards accidentally shoots and kills her. Second, not only is Max risking her life at the behest of a father figure displaced by a powerful woman, but she does so specifically in order to destroy the genetic library that contains her and her family. As one of her sisters points out, "That's us back there." Max's question to herself just before she shoots herself thus seems ironically poignant: "Do you know who I am?" The moment of self-recognition, independent of Logan's gaze, becomes her moment of self-destruction. Although she claims to risk her life on behalf of her "family," she reveals the mission's true motivation when she tells Logan, "You're my family as much as anyone. Only we're never going to be any kind of anything if it keeps on like this." Ultimately, her family, like the series as a whole, centers around him. He is not her "family as much as anyone." The show chooses between families. Her sacrifice then becomes for him and their relationship, which replaces the egalitarian community of "brothers and sisters." The heroic finale is quite literally a suicide mission on behalf of a patriarchal agenda, one that kills Max and a potential feminist community. The next season only furthers this agenda as she pursues the "Father" who created her and starts to fulfill his even more elitist vision, which puts her working-class community at the service of a revolution of the eugenically superior.

If Max returns as the elitist Guevara, why did the writers still insist on killing her? Why not Logan? "The other choice was . . . Logan, but [the writers] didn't want to do that either" because that would violate the true aims of the show. A series cannot "leave the star of the show dead at the end of the season finale."[12] He is our real hero, and the Max–Logan partnership and its constant affirmation is the linchpin of *Dark Angel*'s vision. During the second season, the fans and the network pressured Cameron to shift Max's romantic focus from Logan to Alec, a younger man, fellow soldier, and her social equal. Cameron chose instead to let the television network cancel *Dark Angel*, rather than push his real hero into the background. Logan carries the series' revolutionary argument. He represents the forces of preservation: preservation of culture, of wealth, and seemingly benign patriarchal privilege. By playing the sacrificial heroine on his behalf, Max joins his old revolution, not her own.

Buffy's Gift

Buffy the Vampire Slayer, in contrast to *Dark Angel*, moves further toward a female-identified hero narrative, creating a tough female hero who supports a feminist community. The ultrafeminine name "Buffy," unlike the masculine "Max," identifies our hero unequivocally with women, and *Buffy* creator Joss Whedon's inspiration, instead of coming out of a desire to remasculinize America, stemmed from his empathy with the horror genre's "blonde girl who would always get herself killed." Instead of screaming and dying, he wanted her to "take back the night" and "trounce" the monster. Thus *Buffy* was born as an attempt to undo the equation between woman and weakness by establishing one between woman and toughness, to "create someone who was a hero where she had always been a victim."[13]

Whedon accomplishes this reversal by steering Buffy away from classic patriarchal appropriations such as sexual objectification or isolation within a cast of men. Although a teenage Buffy began with mini minis and cleavage, the camera never sliced her up into fetish-size portions as it did with Max. And Buffy's wardrobe seems less a sop to the heterosexual male gaze and more an indicator of her personal development as a woman getting comfortable in her body. This movement becomes especially clear in later seasons as the adult Buffy wears more mature, comfortable, and concealing clothes, the inverse of the trend in *Xena* and *Dark Angel*. Buffy also surrounds herself with other tough female cohorts who grow into heroism and a feminist community along with her. The show consists of an ensemble cast of powerful women: the witches

(Willow and Tara), the demon/capitalist (Anya), the key to the demon dimension (Dawn), and the phallus-wielding vampire slayer herself.

However, the series displays a noticeable uneasiness with the broader implications of the tough female hero and especially her community. Again, the central question revolves not around whether women and heroic toughness can coexist, but around whether they can mix permanently and without the final snap that forces the tough female hero to relinquish her toughness and heroism. Can Buffy wield phallic power on behalf of a feminist community? Can she grow into, not out of, her gifts? Or, if "that blonde girl" is the real killer in the alley, does she become the chief horror to be extinguished? The overall structure of the show responds to this anxiety by oscillating between the two poles of punishment and transcendence. The series builds around a crescendo of snaps that alternate with affirmations of female empowerment and community.

One of the chief fulcrums for this oscillation is the question of the hero's "gift." Is it power or pain? While Joseph Campbell long ago identified part of the hero's journey as "refusal of the call," eventually, the male hero accepts and embraces his gift as his empowerment.[14] In contrast, the female heroes of *Buffy* often interpret their gifts as curses, and Buffy's journey consists of multiple, guilt-ridden, tortured refusals. Like the ideal republican heroine, she would prefer to be "just a normal girl" who shops, adorns herself, and bakes cookies but, instead, finds herself forced from her "natural" protective cover and discovers mainly misery in the adventure. Describing his narrative formula, which can often seem the psychological equivalent of pulling wings off flies, Whedon claims he wants to "strip" Buffy of her social supports.[15] He wants to examine what happens to a tough female hero who defies her feminine status as protected victim.

This experiment works to a dramatic climax in the fifth season, in which Buffy both comes to terms with her gift and denies it. The show's creators consistently emphasize that Buffy owns the phallus, and Whedon often uses imagery that suggestively positions her in relation to her weapons or makes jokes about it (a stake named Mr. Pointy, for instance) (see figure 6.2). She grows more comfortable with this phallic power and more independent of patriarchal

Figure 6.2. Whedon tells us that Buffy has the phallic power

authority as she grows up, and she claims her heroic toughness most openly in the episode "Checkpoint," when she breaks with the council that has loomed over her. The "watchers' council," which trains and directs the slayer, has arrived in Sunnydale to test her, and they refuse to give her information that she needs to save the world and her sister unless she passes their tests. When the time comes for her final evaluation, Buffy reaches an epiphany. She realizes that the watchers need her, not the reverse. She approaches the dour, gray-haired head of the council, rests the blade of a long sword on the table in front of him, and tells him that she will no longer submit to his authority: "No review. No interrogation. No questions you know I can't answer. No hoops. No jumps. No interruptions. See, I've had a lot of people talking at me in the last few days. Everyone is just lining up to tell me how unimportant I am. And I've finally figured out why. Power. I have it. They don't. This bothers them." Most significantly, she follows this ownership of her own power by acknowledging the essential role played by her egalitarian community. The scene's staging emphasizes her community choice. It places her friends, who clap and cheer for Buffy, in a loft looking down at the watchers. Spatially and ideologically, their approval and authority takes priority over the patriarchal community's. While Max turns away from her potential feminist community toward Logan, Buffy embraces her power and her friends simultaneously.

This impressive step forward precipitates a massive swing back. The watchers inform Buffy that the opponent she faces outdoes the typical demon that Buffy can slay. This female monster is a god, and Buffy eventually discovers that only her suicide will frustrate its apocalyptic ambitions. This episode's validation of the tough female hero and feminist community hinges not just upon Buffy's acceptance of her hero's gift, but also upon the definition of that gift as empowerment. Yet, by the time she reaches her final confrontation with the god, the equation between her gift and power slips into an equation between her gift and suicide. In the final moments of the fifth season's finale, appropriately named "The Gift," Buffy finally figures out what the slayer spirit guide meant when she told Buffy that "death is [Buffy's] gift." She did not mean that, like Conan, the slayer's destiny was killing or that, as "Checkpoint" seemed to promise, her gift was power. Rather, dying, self-sacrifice, Sylvia Plath's suicidal art, is what this tough female hero turned sacrificial heroine does best. The phallic authority, which *Buffy*'s male heroes wield with aplomb, wears heavily on Buffy, wears her out; so when in 2001 she finds herself faced with the sacrificial moment (her life for her sister's and the world's), she releases her friends and embraces her death with relief.

Buffy's last words before she leaps to her death reveal the absolute bankruptcy of this sacrifice. In a breathless statement that seems to affirm community, female strength, bravery, and life, she tells her younger sister, "Give my love to my friends. You have to take care of them now. You have to take care of each other. You have to be strong. Dawn, the hardest thing in this world is to live in it. Be brave. Live . . . for me." In actuality, Buffy's final exhortation tells Dawn that she should live not for herself but for someone else, dooming her to the sacrificial heroine cycle. Buffy wills her younger sister a "strong" and "brave" heritage of misery and self-abnegation cloaked in a life-affirming statement.

This patrimony bears its bitter fruit in the following season, when Willow's spell revives Buffy and snatches her out of heaven into a relative "hell," and the series' female community dissolves into masochistic misery. Even after, according to Whedon, Buffy had "reached some . . . closure" in 2001,[16] the next year saw a number of fans unhappy with the 2002 season and its spiral of humiliation for Buffy, whose happiest moments occurred when she got zapped with an invisibility ray or found out that she might only be a schizophrenic hallucinating her slaying while straitjacketed in a mental hospital. The other female characters also suffered more acutely from their heroic "curses": Dawn, the human-shaped key, feels horribly disconnected and turns kleptomaniac; Anya gets left at the altar and returns despairingly and without any pleasure to her vengeance demon career, and, significantly in her and Willow's bedroom, Tara dies shot through with a stray bullet.

In spite of all the agony a "stripped" Buffy endures, the series does not attack the slayer's pugilistic power. Rather, the show reserves its harshest snap for the archetypal female power, witch-craft.[17] Whereas in early shows Willow finds magic a way toward "individuation," "empowerment," "sexual experimentation," and a female and lesbian "community,"[18] in the 2002 season it suddenly stands in for heroin. Whedon took this opportunity to do a punitive after-school special, complete with a destructive "magicking" buddy that she has to stop seeing, a visit to a back-alley magic crack house, and a drunk-on-magic car wreck. While Willow's male buddy, Xander, derives confidence, independence, and status in the community from the development of his newfound "manly" talent for construction, her "feminine" gift brings her pain and depen-dence, destroys her relationships, and eventually threatens the world with apocalyptic destruction. Although she goes cold turkey for a time, Tara's murder at the end of the 2002 season provokes her into becoming the insane, consuming monster of female power unleashed, which only the reasoning and love of Xander can somehow quench.

We could plausibly interpret these outrageous snaps as Whedon's endorsement of the republican compromise with patriarchy. Willow's descent into the monstrous-feminine implies an equation between female power/feminist community and apocalypse. On the one hand, the guilt, misery, and suicide that Buffy endures betrays the show's lingering investment in sacrificial heroism. On the other hand, *Buffy*'s tough female heroes and their community never snap completely. If they suffer reversals, they also experience feminist apotheoses like "Checkpoint," which expose patriarchal ideology as so much delusional rubbish. The most serious challenge that faces Buffy and her community is not demons or patriarchal watchers but their own failures of faith in themselves and in each other. When they stick together and shove a carping patriarchy out of the inner circle, Buffy can embrace her identity as tough female hero. Her last and greatest effort as a hero fighting on behalf of a feminist community is her deliberate refusal to internalize the patriarchal criminalization of her power.

Xena's Final, Good, Right Thing to Do

Like Buffy, Xena also hesitates between guilty refusal and joyous empowerment, but her end, unfortunately, leaves little space for joy. The series begins by promising to do radical feminist work. As Jessica Amanda Salmonson once wrote, "The very act of women taking up sword and shield . . . is an act of revolution whether performed in fact or in art."[19] When *Xena: Warrior Princess* appropriated the archetypal male hero-form in 1995, it started a small revolution in popular culture. Its tough female hero, even in the eyes of her detractors, became "the preeminent symbol of female empowerment" and the embodied equation between woman and toughness.[20] After having inspired so many and saving the world for six seasons, she earned her revolution. To rein in such a powerful icon, her creators had to betray her with a particularly brutal form of the republican compromise. After years spent prioritizing a feminist community over patriarchy, she abandoned this devotion in order to sacrifice herself to violent misogyny. She accepted guilt for her heroism and bowed to the justice of her punishment, endorsing sexist brutality and the society created by it.

Perhaps Xena received this cataclysmic snap because of her wide-ranging effect. But even more than her popularity, her mission galled: In the words of her co-creator, Rob Tapert, "Xena's story is the story to redeem herself."[21] What made her both important to many women and provoked her final abusive beat-down was her dangerous rewriting of republican paradigms to justify the female hero. She circumvented the inevitable compromise narrative by breaking all its foundational assumptions: She overcame the tough female hero's guilt and took an infectious delight in her martial skill and trickster cleverness. She even denied patriarchy as the only option and enabled her revolution by allowing for the possibility of a feminist community.

Xena's redemption and the show's dynamic ultimately rested upon this ability to negate the compromise's third assumption. Producer Liz Friedman has cited one of the major rules for creating Xena as, "Don't write Xena any differently than if she were a man."[22] One way of interpreting this dictum just dresses Hercules and a dutiful sidekick in leather skirts, but another possible interpretation requires that her creators provide her with the same opportunity for social support and self-actualization, the same personhood, that male heroes receive. Friedman's dictum granted the female hero an enabling feminist community and, in so doing, formed the series as a contest waged for the hero's loyalties to either patriarchy or an emergent feminism. In order to gain this devotion, the communities vied to claim moral authority and priority, and, typically, patriarchy lost. While *Dark Angel* showcased elite rule as civilized and loving, *Xena* picked obsessively at this veil of righteous respectability. Far from being the only reasonable option, patriarchy's ethical pose often appeared irrational, brutal, and criminal, and the feminist community generated by Xena's heroics allowed her to escape its vindictive grasp, if she chose wisely. She made this choice again and again, from the first to the final episode. Xena constantly waffled between feminist priorities, embodied by Gabrielle and the oppressed peoples they saved, and the patriarchal community in its two forms: warlord and resentful villagers, who wanted her either to join their hierarchy or die for transgressing it.

The first episode of the series, "Sins of the Past," establishes this dynamic, in which a village claims the moral authority to judge and punish Xena, while Gabrielle claims that same authority to judge and redeem her. Xena returns to her hometown to seek forgiveness, but they instead try to lynch her. They want to punish her for her original crime, which we learn happened not when she went a-warlording but when she "played the hero" and successfully defended the town against invading mercenaries. Because her brother and other young men died as she led them into battle, her family and village reviled and cast her out. Only then did she turn to the other patriarchal option, the bloodthirsty society of warlords. Though the villagers blame her for this second decision as well and plan to punish her for it, Gabrielle defends Xena. Her witty justification convinces them to stop and diverts Xena from a masochistic sacrificial snap, allowing her to choose female partnership and a heroic journey instead.

Although Xena escapes the rubber band's recoil by choosing Gabrielle and heroism repeatedly throughout the series, she makes the clearest decision at the high point of the show's popularity, the second episode of the second season, "Remember Nothing." In this episode, she receives the opportunity to merit the town's forgiveness by undoing the original act of her tough female heroism and returning to her status as passive village girl. When, after accidentally killing a young male soldier who was attacking a defenseless temple, she wishes that she had "never followed the sword in the first place," the Fates grant her an *It's a Wonderful Life* chance to be that innocent girl her town loved. The Fates tell her that as long as she relinquishes her role as a warrior and never "draw[s] blood in anger," she can preserve that alternate reality in which she never became a tough female hero and thus avoid the young soldier's and her brother's deaths. Although joyfully reunited with her brother Lyceus, she soon realizes that this "innocent" world is not necessarily a just one. Overrun with warlord gangs, Greece labors under the heel of its new masters, and society has become an even more reactionary dystopia for many women. The warlords have decimated and enslaved the Amazon nation and gleefully anticipate "break[ing] them." Her mother has died of heartbreak after her village was conquered, and Gabrielle cringes through life under the lash and rape that shapes her totally functionalized nonexistence as a slave.

Xena realizes that although the sacrifice of her toughness might satisfy resentful villagers and save some young men's lives, it does so by creating a reactionary male community at the expense of her partner and a feminist community. Faced with the choice between them, she says a painful good-bye to her brother and picks up the sword again to find forgiveness not in the past but in the future and in an emergent feminism. Thereafter, whenever she despairs under the resentment of frightened villagers or old enemies, whenever the guilt of "taking up the sword" weighs too heavily and she wants to toss it aside or fall upon it, Gabrielle comes to her rescue with the refrain "Xena, it's not your fault." Xena reciprocates by listening to and empowering her friend. Once she prioritizes Gabrielle's authority, they can embark on their heroic mission with new vigor, crossing the ancient world to extend their community, helping out defenseless patriarchal villages, galvanizing the Amazon nation, and coming to the aid of Cleopatra and Helen.

The series finale, "A Friend in Need I and II," self-consciously repeats the structure of "Sins of the Past" and "Remember Nothing," but its conclusions do not actually make the proclaimed "full circle" so much as a 180-degree snap. As in the previous episodes, Xena comes to a question mark in her journey. She revisits another point of heroic origin. Again the locals want her dead because of a crime committed during her heroic act, but this time she does not listen to her friend and instead capitulates and devotes herself to the vengeful patriarchal community. Instead of the forward-moving heroism established by her previous feminist loyalties, she traps herself and Gabrielle in the backward-turning cycle of the sacrificial heroine.

The finale begins with a cosmic moment of choice when the heroes could confirm their feminist mission or snap. Gabrielle is lounging by their campfire, pondering the aurora borealis, and wondering aloud about their larger future path together. When Xena responds enthusiastically to her comments, suggesting they push further into new territory, continuing the progressive heroic journey, Gabrielle smiles with delight and says, "I can't believe you're awake, much less listening to me." This moment marks the last time Xena listens to Gabrielle about a defining moral issue (see figure 6.3). The next instant, a monk, the celibate icon of woman-excluding patriarchy, intrudes with an old mission for Xena. He brings a cry for help from the ghost of Akemi, a sacrificial heroine whose suicide "broke [Xena's] heart," a call that will draw her into

Figure 6.3. Xena and Gabrielle enjoy their final moment of heroism and community before the snap

a repetition of Akemi's suicidal "duty" to patriarchy and turn her from a heroic future with Gabrielle.

Boiled down to its essential details, Xena's relationship with Akemi provided Xena with her first feminist community and instigated her second act of true heroism. Akemi seduced her from her male-identified warlord affinities and taught her to identify with her own authority as a woman and claim forbidden phallic power as a woman. But she betrayed Xena and their emerging hero–hero dynamic by metamorphosing into the sacrificial heroine and stabbing herself, the penalty she paid for the ultimate patriarchal transgression: killing her father, a monstrous warlord named Yodoshi. When Xena tried to fulfill Akemi's last wish to "restore [her] honor" and bring her remains to her family's cemetery in Higuchi, "word got out that I was honoring the ashes of a girl who had killed her father. The townsfolk felt that I would be defiling their graveyard. They banded together to stop me." The villagers attacked her and scattered Akemi's ashes in order to protect the *pater*'s privilege at the expense of a woman's last wishes, her heroic "honor," her individualism.

If Xena were a male hero (and here is where the writers ignore Friedman's proviso), her guilt would stem from the spilt ashes of her friend, her failed heroism, but, instead, the narrative contorts itself and violates all plausibility to make her guilty because of her heroism. In fact, we find that her defense of Akemi somehow turned into her most horrible crime, the one she must "atone for" by becoming a sacrificial heroine herself. After Xena and Gabrielle save Higuchi from the fire set by now phantom Yodoshi's invading army, instead of cheering them, the local "ghost-killer," Harukata, lambastes Xena. He informs them that her tussle with the villagers inadvertently started a fire that killed 40,000 (very slow or oblivious) people, whose souls were then swallowed by the ghost warlord. Harukata passes over Gabrielle's exclamation that "Xena saved your city" by barking "But that does nothing to atone—for what happened—when last she was here," an ethic completely at odds with the pay-it-forward moral of "Remember Nothing."

Shockingly, Xena accepts his logic and proceeds to ignore Gabrielle's arguments and desires to the contrary. Fatally deaf to her partner's moral authority, Xena internalizes the patriarchal assumptions she had earlier rejected. Accepting her guilt, she no longer wants her heroism. She puts down her sword and allows herself to be perforated by a dozen arrows, beheaded, and symbolically raped before her ghost body defeats Yodoshi (see figure 6.4). But even that punishment fails to satisfy. She needs to make her final choice of community clear. As she tells Gabrielle in their last scene together, "for those souls to be released into a state of grace, they must be avenged. I must stay dead." Having internalized the patriarchal community's need to punish the female hero, Xena repeats their cruelty and thwarts Gabrielle's heroic mission to retrieve her ashes and resurrect her. She must disempower her partner, and she literally and figuratively turns away from her and their feminist community toward patriarchy. She devotes her death, her final heroism to it.

Xena's rationale for this decision encapsulates the logical contradiction between individualism and patriarchy at the heart of the republican compromise. She explains to Gabrielle, "If there is

Figure 6.4. Deprived of armor and sword, Xena disappears beneath a phallic barrage

a reason for our travels together, it's because I had to learn from you the final, the good, the right thing to do. I can't come back." But Xena, the female hero, is already gone. Xena, the sacrificial heroine, is not learning from her feminist community, which is pleading with her to "Stop it!" Within the compromise's logic the purpose of the tough female hero's journey, "the reason for our travels together," must ultimately be devotion to its antithesis. She empowers women and a feminist community only in order to subvert them and reaffirm patriarchal privilege as "the final, the good, the right thing to do." Gabrielle, unconvinced but silent now, collapses against her friend. The tough female hero is no longer her partner or an option for herself, and she cannot continue as a heroic full person, finding love and freedom and bringing this empowerment to other women. In the last scene, when she finally scatters Xena's ashes instead of revivifying them, she reveals that, like her former hero, she too has internalized the misogyny that dispersed Akemi's remains. Once Gabrielle accepts Xena's sacrifice, the feminist community dissolves back into patriarchy, and the possibility for revolutionary redemption disappears with it.

Although Xena finally embraced sacrificial heroinism, the rubber band had to strain to make this snap. The finale's version of the compromise seemed forced and irrational, not natural, as convincing ideologies should be. The ideal transformation from tough female hero to sacrificial heroine should snap so smoothly that the audience can hardly notice its workings, but the fans saw the contradiction and reacted with confusion and outrage. When the lights went up on the sneak preview's screening, the guest speakers ducked equally distributed "polite" clapping and booing and a shout expressing how the ending "sucked!" This less than enthusiastic reaction mirrored the general fan response to Xena's end.

The radical disjuncture between creators and fans revealed by the post-screening Q&A session and later fan essays exposes the republican compromise as the sacrifice's motivating rationale. When fans fired angry "whys" at Rob Tapert and R. J. Stewart, they responded by insisting on the logic of their hero's sacrifice: "Xena's story is the story to redeem herself" (Tapert), and "the ultimate redemption for Xena here is not to be brought back to life" (Stewart). They further claimed that Xena was and had always been a "war criminal" and had to be punished like one.[23] Threading the needle between the transcendent/criminal explanations of the tough female's death, they interpreted her suicide as a reconciliation between the hero's need for "ultimate redemption" and the community's need to punish a threat on par with crimes against humanity. In other words, they repeated the republican compromise between the ethic of heroic individualism and the patriarchal community's need to criminalize the apocalyptic threat of female power. Xena's guilt-driven transformation from tough female hero to sacrificial heroine, her snap, atoned for her toughness and power without violating the individual choice that rhetorically grounds American republicanism.

Xena's creators rationalize her suicidal snap by recurring to the republican compromise's three main assumptions. They assume the tough female hero's guilt and her genuine desire to put down the sword in order to assuage this guilt, but, most importantly, they equate community with patriarchy. Only this identification allowed them to perceive the tough female hero's sacrifice to patriarchy as a transcendent and freeing expression of republicanism's individual heroic journey.

Revolutionary Resurrections

Although her creators' inculcation into the compromise's ideology means that Xena cannot come back except for a last bow, some tough female heroes do return more permanently. Suicide narratives that resurrect the tough female hero might allow us an alternative to the female hero-sacrificial heroine cycle. Could her suicide-resurrection imply a movement through and beyond the republican rubber band? Could her return from sacrificial heroinism model an American feminist identity and challenge the antidemocratic structures of our political culture?

Literary critic Teresa Goddu's discussion of the American gothic may help to frame an answer. She claims that "resurrecting what [national] narratives repress . . . can strengthen as well as critique an idealized national identity" and that this American identity poses as "innocent" and free from oppressive power.[24] Or, to put her assertions in this chapter's terms, the "idealized national identity" imagines America as enabling republican individualism rather than patriarchal control. If the repressed powerful female returns as the monstrous-feminine or the pliable heroine, she only perpetuates and strengthens this pose. Like the "war criminal" Xena, she naturalizes patriarchy as a pragmatic response to the criminal. Or, like Max, she returns to ally herself with a seemingly benign paternalistic guide and protector. Because both these options join seamlessly with innocent individualism, the compromise that should cause profound dissonance disappears from view. Patriarchy continues to appropriate and undermine feminist-democratic politics.

In contrast, a resurrection narrative that critiqued this rhetorical subterfuge would expose the compromise's dissonance with the avowed principles of republican individualism. It would reveal the tough female's death as unnecessary and morally bankrupt. Its revived protagonist would refuse criminalization and appropriation and combine the toughness of the monstrous-feminine with the heroine's moral righteousness. In other words, this resurrection would tell the story of a tough female hero who returns to reject the three patriarchal assumptions that underpin the compromise. She would deny the criminalization of her toughness, embrace her power as a moral good for the feminist community, and thus claim the hero's ultimate goal: political authority.

Buffy tends toward such a narrative. She raises suffering to a high art, and she marches through all the republican compromise's snaps on her way to resurrection. Yet the season following her suicide challenges the rubber band cycle and posits the possibility of progress rather than inevitable return. The question, "Where do we go from here?" is the final refrain of 2002's most popular episode, the musical "Once More, With Feeling." This query extends through the entire season and becomes its central issue. As discussed earlier in this chapter, Buffy can deny the moral priority of patriarchy, and, unlike Xena and her "full circle," Buffy appears capable of resisting without return. She can grow and move forward. As she evolves beyond patriarchy, she is finding a way to embrace her power without engaging in a corrupt desire to dominate. She refutes the patriarchal justifications that characterize female strength as monstrous and tyrannical, and, as she and her friends uncover the ugly self-hatred that motivates her preference for playing the sacrificial heroine, she exposes the fallacy of the happy or transcendent suicide.

The series suggests that the key to this progression through the republican compromise lies in identification with a feminist community. In order to claim moral authority, heroes must act for a community that they can shape and be shaped by in empowering ways. Otherwise, they just flicker on the margins of society without access to political power. In spite of American republicanism's rugged lone cowboy imagery, the tough hero's journey is always a communal effort. Patriarchy's ubiquitousness simply makes its partnership silent and almost invisible. In contrast, when a radically marginalized leader, such as the tough female hero, constructs her own enabling community, its centrality suddenly becomes apparent. Buffy and her friends ask, "Where do *we* go from here?" as part of their acknowledgment of a communal heroism. They formulate Buffy's embrace of suicidal guilt and sacrifice as everyone's problem. They respond by bemoaning that the "path . . . home" to a feminist community appears "unclear" and uncharted, but they strive to walk it "hand in hand." As long as they maintain their grip, externalize patriarchal ideology, and justify their tough female hero, they open up space for an alternative to America's compromised identity. The series finale in 2003 sees them succeed as the episode creates this space for a permanent feminist community and heroic female identity. Using her renewed magic, Willow extends Buffy's power to all the potential slayers everywhere. With their help, Buffy finally annihilates the forces of apocalypse, and the town of Sunnydale sinks into the shattered Hellmouth. As metaphysical evil collapses, so does the banal patriarchal community it supported. Freed of its burden, Buffy ends the series smiling (we are led to believe) over dreams she can now pursue in an America transformed by newly empowered girls. The tough female hero's transformation into sacrificial heroine endorsed patriarchal oppression. Yet, her resurrection suggests possibilities for a feminist-democratic social order that recovers a repressed republican individualism.

Notes

1. *Farscape*'s Zhaan and *Star Trek: Voyager*'s Captain Janeway also committed suicide that spring, and *Charmed*'s aggressive alpha witch, Prue, died in place of her more feminine sister.
2. Barbara Creed, *The Monstrous-Feminine: Film, Feminism, and Psychoanalysis* (London: Routledge, 1993) and Sherrie A. Inness, *Tough Girls: Women Warriors and Wonder Women in Popular Culture* (Philadelphia: University of Pennsylvania Press, 1999), 80–81. See also Robin Roberts, *A New Species: Gender and Science in Science Fiction* (Urbana: University of Illinois Press, 1993), 15–65; and Sarah Lefanu, *Feminism and Science Fiction* (Bloomington: Indiana University Press, 1988), 37–52.
3. Jack Boozer, "Seduction and Betrayal in the Heartland: *Thelma & Louise*," *Literature Film Quarterly* 23, no. 3 (1995): 188–196.
4. See Gillian Brown, *The Consent of the Governed: The Lockean Legacy in Early American Culture* (Cambridge, MA: Harvard University Press, 2001); Carole Pateman, *The Sexual Contract* (Stanford, CA: Stanford University Press, 1988). For recent historical arguments covering the extent of women's freedoms and political roles in early America, see Susan Branson, *These Fiery Frenchified Dames: Women and Political Culture in Early National Philadelphia* (Philadelphia: University of Pennsylvania Press, 2001); Shirley Samuels, *Romances of the Republic: Women, the Family, and Violence in the Literature of the Early American Nation* (New York: Oxford University Press, 1996); Mary Beth Norton, *Founding Mothers & Fathers: Gendered Power and the Forming of American Society* (New York: Alfred A. Knopf, 1996). The work of Linda Kerber and Nancy Cott also provides groundbreaking insight into this issue.

5. Although institutional amnesia constantly forgets their stories, tough female heroes have been generating great popular enthusiasm throughout American history, from Hannah Dustan's Puritan Indian-killer to Deborah Sampson's Revolutionary war soldier to the dime novel's Calamity Jane. In fact, Harriet Beecher Stowe's depiction of super-mom Eliza leaping across an icy river to freedom became one of the most influential and reproduced images in the nineteenth century.

6. Lee R. Edwards, *Psyche as Hero: Female Heroism and Fictional Form* (Middletown, CT: Wesleyan University Press, 1984), 9.

7. Carol Pearson and Katherine Pope make a similar distinction between the central, feminist "female hero" and the supporting, male-identified "heroine." See *The Female Hero in American and British Literature* (New York: R. R. Bowker Co., 1981).

8. Michael Weatherly (Logan) once said without apparent irony, "Once in awhile, I look for that microchip in [Max/Alba's] head, because I think James Cameron might have created her. She might be the Billion Dollar Woman. It's like, 'What did you do with all that *Titanic* money, Jim?' 'I created the perfect female . . . and her name is Jessica Alba!' " See this interview in *Entertainment Weekly* (March 28, 2001); available at http://www.ew.com/ew/report/0,6115, 277846~7/22443//0~,00.html; accessed December 4, 2002.

9. Josh Rottenberg, "Dark Victory," *TV Guide*, November 25, 2000, 21–26; Dan Snierson, "The Terminatrix," *Entertainment Weekly* (March 16, 2001); available at http://www.ew.com/ew/report/0,6115,280327~7~~,00.html; accessed December 4, 2002. Joyce Millman claims that "something snapped" in Cameron that shifted his work from truly tough women, "buffed up, fearless, kick-ass . . . grown-up . . . feminist action heroines" like Ellen Ripley of *Aliens* or Sarah Conner of *Terminator*, to "jailbait fetishism [and] . . . wish-fulfillment . . . for every guy who's had all he can *stand* of mature heroines with mommy power and big muscles." See "Be Afraid, Be Very Afraid . . .," Salon.com, October 3, 2000; available at http://dir.salon.com/ent/col/mill/2000/10/3/dark_angel/index.html; accessed December 4, 2002.

10. *Dark Angel* creator James Cameron admitted that the rail-thin Alba "wasn't particularly physically fit." Snierson, "The Terminatrix." He explained the logic behind Max's weakness: "You always have to balance that [strength] with vulnerability, so they're real." (I have not been able to find Cameron making similar statements about another of his cinematic projects, *Rambo*.) See Gloria Goodale, "Director's Answer to 'Xena,' 'Buffy,' " *Christian Science Monitor*, August 25, 2000, 19.

11. See the interview with William Gregory Lee. "Dreamwatch: Zack-rifice!" October 25, 2001; available from www.darkangelfan.com//news/1179.shtml; accessed December 4, 2002.

12. Lee, "Dreamwatch: Zack-rifice."

13. "Joss Whedon on 'Welcome to the Hellmouth' and 'The Harvest' " and "Audio Commentary by Joss Whedon," *Buffy the Vampire Slayer: The Complete First Season on DVD* (Twentieth Century Fox Inc., 2001).

14. Joseph Campbell, *The Hero with a Thousand Faces* (New York: Meridian Books, 1958), 59–68.

15. Joss Whedon, "Commentary," *Buffy the Vampire Slayer: The Complete Second Season on DVD* (Twentieth Century Fox Inc., 2002).

16. Joss Whedon, Buffy: Bronze V.I.P. Posting Board Archive, http://www. cise.ufl.edu/ cgi-bin/cgiwrap/hsiao/buffy/get_archive?date= 20010523 (the address for just the site—not the specific reference—is http://www.cis.ufl.edu/ hsiao/media/ tv/buffy/bronze) May 23, 2001.
17. Robin Roberts examines magic as the embodiment of women's special knowledge or science, A New Species, 92–101.
18. J. Lawton Winslade, "Teen Witches, Wiccans, and 'Wanna-Blessed-Be's': Pop-Culture Magic in Buffy the Vampire Slayer," Slayage: The Online International Journal of Buffy Studies; available at http://www.middleenglish.org/ slayage/essays/ slayage1/winslade.html; accessed August 19, 2002.
19. Jessica Amanda Salmonson, Amazons! (New York: DAW Books, 1979), 14.
20. Andrew Stuttaford, "Dressed to Kill," National Review, October 13, 1999, 69.
21. See Rob Tapert, interview in Paddy Fitz, "Slumming (and Slimming) in Beverly Hills," Whoosh! On the Road, June 19, 2001; available at http://www.whoosh. org/road/mtr2001/paddy.html; accessed August 25, 2002.
22. Robert Weisbrot, Xena: Warrior Princess: The Official Guide to the Xenaverse (New York: Doubleday, 1998), 160.
23. Chris Clogston, "MTR Event," Whoosh! On the Road; available at http://www.whoosh.org/road/mtr2001/clogston.html; original date, June 19, 2001; accessed August 25, 2002.
24. Teresa Goddu, Gothic America: Narrative, History, and Nation (New York: Columbia University Press, 1997), 10.

Part II

New Images of Toughness

Chapter 7

No Cage Can Hold Her Rage? Gender, Transgression, and the World Wrestling Federation's Chyna

Dawn Heinecken

The November 2000 issue of *Playboy* features a muscular woman dressed in black leather, standing with hands on hips, glaring out at the reader. She is not the typical cover girl. Her aggressive stance, her confident and direct gaze out at the reader, and her muscular body do not conform to the ideal of femininity usually promoted by *Playboy*. The woman is Joanie Laurer, otherwise known as World Wrestling Federation superstar Chyna. Since her first appearance on the WWF in February 1997, Chyna made the transition from an oddity in the traveling freak show of the WWF to a household name. As professional wrestling moved from alternative entertainment to the mainstream during the last few years, she also traveled from the fringes to the center, appearing on mainstream magazine covers, prime-time TV series like *Third Rock from the Sun*, and even *The Tonight Show*. Her best-selling autobiography, *If They Only Knew*, was published in 2001.[1] Chyna, like other "powerful" women in the media such as Xena and Buffy, is "cool."

Television series like *Buffy the Vampire Slayer* and *Xena: Warrior Princess* have been widely discussed in recent years because of the ways their heroes transgress traditional media representations of passive femininity.[2] Such transgression has a long history. In *The Unruly Woman: Gender and the Genres of Laughter* (1995), Kathleen Rowe examines how the stock character of "the unruly woman" has been incorporated into popular culture in diverse forms such as comedienne Roseanne and Miss Piggy. The unruly woman is one who, through various means, rebels against her "proper place" and "unsettles one of the most fundamental of social distinctions—that between male and female," through excess and outrageousness. The most apparent qualities of the unruly woman include her large size, her masculine or androgynous appearance, and her domination of, or attempted domination of men.[3] Rowe argues that the unruly woman is a "prototype of woman as subject" who is transgressive because she "lays claim to her own desire."[4] The unruly woman makes a spectacle of herself, claiming the power that comes from visibility in the public realm. However, at the same time that she is a powerful figure she is often reviled.[5]

Chyna possesses many of the qualities of the unruly woman. As a wrestler, she is often literally "on top" of men. Her transgression of female passivity and her excessively muscular body have likewise helped her claim a high degree of public visibility. However, her appearances, like those of the unruly woman, are often complex and conflicting. As Patricia Pender argues about *Buffy*, the often-contradictory representations of active women within popular media operate as sites of cultural negotiation where the meaning of ideas like feminism and transgression can be worked out.[6] As part of a media trend of women who defy conventional notions of female passivity, an examination of the way in which Chyna has been represented helps unravel current discourses concerning gender and power in the media.

In such an examination, it is important to look at the process by which Chyna has made her transition from the margins to the center. A close reading of her performances in the WWF shows the rhetorical strategies by which her unconventional appearance was explained, maintained, and promoted. When she first emerged, she was a reviled, contested figure because of her muscular body and the way she transgressed gender norms. She was described as a monster and not a "real" woman. Her marginalization continued when she was demonized as a feminist who challenged male dominance. Her latest, and most popular incarnation, was that of a sex symbol, a role that required substantial body modification. The different framing of her various incarnations is telling. While Chyna ostensibly projects an image of rebellion, a figure that threatens to melt down the male-dominated world of professional wrestling, her popularity, may, in fact, be due more to a process of normalization than to her transgressive qualities. Thus, her case is useful for what it has to tell us about the ways in which female unruliness is framed by popular media.

WWF: Carnival and Masculinity

To understand the significance of Chyna's presence in the WWF, it is necessary to understand the context in which she appeared. Professional wrestling is a site that welcomes disruptive images. In his 1989 study of professional wrestling, John Fiske linked wrestling to carnival. Both are concerned with inverting the "norms" of the social order:

> Carnival is an exaggeration of sport, the space for freedom and control that games offer is opened up even further by the weakening of the rules that give it a pattern, but unlike sports (whose rules tend to replicate the social), carnival inverts those rules and builds a world upside down, one structured according to the logic of the "inside out" that provides a parody of the extra carnival life.[7]

One way in which norms are disrupted in carnival is through the behavior of, and focus upon, the body. By placing extreme emphasis on the level of the body, the level "on which all are equal," Fiske asserts that the social hierarchy, in which one class has power over another, is disrupted.[8] Drawing on Foucault, Fiske notes that control over the body's appearance is inherently political. The social order is disrupted by the "grotesque" bodies of the wrestlers that defy the ordered aesthetic world of the bourgeoisie. The often fat, flabby bodies and ugly appearance of many wrestlers suggests their liberation "from the social construction and evaluation of the body."[9] In a world in which the middle class emphasizes the ideal of slenderness and beauty, being fat or ugly is an act of resistance.[10] In addition to the wrestler's excessive bodies, professional wrestling displays "excess" through its intense focus on physical pain and suffering. Such excess "opens a space for oppositional and contradictory readings of masculinity" to emerge.[11]

While the inversion of social order and middle-class respectability is very much the same in today's wrestling, it is notable that changes have taken place within the sport since Fiske's analysis. Professional wrestling has moved from being a marginal form of entertainment, associated with the working classes, to mainstream entertainment. It is "cool" to admire the kinds of rebellion and parody at play in wrestling. Professional wrestling has reached an all-time high in appeal, even serving as the setting for a major motion picture, *Ready to Rumble*, and wrestlers regularly appear on prime time and talk shows.[12] The WWF alone performs six shows a week, and there are at least three primetime spectacles fans can tune into, including *Raw*, *Heat*, and *Smackdown*.

The physical appearance of male wrestlers has, for the most part, changed since Fiske's analysis. The bodies of today's wrestlers, like those of The Rock, Hunter Hearst Helmsley, and Stone Cold Steve Austin, are no longer flabby but excessively hard and chiseled. The commentators' dialogues emphasize the wrestlers' brute strength, size, and athletic prowess. It could be argued that the excessive, exaggerated nature of this masculinity is one that as much mocks such macho notions as validates them. While now based on hardness and extreme muscularity rather than flab, wrestlers' bodies are still excessive. Highly developed bodies point to the fact that they are labor intensive, suggesting the performative nature of gender.[13] Yvonne Tasker similarly suggests that such "postmodern" trends in representing the muscular male body, may, like carnival, be seen as a way to express oppositional points of view. She argues that such male figures offer "a parodic performance of 'masculinity,' which both enacts and calls into question the qualities they embody."[14] Thus, images of muscular men may simultaneously represent an assertion of male power at the same time that they express anxiety over its loss.

However, while they occasionally suggest the constructed nature of masculinity, the excessively muscular bodies that are currently the norm within the world of wrestling really work to enforce the status quo. The general mainstreaming of professional wrestling, like the hypermasculinity of wrestlers' bodies, must be viewed against the larger cultural context in which we see increasingly large, muscled bodies as "the norm."[15] While a few flabby wrestlers like Rikishi exist, their flabbiness is their shtick—Rikishi stands out from other wrestlers because his flabby appearance is so different from the excessively muscular, hard, and chiseled norm of the WWF. His signature move—rubbing his thong-clad buttocks into the faces of his opponents—is viewed as repulsive and deadly precisely because his flabby body is outside the norm.

Masculinity in pro wrestling is further defined through its opposite: femininity. Wrestlers who fail or are "heels" (take the role of the bad guy) are associated with the feminine. Commentators impugn the manhood of these wrestlers, and "heels" wear clothing that is sexually suspect—pink tights or earrings, for example. Above all, the masculinity of the wrestlers is established by the presence of extremely feminine women.

Four of the most visible women in recent years—Sunny, Sable, Marlena, and Debra—are petite, large-breasted women with long flowing blond hair who dress in extremely provocative clothing. Frequently designated as "managers" or wives, these women take a subservient role to the men and often have a clearly sexual relationship with them. Female managers function as damsels in distress; for example, rivals attack each other's female managers in order to distract their opponents. In the world of the WWF, women have historically functioned as sexual spectacle.

Such spectacles of femininity not only provide pleasure for the male gaze but also reassure the viewer as to the wrestlers' heterosexuality. The managers function in a way that is no different from that of female cheerleaders in real sports, distracting fans from the homosocial element and the fact that men are placing their hands all over each other in very intimate ways. Although a few wrestlers like Gold Dust are coded as gay (he is painted gold, wears a long blonde wig, and makes lascivious comments to his opponents), heterosexuality is reinforced in many ways. Gold Dust is reviled by the commentators and other wrestlers, and his behavior is repeatedly described as "bizarre." Most importantly, his threat to heterosexuality is contained by his highly sexual, romantic relationship with his manager Marlena. The two kiss and cuddle in the ring. Marlena, puffing on her cigar, constantly reassures viewers she "knows" Gold Dust is "all man." Further, the tiny, buxom, all-but-naked bodies of the female managers contrast sharply with the enormous, muscular, all-but-naked male bodies, providing visual affirmation of a "natural" gender difference.

Chyna: The "Monster"

When Chyna first appeared, the athletic realm of wrestling was occupied *only* by men, since the WWF at that time no longer sponsored female matches. As noted earlier, the excessive muscularity of wrestlers suggests that masculinity is unstable. The petite, thin, white, buxom feminine bodies of the managers thus work to help define and contain masculinity. As Sharon Mazer writes, "Whatever a woman's formal role in the wrestling event might be, as spectator, manager, or wrestler, her function is always to affirm male heterosexual orthodoxy."[16] Chyna, with her large, muscular body and aggressive behavior, created a disruption in the social fabric of wrestling by throwing ideas of "natural" sex differences into confusion. As wrestler X-Pac told her, "I swore I'd never hit a woman. But I'm man enough, and I think you are too."

As Abigail Feder notes, even with the recent fitness craze, women are supposed to keep all signs of their athleticism invisible because "[F]emininity and athleticism are mutually exclusive concepts in American culture."[17] This is not surprising since athletic success and visible musculature are primary ways in which men confirm their masculinity in American society. In particular, muscles are seen as signifying the natural sex differences between men and women. As a result, muscular women, particularly excessively muscled women like body builders, have had their sex questioned.[18] Since female bodies are defined as passive and small in our culture, large, active bodies that do not fit that mold are perceived as transgressive and disruptive of the social norms.[19]

It is thus likely that the presence and history of muscular women in professional wrestling—female wrestlers have existed since the forties—can be explained because of wrestling's status as carnival: It is about the disruption of the norm. However, wrestling's welcoming of disruption has its limits: Women's matches have never enjoyed equal status to men's matches but have essentially functioned as novelty acts.[20] Women wrestlers prior to Chyna only wrestled each other in segregated female matches and never posed a direct threat to the masculinity of male wrestlers. Moreover, wrestling has always worked to define the femininity of female wrestlers in traditional ways. Mazer observes that female wrestlers, like male wrestlers, have been characterized as "good" and "bad," but their morality has been tied to their sexual behavior, replicating the virgin/whore dichotomy.[21] In the late 1980s and early nineties, the appearance of women in the WWF was extremely limited. Two of the most well-known women, for example, were the virtuous "Miss Elizabeth" and the trampy "Sensational Sherri," who functioned as manager/consorts for male wrestlers.[22] When Chyna emerged in 1997, these sexualized roles were the only ones open to women.

With her emergence, Chyna destabilized the social fabric of professional wrestling. The unruly woman, Chyna, is "neither where she belongs nor in any other legitimate position. When she rises above the male, she neither becomes a 'man' nor quite remains a 'woman.'"[23] Consequently, during her first year with the WWF, questions about the "truth" of her sex and the social disruption she caused provided the framework for every appearance she made. She was set in opposition to the traditional feminine, which is "silent, static and invisible."[24] Her introduction to the WWF was connected to images of female madness and aggressive sexuality, which have historically been associated with the figure of the unruly woman.[25] Her transgression in the physical arena was thus explained by her deviance from the norm.

Chyna first appeared during a match between Gold Dust and Hunter Hearst Helmsley. Apparently a crazed fan, she emerged from the crowd to throttle tiny blonde Marlena. In the recaps, Chyna, referred to only as "that woman" and as "huge" and "crazed," was contrasted to "little Marlena" by the commentators. This established the women as representing two ends of the spectrum, one embodying the extreme of femininity, the other of masculine aggression. This opposition was also made by the sharp contrast in the two women's appearance. Chyna was extremely large, had an excessively bulky, muscular body, dressed all in black, and wore pants similar to that of the male wrestlers. She had a prominent underbite. She was stoic, unsmiling, and silent. Marlena, a voluble, tiny blonde, was dressed in a tight gold minidress.

In our culture, status and a certain amount of power are granted to women who fit the "feminine" mold. Chyna's attack against the beautiful Marlena functions as a moment of social inversion. Chyna, marked as a social underdog due to her unfeminine appearance, claims the power usually granted to beautiful women. Future WWF broadcasts repeatedly replayed the attack, zooming in for slow-motion close-ups of Marlena's agonized face. The repetition of this image, the fetishization of Marlena's pain, is significant. It suggests pleasure in seeing Marlena knocked from her privileged position as well as expresses contempt for the feminine qualities that she represents.

Although Chyna's aggression against Marlena was met with fan approval, her place among the male wrestlers was more problematic. During this time, Chyna was characterized as a crazed fan or stalker. Her "stalking" of Helmsley suggested her sexual frustration and anger at men. At the same time, it connoted an unbridled and uncontrollable lust. By offering viewers this stereotypical explanation for her behavior, the threat of her transgression was contained. Throughout her career, Chyna's anger at men was evoked by her trademark move—the "low blow" in which she attacked men's genitals—and by the popular fan slogan "Chyna, No Cage Can Hold Your Rage."

During her first six months, she was described by WWF announcers in mainly pejorative terms, sometimes as an "Amazon," or "Bionic Woman" but chiefly as a "monster" and even as "a dangerous and evil woman." Her looks were laughed at: "Nice chin. Jay Leno, eat your heart out." She was dissected by the language of the commentators, who said, "Look at the shoulders. Look at the delts," "Look at the size of her. Look at her. What a specimen," "She's massive. She's huge. Have you ever seen anything like that?" "Hunter Hearst Helmsley has a cyborg female on his hands." Chyna was described by the commentators as an object, a thing, something not quite human.

At the same time that the language placed her as despised Other, however, the camera work consistently highlighted her strength. In one episode of *Raw* in 1997, she stood in sharp contrast to the "Funkettes," a pair of thong-clad dancing girls escorting one of the wrestlers. She was shot from behind, as she stood overlooking the crowd, arms folded on her chest, emphasizing the strength and power of her body. In her first two years of wrestling, she was repeatedly shot from extremely low angles that emphasized her height as she glared straight into the camera, aggressively returning the gaze.

She was truly problematic at this point because she destabilized the balance between male wrestlers and female managers and the "natural" difference of gender. The conflict her masculine appearance and behavior caused in her first appearance was crystallized by the comments of one announcer who asked, his voice breaking as if he were emasculated by her very appearance, "is that a woman?"

While Chyna was admired, there were attempts to control the threat of emasculation she posed. For example, in one episode of *Raw* in 1997 she punched out Phineas Godwinn, a hillbilly character who wrestled in overalls, wore a long, unkempt beard, and had a pet pig. This punch was met with great excitement by the commentators:

> Ross: (Admiringly) Straight right by Chyna! She weighs close to two-hundred pounds. This woman is Helmsley's bodyguard. She of the three-hundred pound bench press strength.
> McMahon: And she is absolutely fearless. I wonder if—as a male— what you would do J. R. if she hit you? I mean she is a lady. Well, no wait a minute, she's a woman, not necessarily a lady.

The commentators admired her strength and skill at the same time that they recognized that she did not fit "feminine modes of behavior." They wondered what the proper male response to such a woman should be. A possible response was suggested just moments later: Phineas grabbed her and kissed her. She pushed away from him and wiped her mouth, looking, as the announcers noted, like she was "going to regurgitate." This scene has a variety of possible readings associated with gender and class. Phineas the hillbilly was possibly too stupid to know what "real" women were supposed to look like, or perhaps he was practical and appreciated a strong women who might plow his fields. In either case, the lower-class Phineas rejected the middle-class notion of a slender, useless woman. This was a moment when Chyna was simultaneously desired for and punished for her transgression of gender roles. His kiss was a symbolic rape that worked to "put Chyna in her place." Despite this, the moment remains ambivalent. She was disgusted, angered perhaps by his appearance, but she also appeared unfazed by the experience.

The tension between Chyna as a sexual object or an active subject was clearly articulated at the 1997 Slammy Awards, the yearly "Oscars" of the WWF, during which the WWF women competed for the title of Miss Slammy. The competition included a talent and swimsuit competition. For the talent section, some women danced and Sunny modeled, while Marlena showed how she smoked a cigar. Chyna's talent was a clip of her pumping iron in the gym. During this clip, she was filmed in the way that men usually are, as a figure in a landscape.[26] The camera angles were low and showed her whole body, emphasizing her physical power and strength. The clip ended with Chyna flicking sweat into the camera and sneering directly at the viewer. This kind of direct address has been seen as a break from the representation of women as passive objects of the male gaze and as a way for women to assert visual power.[27]

During the swimsuit competition, Sunny, Sable, and Marlena paraded around in provocative, thong-backed swimsuits and high heels. Camera angles changed repeatedly, focusing on individual body parts, a technique that sexualizes and objectifies women.[28] The commentators made appreciative and salacious comments about the women's specific body parts. Sable, for example, was described as having "an end to end all ends" as she bent over in front of the camera. The importance of women as visual objects was underscored by intermixing reaction shots of the approving male audience.

When Chyna's name was called for the swimsuit portion, however, Hunter appeared in her place and explained that he had withdrawn her from the competition because:

> She doesn't belong on stage in the valley of the silicon queens. What she is is a rock hard killer. She's not here to entertain you. She's here to take care of business. And as far as talent goes—people like Sunny—we know what her talent is and you can't show it on national TV.

Chyna, unlike the "feminine" women who were useful only for their sexual parts, had a highly valuable identity as a "rock hard killer" who "take[s] care of business." Chyna, unlike the despised "real" women, is one of the guys.

Yet the question remains—can she be one of the guys and be a woman? One announcer commented, "I know why Chyna's not (at the swimsuit competition). You ever seen the movie *The Crying Game*? That may be Chyna's problem." Obviously, Chyna's female sex is questioned because she possesses muscles. Since muscles are seen as physical "proof" of masculinity, she must be a man. In addition, she refuses to offer "proof" about both her female sex and feminine gender. She refuses to conform to feminine behavior by displaying her body for male approval, and she does not expose body parts like her breasts, which might be read as "proof" of her female sex. Her punishment is thus to be accused, like most females who transgress against accepted notions of femininity, of being a man rather than a woman. This theme continued for her first two years in the WWF and was reflected in fan signs that read "Chyna is a man," "Chyna does viagra," and "Chyna is Cartman's Dad."

As Christine Holmlund has observed, there is a tendency in American society to equate muscularity in women to lesbianism.[29] Muscular women, like lesbians, deviate from the norm and may be seen as transgressing against biology. Undoubtedly, Chyna's physique threatened both male and female viewers for this very reason. Interestingly, while her gender was frequently called into question by WWF commentators, she was never accused of being a lesbian. Possibly, the threat of same-sex attraction was too unsettling for the precariously balanced sex-gender system of the

WWF.[30] A strong evocation of lesbianism—particularly lesbianism without benefit to men—might raise awareness that male wrestlers might also desire each other.

A sign that Chyna was not completely a figure of scorn was her assimilation into the popular wrestling group Degeneration X. Male members of the group frequently pointed out her strength: Helmsley several times credited his wins to Chyna's help. In a broadcast of *In Your House*, Shawn Michaels told the crowd that Chyna was training him to increase his tolerance for pain. During his speech, she flexed for the crowd, while Helmsley poked her arm to show its hardness as the camera zoomed in to focus on the muscle. In a 1998 episode of *Raw*, Chyna flexed while guest Mike Tyson admiringly felt her muscles. She was admired for her ability to meet masculine standards of hardness and strength.

However, femininity was literally implanted into Chyna only a few short months into her career. She appeared on *Raw* wearing a low-cut bra top with a leather dog collar, and with a new, softer, hairstyle as Shawn Michaels took the center of the ring, saying: "I'd like to introduce the two newest members of Degeneration X." Michaels pushed his head toward Chyna's breasts, and as the camera zoomed in to her cleavage, he exclaimed "They are right *here*! Oooooooh!" As Michaels and Helmsley continued to make a series of breast jokes, Michaels even rubbed his head against her cleavage. This was the moment in which the certainty of Chyna's gender was solidified and could no longer be questioned. Female bodybuilders have similarly been forced to confirm their femininity via breast size.[31] One of the ways in which femininity is constructed is through visibility. Women are assumed to be constantly available for public display and comment.[32] Chyna's breasts not only were visible signs of her femininity, but in the "proper" treatment of the feminine, were made into a spectacle, openly discussed, and joked about.

Chyna Talks!

Chyna's breast implants were the first step in her move from being a supporting player in the WWF to a headliner. Thoroughly gendered as female by her second year in the WWF, her gender became the central "problem" of her character. Despite finally being acknowledged as a "real" woman, Chyna did not adhere to proper feminine behavior but continued to confront men. While a deviant "monster" might have gotten away with this, it was clearly not acceptable behavior for someone within the sex-gender system of the WWF. Not coincidentally, at the same time that Chyna was finally accorded the status of "woman," she was also made into a "heel"— a villain—when she began to articulate a liberal feminist stance.

Chyna's feminism is framed as a betrayal against men. She turns "heel" when she betrays her mentor, Hunter Hearst Helmsley. Her villanization can be read as part of a backlash against feminism and echoes the demonization of feminists within the mainstream media.[33] Jackson Katz asserts that the popular acceptance of antifeminist and even misogynist voices within the media is a sign that the cultural changes wrought by feminism threaten the power of certain groups of men.[34] Moira Ferguson, Ketu H. Katrak, and Valerie Miner likewise argue that it is now acceptable to challenge women's struggles for equality because feminism has been framed by the New Right as "tyrannical, undemocratic ideology, bearing the nebulous and rather ambiguous label of 'political correctness.'"[35] In the carnivalesque, rule-breaking atmosphere of the WWF, being "correct" in any way is clearly the act of a villain.

Chyna's stint as a feminist demonstrates both the ways that feminism has been demonized and how thoroughly cultural changes wrought by feminism have been accepted as part of our larger culture. For example, she battled for the title of Intercontinental Champion against Jeff Jarrett in a series of comical matches labeled the "Battle of the Sexes." In contrast to the majority of Chyna's characterization during this time, the preferred slant of these fights was very much "pro-Chyna" and supported the liberal feminist position she espoused. Nevertheless, the matches also provided ample opportunity for women to be mocked and belittled. The "Battle of the Sexes" began when Hardcore Holly and Jeff Jarrett refused to fight Chyna. Calling her "sweetheart" and "honey," Holly said, "You're a woman. I'm a man, and I don't wrestle women." Chyna got them to fight her but was knocked unconscious by Jarrett with a frying pan. He then draped an apron over her inert body, placed a pan and a soup ladle in her hands, and shouted, "Get your ass in the kitchen and start fixing my supper." Later, Chyna attacked Jarrett with a frying pan. While the crowd cheered, she covered him with an apron, removed his pants and put them on herself.

In the promo for the Intercontinental Title match, Jarrett was revealed as not only a sexist but also a downright cad. As he proclaimed "women are weak, and men are the dominant species," a montage showed him attacking various women—including non-wrestlers like model Cindy Margolies and even the make-up woman from back stage. During the match, the Fabulous Moolah and Mae Young—two legendary female geriatric wrestlers—watched from the sidelines as "Chyna's cheerleaders," while Jarrett and Chyna belted each other with domestic items, including pots and pans, an ironing board, and even a kitchen sink.

In another match, Jarrett was about to claim victory when Young and Moolah jumped into the ring. Despite the horrified announcer, who could not believe Jarrett was fighting women "old enough to be his grandma," he body slammed and clotheslined them, eventually knocking them from the ring. Chyna was finally saved by "spitfire" Debra, Jarrett's manager, who betrayed Jarrett by knocking him out with a guitar. The Chyna-Jarrett matches culminated when all the women Jarrett had attacked entered with brooms, pans, and mops and beat him up.

Chyna's victory in the Intercontinental Title acknowledges the ways that women's roles have changed over the years. Since the second-wave feminist movement of the seventies, the culture at large has increasingly accepted women's movement into the public sphere and has also gained an increased awareness of issues related to violence against women.[36] Jarrett's demand for complete subservience from women and his desire for women to be barefoot and pregnant in the kitchen was clearly laughable in a culture in which most women work outside the home. Similarly, his violence against women was presented as inexcusable.

It is important to note that at the same time viewers were invited to jeer at Jarrett, they were being treated to multiple images of women being beaten. Similarly, while the WWF presented overt misogyny as unacceptable, indirect misogyny flourished through the use of humor. The humorous framing of the matches allowed viewers to take pleasure in Jarrett's voicing of his misogynist opinions and to read them as "just" a joke. According to Kathleen Rowe, this is typical of representations of the unruly woman, who is "poised between serving as a target of hostile laughter herself and hurling that laughter back at its sources."[37] Following Freud, she points out that jokes actually "veil and make acceptable an underlying aggression" toward women.[38] The sexual aggression inherent in jokes is evident in the way that much of the humor directed at Chyna took a sexual and violent form.

For example, as noted earlier, Phineas Godwinn's kiss was a symbolic rape used to put Chyna in her place. This metaphor recurred in a more threatening way two years later when she attempted to attack The Rock. She was surrounded and brought down to her knees by several of his henchmen as he held her face near his groin. During this scene, the camera stayed in a tight close up of her twisted, agonized face, framed by The Rock's huge hand suggesting forced oral sex. To make the sexual threat more obvious, he said: "You're just itching to get some. . . . Tell you what, you look pretty damn good on your knees Chyna. It almost looks like a natural position."

During this sequence, the announcers commented frenziedly on how "humiliated" Chyna was. Her humiliation stemmed not just from her physical defeat but from the fact that, for the first time, she was in a powerless position coded with explicit references to female sexual submission. At this point, the crowd was going wild. Whether this was due to the fact that it was an exciting development that might lead to Chyna retaliating in some deadly way, or due to pleasure in her punishment, was unclear. Ultimately, the Rock released her, saying: "There ain't no way . . . The Rock would ever kiss a piece of trash like you." This rejection was also a violation—denying her status as a woman, she was dehumanized, trash.

Similar antiwoman attitudes are expressed by a wide range of contemporary media figures. They reveal the ways in which violence against women is normalized within mainstream culture and may be read as reflective of a backlash against feminism.[39] This cultural tension is apparent in the contradictory ways in which Chyna functioned during her incarnation as a feminist. At times, she helped to express feminist ideas such as the right for women to have an "equal playing field" and compete equally with men. More often, her position as a feminist was equated to her status as a heel and her appearances were used to articulate deeply misogynist attitudes.

Suddenly Sexy

The contemporary emphasis on toned bodies, currently expressed by media figures such as Madonna, Janet Jackson, and Gabrielle Reese and magazines like *Self*, reflects larger cultural attitudes about the need for self-management. As Susan Bordo writes, "the firm, developed body has become a symbol of a correct *attitude*; it means that one 'cares' about oneself and how one appears to others, suggesting willpower, energy, control over infantile impulses."[40] The emphasis on self-control reflects the paradoxical nature of modern consumer culture in which we are constantly encouraged to indulge our desires and consume. At the same time, we need to maintain discipline and self-control in order to keep producing goods and services.[41] The toned body is also related to social mobility since the self-control it represents means that one has the managerial qualities needed to succeed.[42]

While muscles are a sign of self-discipline, in her early years in the WWF Chyna's body transgressed the cultural values expressed by the ideal of the toned body. Particularly because she was a woman and, therefore, not supposed to be naturally muscular, her extreme, excessive musculature read like an overindulgence: She had overdosed on working out to the point where she blurred the gender lines and no longer appeared to be a "real" woman. Her body read as a body out of control because it violated the biological laws of nature and suggested a disregard for social laws. Chyna transgressed further by refusing to position herself as a sexual object through her appearance and behavior. It is telling that her popularity expanded enormously when she adopted the role of the sex symbol and began to adhere to contemporary beauty norms. The discourse surrounding her changing appearance and sexualization reveals how her potential to disrupt gender lines was muted and contained.

The later discussion surrounding Chyna's body and sex appeal was notable for the fact that male figures in the WWF and promotional material made no mention of her prior history as a figure of fun. WWF commentators, who gushed over her scxiness, never mentioned their past doubts about her gender and their labeling of her as a monster. To a certain extent, this is part of the tradition of wrestling, where villains regularly turn into heroes and vice-versa. Though others chose not to speak of it, Chyna spent a lot of time talking about her painful past experiences of her body as being too transgressive for toleration.

For example, during a *Playboy* online chat, when asked what were the most difficult obstacles in her life Chyna replied: "One, my physique; two my home life with my parents." In a 2000 broadcast of *Raw*, she confessed: "for some years people ridiculed me, they called me names, ugly, um freak, some very cruel things." She expressed an awareness in this broadcast that her body was still suspect. "People always accuse me of either being on drugs or not being normal for the amount of muscle I have. I think they don't realize the many hard years of work I've put into my body and the dedication that I've had."[43] Despite her awareness of how others reacted to her body, she positioned her physique as a sign of and product of her character and determination.

Chyna/Laurer overtly situated her appearance as a sex symbol who was also muscular as a transgressive act against oppressive norms and saw herself as a role model helping other women: "I think we show too much of the same type of woman. There are women of all different shapes and sizes. And it also allowed me to show my feminine side." *Playboy* allowed her to show herself as a "power beauty."[44] She told Regis Philbin that "I fccl that I am really a pioneer as a female to be in this completely male-dominated entertainment field."[45] She also stated that "I know for a fact that I'm an inspiration for many women out there."[46]

She argued that women need to "look how they want to." In an online *Playboy* interview she wrote,

> I had to show people that you have to be your own woman. And by the way the magazine has been selling, it looks like there are many men out there who like built women. . . . There are so many women who would like to have built bodies but are afraid of how people will look at them and what they'll think. . . . By posing for *Playboy*

magazine, I've really broken the ice for a lot of other women to look how they want to look.[47]

Her language implies that while it is important for women to own themselves, it remains essential that men find this look appealing. Laurer has a point. Images gain their meaning from context—from their relationship to other images as well as their relationship to the larger world. As Sut Jhally has observed, nothing is inherently bad in visual objectification. It is part of human nature to objectify and to want to be objectified at times.[48] The evaluation of that objectification as positive or negative comes from the image's relationship to other images in a system. Thus, in a sign system in which female sexuality and objectification are signs of female success, women who are not sexually objectified by the mainstream because they are too fat or too muscular experience a symbolic annihilation as sexual beings. As a result, they are no longer able to claim the privileges that objectification sometimes brings, such as love, marriage, economic security, and other signs of feminine success.[49]

What was *not* acknowledged in all Laurer's and the press's talk about Chyna as a transgressive role model was the fact that Laurer, in order to achieve her success, changed her body considerably. Her transformation from being called "freak" to being called the "Ninth Wonder of the World" by commentators was contingent on her increasing adherence to traditional feminine norms of appearance. Once threatening the social hierarchy with her large and androgynous appearance, her unruliness was subdued through a rhetoric of overt sexualization and bodily normalization, particularly the shrinking of her muscular body.

For example, her sexual appeal was contained by framing her sexuality in particular ways. Obviously, her later sexual appeal was tied to the image of the dominatrix, a figure drawn from male pornography. She wore black leather, thongs, studded bra tops, and dog collars. Her entrance to the WWF ring was marked by her firing off of a giant bazooka into the crowd, a sign of her claiming phallic power through her sexiness. Within the WWF and in the outside press, her sex appeal was almost always linked to either some threat of violence or to "animal" appeal. In her appearance on *The Tonight Show*, for example, Chyna wore a leopard-skin pantsuit and kissed band leader Kevin Eubanks aggressively. Her photographs in *Playboy* stress her "animal" side. One features her reclining on animal-print sheets. In another, she is photographed from the side as she tosses her head back, back arched, while her long hair takes up much of the page, fanning out behind her like a mane. These images represent a kind of sexual othering, consistent with representations of those, like black women, whose sexuality is marketed as particularly dangerous.[50] Such images provide a way for audiences to make sense of Chyna. She is no longer a new and threatening figure but can be categorized into traditional ways of viewing female aggression that do not disrupt notions of male power.

Another mode of containment was to romantically link her with men like Hillbilly Phineas Godwinn or Latino Eddie Guerrero, who were already marked as emasculated by racist and classist stereotypes. Another tactic was to deny or excuse her toughness. The press coverage around her, for example, frequently worked to distract from her potential physical threat: "Tough Chyna's also feminine Joanie Laurer," "I like to be romanced," "I am Chyna, but I still love make-up and I still love feminine things."[51]

The most noticeable and important change was in Chyna's body. She had extensive plastic surgery, including breast implants and facial reconstruction. Chyna, who once had her chin compared to Jay Leno's, had plastic surgery to fix her underbite and appears to have had cheekbone implants as well. Her appearance was also softened. Her hair, initially pulled back tightly in a ponytail and worn with bangs, was later styled and worn long and unbound. She wore more glamorous makeup. While once she had the dark-orange tan skin of the body builder, her skin increasingly grew lighter, more reflective of the white feminine ideal.

She shed a large part of the muscular bulk that made her so troublesome just three years earlier.[52] This change was most noticeable about her arms and shoulders. Where once she had to walk with her arms jutting out at her side—the gorilla-like stance of many large wrestlers or weight lifters—in her new sexy guise she walked in the familiar feminine manner, with arms swaying side to side across her body. Her arms and shoulders, while still possessing muscular definition few women have, were far less bulky. She had moved closer to the sculpted muscular appearance that is the norm in today's culture. In reducing her body this way, Chyna was conforming to contemporary dictates urging women to be smaller.[53]

She defended her change in appearance as "choice," remarking, "I've been trying to streamline my body."[54] She defended her breast implants as a choice made for herself, denying that WWF owner Vince McMahon paid for her breast job and saying the implants were her Christmas and birthday presents to herself. "That was the one part of my body. . . . Although I could sculpt everything else, I couldn't sculpt those. So I bought myself a pair."[55] Chyna described herself as actively shaping her own body, positioning it as an object to be controlled and manipulated at will.

As Susan Bordo has noted, the rhetoric of such bodily transformation and body sculpting is one that is based on an idea of the body as plastic and on an ideology that is

> fueled by fantasies of rearranging, transforming, and correcting, an ideology of limitless improvement and change, defying the historicity, the mortality, and, indeed, the very materiality of the body. In place of that materiality, we now have what I will call cultural plastic. In place of God, the Watchmaker, we now have ourselves the master sculptors of that plastic.[56]

The term sculpting also ignores the homogenizing and normalizing effects of plastic surgery. As Bordo observes, focus on choice obscures the fact that the images we aspire to have a content that is "far from arbitrary, but is instead suffused with the dominance of gendered, racial, class, and other cultural iconography."[57] Like many plastic surgery or exercise advertisements, Chyna's discussion about her body focused on empowerment and choice, but she ignored the fact that the changes she made to her body were "choices" made within the narrow constraints of a society that deemed her a nonwoman and monster because of her flat-chested, muscular appearance. Just as black women's choice to straighten their hair reflects the racist society in which they live, Chyna's plastic surgery must be placed against a social context in which only a limited range of women are deemed acceptable.

While it is probably likely that Laurer's facial surgery was at least partly motivated, as she claimed, by medical problems caused by her severe underbite, she could be thought of as a poster child for the social benefits of plastic surgery. It is through such physical changes that she sculpted a new sexy persona that reaped her many rewards. She had nowhere near the notoriety in the outside world or as prominent a role in the WWF until surgery literally implanted her with femininity. Not surprisingly, it is her surgically enhanced breasts, as easily visible signs of femininity, that tended to be the subject of many of her interviews and wrestling appearances. *Regis and Kathie Lee*, for example, discussed her "awesome icebergs," while Jay Leno's interview focused on how many times Chyna's breasts had popped out of her top during matches.

In fact, whereas in the past her body was the focus of WWF storylines because it transgressed feminine norms, her newly sexual, desirable body was the focus of many later storylines for being "too" feminine, too sexy. One recent feud was with the wrestling group "Right To Censor," whose villainous members wear costumes modeled after the Mormons' white shirts and black ties. The group's conflict with Chyna focused on her posing in *Playboy* and her "flaunting" of her body and is illustrated in this excerpt from the October 26, 2000, broadcast of *Smackdown*:

> Ivory: I want to speak up for all the women in the world. . . . Now
> I find, personally, the most reprehensible of The Rock's
> remarks concerning pie. I'm disgusted by these remarks. . . .
> We are not here for you to—we're not incredible edibles. We
> are not pieces of meat. . . .
> Chyna: Now Ivory. We—meaning myself and probably the rest of
> the women in attendance tonight—don't really appreciate a
> self-righteous, uptight *librarian* woman who really—
> Ivory: Chyna. I understand. I understand you're angry. And I feel
> your pain. I feel your pain because you of *all* women in the
> WWF, you have been exploited the most. Posing nude doesn't
> make you beautiful! It just makes you *cheap* (crowd boos).

Ivory voices the feminist viewpoint, which, in the world of the WWF, was collapsed into the same position as religious conservatives and others who wish to censor free speech. By accepting and welcoming her place as "pie," Chyna helped turn the joke against those women who are truly unruly, like Ivory, or feminists. Such women were clearly labeled as nonwomen. Ivory was criticized for being sexually repressed, shrill, and "running on," all signs that she was a sexually deviant lesbian feminist. In contrast, Chyna became a "real" woman, a woman who was happy to be pie. This exchange demonstrates, over the last three years, the inversion of her character and position within the masculine world of the WWF.

The fact that a muscular woman was being presented as worthy of sexual esteem is a sign of an expansion of normative beauty standards, but at what cost? Tellingly, Chyna is no more. Laurer announced her departure from the WWF in July 2001. Although she maintained that her decision to leave the WWF was mutual, it is clear that part of the difficulty lay in her character. Thoroughly feminized by this time, Chyna, whose fame was originally based upon the fact that she only fought men, had begun to fight women more frequently. Laurer described this as a disservice to herself as well as the fans.[58] While she said that she left for greater economic and professional gain (she wants to be an actress), it is hard to ignore the possibility that she had run through the gamut of acceptable roles for women within the conceptual world of the WWF. Her character was played out. Once the monstrous woman had been tamed, caged inside the box of female sex kitten, there was no more use for her. She had become just like all the other WWF women: expendable.

Making Grown Men Cry: The Power of Spectacle

Chyna's violence against men, the fighting of her "feminist" battles, such as the matches against Jeff Jarrett, gave voice to oppositional perspectives on gender relations and women's power. Her appearances simultaneously demonstrate the widespread acceptance of some feminist ideas in mainstream culture as well as discomfort with these ideas. At times Chyna offered an appealing image of rebellion. She disrupted the ways in which gender norms are constructed within the world of wrestling. She also broke from traditional depictions of female bodies as purely sexual objects and challenged notions of gender as natural through her muscular physique. At the same time, she frequently suffered a backlash, becoming the brunt of sexualized humor and violence and being labeled a villain for her feminist views. Ultimately, the rebellion she provided to viewers must be situated against the context of her changing body. Her muscular body, once a clear sign of resistance to the masculine norm of the WWF, was assimilated, changed from a threat to a fetish object. Like female bodybuilders, Chyna's appearances were discursively framed and assimilated into traditional ways of thinking about femininity and the female body.[59] While she was once a problematic figure offering a challenge to established gender roles and correct feminine behavior, she increasingly assumed a more acceptable form: a woman who enjoys making a sexual spectacle of herself.

While those committed to a feminist utopian ideal might cringe at the way Chyna's presence has been contained, it would be inaccurate to state that her muscular body has had all signs of resistance erased from it. It is important to bear in mind the power of the spectacle her diminished yet still powerful body creates for audiences largely unaccustomed to *any* images of physically powerful women.

Although body sculpting is certainly a process by which the unruly body is disciplined, the effectiveness of such discipline is contingent upon the processes of discipline being erased from view. The muscular, sculpted body cannot reveal the effort that goes into it. In contrast, wrestling is a medium that revolves around making a spectacle of sweat and pain. It constantly reminds the audience of the extreme strength and skill participants must have in order to withstand such punishment. Similarly, Laurer's personal discourse surrounding her body is full of references to how hard she has had to work and train to develop her physique in order to compete with men.

In addition, spectacle is a way that women can claim visibility in the public sphere and, through public visibility, power. Women can secure power "not only by looking—but by being seen—or rather, by fashioning, as author, a spectacle of themselves."[60] As a wrestler, Chyna differs from other "built" women like female bodybuilders. She has authored a body that is to be *used*, a kicking, fighting body that she has designed for motion and function, not for static display. Her muscles are highly visible signifiers of her willingness to transgress.

Chyna still provides a spectacle of wonder for audiences who are unaccustomed to any sort of musculature on women. For example, when she appeared on *Regis and Kathy Lee* the two hosts could not take their eyes off of her as she proudly displayed her body as an object of awe and fear.

> Regis: You're an awesome looking woman. I can't take my eyes off. . . .
> Kathie Lee: You're glittering. . . .
> Chyna: Look at this (flexes arm).
> Regis: Look at that!
> Kathie Lee: Oh my. . . .
> Regis: Oh my god!
> Chyna: It's like an onion. . . . You peel this back and it makes a grown man cry.

Although she has diminished in size and powdered her nose, for many people, Laurer's physique retains the visceral power to disturb and excite.

Notes

1. Chyna with Michael Angeli, *If They Only Knew* (New York: Regan Books, 2001).
2. Rhonda V. Wilcox and David Lavery, *Fighting the Forces: What's at Stake in Buffy the Vampire Slayer* (New York: Rowman & Littlefield, 2002); Sherrie A. Inness, *Tough Girls: Women Warriors and Wonder Women in Popular Culture* (Philadelphia: University of Pennsylvania Press, 1999).
3. Kathleen Rowe, *The Unruly Woman: Gender, and the Genres of Laughter* (Austin: University of Texas Press, 1995), 31.
4. Rowe, 31.
5. Rowe, 31.
6. Patricia Pender, "'I'm Buffy and You're History': The Postmodern Politics of *Buffy*," in *Fighting the Forces: What's at Stake in Buffy the Vampire Slayer*, ed. Rhonda V. Wilcox and David Lavery (New York: Rowman & Littlefield, 2002), 43.
7. John Fiske, *Understanding Popular Culture* (Boston: Unwin Hyman, 1989), 82.
8. Fiske, 83.
9. Fiske, 88.
10. Fiske, 92–93.
11. Fiske, 89.
12. Gemma Tarlach, "Wrestling: An American Way of Life," *Milwaukee Journal Sentinel*, August 11, 2000.
13. Richard Dyer, "Don't Look Now," *Screen* 23 (1982): 71.

14. Yvonne Tasker, *Spectacular Bodies: Gender, Genre and the Action Cinema* (New York: Routledge, 1993), 111.
15. Richard Majors, *Cool Pose: The Dilemma of Black Manhood in America* (New York: Lexington Books, 1992); Jackson Katz and Jeremy Earp, *Tough Guise: Violence, Media and the Crisis in Masculinity*, dir. Sut Jhally, Media Education Foundation, 1999, videocassette.
16. Sharon Mazer, *Professional Wrestling: Sport and Spectacle* (Jackson: University Press of Mississippi, 1998), 128.
17. Abigail M. Feder, "A Radiant Smile from the Lovely Lady: Overdetermined Femininity in 'Ladies' Figure Skating," in *Women on Ice*, ed. Cynthia Baughman (New York: Routledge, 1995), 22.
18. Laurie Schulze, "On the Muscle," in *Building Bodies*, ed. Pamela L. Moore (New Brunswick, NJ: Rutgers University Press, 1997), 9–30.
19. Vickie Rutledge Shields with Dawn Heinecken, *Measuring Up: How Advertising Affects Self-Image* (Philadelphia: University of Pennsylvania Press, 2002), 95–97; Rowe, 65.
20. Mazer, 123.
21. Mazer, 123, 134.
22. Mazer, 136–137.
23. Rowe, *The Unruly Woman*, 43.
24. Rowe, 31.
25. Rowe, 31.
26. Laura Mulvey, "Visual Pleasure and Narrative Cinema," in *Feminist Film Theory: A Reader*, ed. Sue Thornham (New York: New York University Press, 1999), 64.
27. Beverly Skeggs, "A Good Time for Women Only," in *Deconstructing Madonna*, ed. Fran Lloyd (London: B.T. Batsford, Ltd., 1993), 67.
28. Mulvey, 65–66.
29. Christine Holmlund, "Visible Difference and Flex Appeal: The Body, Sex, Sexuality and Race in the 'Pumping Iron' Films," *Cinema Journal* 28, no. 4 (1989): 43.
30. There has been only one moment where the possibility of lesbianism for the benefit of women—not men—has been suggested. It was implicitly referenced when Miss Kitty defected from Jeff Jarrett to Chyna's side. Kitty appeared in the next match, dressed in a Chyna costume, rooting for Chyna at ringside, as the female escorts typically do for their male wrestlers. This angle was dropped after only two broadcasts, suggesting it was too transgressive even for the WWF.
31. *Pumping Iron II: The Women*, prod. and dir. George Butler, Bar Belle Productions, Inc., 1985, videocassette.
32. Shields with Heinecken, *Measuring Up*, 73–75.
33. Rebecca Ann Lind and Colleen Sabo, "The Framing of Feminists and Feminism in News and Public Affairs Programs in U.S. Electronic Media," *Journal of Communication* 52, no. 1 (2002): 211–224; Rhonda Hammer, "Anti-feminists as Media Celebrities," *Review of Education/Pedagogy/Cultural Studies* 22, no. 3 (2000), Academic Search Premier, available at http://web11.epnet.com/citation. asp?tb=1&_ug=dbs+1+1n+en%2Dus+sid+497270F2%2D.
34. Katz and Earp, *Tough Guise*.
35. Moira Ferguson, Ketu H. Katrak, and Valerie Miner, "Feminism and Antifeminism: From Civil Rights to Culture Wars," in *Antifeminism in the Academy*, ed. Shirley Nelson Garner, Margaret Higonnet, and Ketu H. Katrak

(New York: Routledge, 1996), 35–65, quoted in Hammer, "Anti-feminists as Media Celebrities."

36. David Kallick, "Gender Politics," *Social Policy* 23, no. 4 (1993), Academic Search Premier, available at http:// web11.epnet.com/citation.asp?tb=1&_ug=dbs+1+1n+en%2Dus+sid+497270F2%2D.

37. Rowe, 69.

38. Rowe, 68.

39. Jackson Katz, "Advertising and the Construction of Violent White Masculinity: From Eminem to Clinique for Men," in *Gender, Race, Class in Media: A Text Reader*, 2d. ed., ed. Gail Dines and Jean Humez (London: Sage, 2002), 349–358.

40. Susan Bordo, *Unbearable Weight: Feminism, Western Culture, and the Body* (Berkeley: University of California Press, 1993), 195.

41. Bordo, 201; Bryan S. Turner, *The Body and Society: Explorations in Social Theory*, 2d. ed. (London: Sage, 1996), 24.

42. Bordo, 201.

43. Chyna interview, *Playboy* online chat available at http:// www.Playboy.com/magazine. Nov. 2000.

44. Chyna, Interview, *Playboy* online chat.

45. Chyna, interview, *Live with Regis and Kathie Lee*, May 6, 1999.

46. Chyna, interview, *Fox News Live*, Fox, September 28, 2000.

47. Chyna, interview, *Playboy* online chat.

48. Sut Jhally, *Dreamworlds II*, dir. Sut Jhally, Media Education Foundation, 1995, videocassette.

49. Shields with Heinecken, *Measuring Up*, 165.

50. Patricia Hill Collins, "Pornography and Black Women's Bodies," in *Gender, Race and Class in Media*, ed. Gail Dines and Jean M. Humez (London: Sage, 1995), 282–283.

51. Chyna, interview, *Playboy* online chat; Chyna, interview, *Jane Hawtin Live*, WTN, April 23, 1999.

52. Chaunce Hayden, "Joanie Laurer: Still Rockin' After Leaving the WWF," *Steppin'Out Magazine: New York and New Jersey's #1 Entertainment Magazine* (July 25, 2001), available at http:// www.steppinoutmagazine.com/07_25_01/archive_index.html.

53. Jean Kilbourne, " 'The More You Subtract, the More You Add': Cutting Girls Down to Size," in *Gender, Race, Class in Media: A Text Reader*, 2d. ed., ed. Gail Dines and Jean Humez (London: Sage, 2002), 258–267.

54. Chyna, interview, *Playboy* online chat.

55. Chyna, interview, *Jane Hawtin Live*.

56. Bordo, *Unbearable Weight*, 245–246.

57. Bordo, 246.

58. Hayden, "Joanie Laurer."

59. Schulze, "On the Muscle," 9–30.

60. Kathleen Rowe, "Roseanne: Unruly Woman as Domestic Goddess," in *Feminist Television Criticism: A Reader*, ed. Charlotte Brunsdon, Julie D'Acci, and Lynn Spigel (Oxford: Clarendon Press, 1997), 77.

Chapter 8

Tough Love: Mamas, Molls, and Mob Wives

Marilyn Yaquinto

The label "tough" is routinely linked to women who "act" like men, which usually means waving a gun around. Ironically, women as police officers and soldiers, despite their increasing numbers in actuality, remain rare onscreen. The gun-toting "toughness" of Demi Moore's *G.I. Jane* or Halle Berry's secret agent (and latest Bond girl) in *Die Another Day* is often chided for being too fantastic (as compared to the "realism" of John McClane, returning soon in *Die Hard IV*). Moreover, the toughness of pistol-packing women is frequently linked to an ascribed maternal instinct, which does not destabilize traditional gender roles but reaffirms them. As Yvonne Tasker notes, "The maternal recurs as a motivating factor, with female heroes acting to protect their children, whether biological or adoptive (*Terminator 2, Aliens, Strange Days*) or in memory of them *(Fatal Beauty)*."[1] Even the more complex heroine in *The Long Kiss Goodnight* is split in two, emphasized "through the codes of costume and behaviour": the tough, cross-dressing Charly who kicks ass and the "feminine" Samantha who is "defined by her motherhood, community role, and thence by the needs of others."[2] Aside from this kind of marauding mom or Berry's sultry assassin, contemporary cinema limits its run of tough gals with guns (smoking or symbolic) and leaves it to the boys with toys to portray toughness as gun play.

Besides brandishing a gun, another way for a woman to be labeled "tough" is to use her body as a weapon—especially if she makes it available to Hollywood's baddest boys. Having sex with outlaws, fugitives, gangsters, and rebels is what turns good girls into hard-boiled dames, villainous vamps, and smart-mouthed molls. The best place to find these characters is within gangster films, where there are two ways to earn tough-girl status via the bedroom: to marry a mobster or to be a mobster's moll.

At first glance, the gangster film seems an unlikely environment in which to map progressive, even oppositional, women because of the genre's misogyny. But women in gangster stories—from classic cinema to contemporary television—are enlightening for what they reveal about gender constructions, identity formations, and cultural containment. They also provide glimpses into transgressive fantasies and illuminate portraits of women who often appear daring and rebellious. Like the gangster, who seems thrilling while he lasts (though he usually ends up physically or morally dead in the end), his female partner seems bold and liberating while she lasts as well.

Scholars have long argued that the gangster film, an American invention, represents a shared anxiety between moviemakers and moviegoers about the culture's tendency to question authority, celebrate lawlessness, and grow impatient with the promise of the American dream, which can breed serious challenges to the social order. Gangsters, like other cinematic outlaws who subvert the system, are idolized and vilified. Yet their doomed ends fail to effectively eclipse the potent image of resistance their riveting lives sometimes represent. Moreover, they keep returning to the screen, resurrected each time Americans feel under siege or grow anxious about perceived threats to law and order.[3] Each time the gangster is updated, so is his female companion; she proves to be as enduring as he is, able to survive and adapt to changing circumstances despite the hypermasculinized and violent environment in which she lives. Although her toughness often marks her sexuality, it also can epitomize her survivability. Toughness in women, particularly within gangster films, is increasingly featured as an empowering quality, as it usually has been for men. In recent years, women in gangster dramas can assert themselves; they talk back and demand their share of the spoils. The female characters displaying this type of gender-bending toughness in gangster films are, surprisingly, no longer the intrepid molls but, of all women, the Mob wives and mothers who used to cringe at the corners of the screen.

This chapter first tracks the rise and fall of the moll's "liberating" influence. Although usually considered more of an opportunist than a victim, she increasingly flies in the face of modern sensibilities by using sex to get what she wants, which now makes her seem more regressive than rebellious. Second, the chapter analyzes how Mob wives, mothers, and sisters—once the doormats of the screen underworld—are now the tough ones. The two halves of the Madonnawhore binary, which the molls and their virtuous counterparts once represented, have begun to merge and, in the process, are helping to destabilize fixed notions of identities. Mob women such as Connie Corleone (*The Godfather, Part III*), Karen Hill (*GoodFellas*), and Carmela Soprano represent changing concepts of femininity. Notions of masculinity and femininity as wedded, respectively, to males and females, have eroded in the wake of the modern women's movement, among other social challenges. There has been a degree of conflation between the two polarities, each adopting attributes of the other: masculinity reflecting greater vulnerability and femininity exhibiting more emotional control. This gender blurring is evident in the new Mob women appearing onscreen.

Third, this chapter investigates the more recent phenomenon of Mob mothers who display toughness not just to protect children but also to protect themselves, defying conventional representations of selfless and other-directed moms in popular culture. Carmela Soprano best reflects the sea change that perceives women as equal partners in family affairs, even when the family is a collection of criminals and its business is organized crime. She also represents shifts within the real underworld, where women are being held more accountable as players, partners, and accomplices, facing prosecution for knowingly helping to earn, shield, or spend the criminal spoils.[4] Such women who "partner" with bad boys— whether confined to the speakeasies, exploited in the bedrooms, or bullied in the courtrooms—are worth studying because they represent the worst and best of female characterizations, women who survive and flourish in a flagrantly misogynistic universe, yesterday and today. Women's progress within that realm is as instructional as it is fascinating.

During the last few decades, scholars have brought to the study of popular culture fresh approaches to analyzing how women are portrayed in the media and what cultural work such portraits do. To conduct the search for patterns and meanings behind the representations, scholars use a variety of methods, including genre study and textual analysis, along with semiotics and psychoanalytical approaches. I blend together many of these approaches but limit my use of psychoanalytical tools, despite their prevailing popularity as first enunciated and applied to film studies by Laura Mulvey.[5] Her observations about the "male gaze" remain useful, in their broadest strokes, given that most Hollywood productions continue to be male-dominated, largely highlighting male crises. But I have concerns over Mulvey's strict descriptions of males as active agents and females as passive objects, categorizations that have been complicated (by Mulvey herself, among others) since she first published her influential essay in 1975.

Critics and moviegoers alike now accept more complicated representations of women, however limited they remain. Yet scholars still grapple with what Teresa de Lauretis identified as a problem in 1984: "[S]ince the historical innocence of women is no longer a tenable critical category for feminism, we should rather think of images as (potentially) productive of contradictions in both subjective and social processes."[6] Judith Mayne concurs with de Lauretis that the goal of contemporary scholarship should be to strive for the articulation of what the "contradictions in the name of women as historical subjects have to tell us."[7] My essay focuses on contradictions embedded in female characters within gangster films and contemplates what the women can tell us as historical subjects and as embodiments of social processes.

Unfortunately, the patterns of female toughness this essay focuses on only work for white women within gangster films, as the effectiveness of their challenges to patriarchy is heavily dependent on their whiteness. As many scholars point out, the racialized gaze of white Hollywood produces a gender effect that cuts across race and a racial effect that complicates notions of gender.[8] Robyn Wiegman notes that blacks are persistently trapped by limiting stereotypes, with black women still drawn too narrowly because, as bell hooks notes, "black female sexuality has been . . . synonymous with wild animalistic lust."[9] This usually limits a black female character to the whore's end of the binary, denying her the starting point of sexual innocence, which is essential to representations of Mob wives and mothers. The dearth of black female representations within gangster films remains a troubling omission and reflects the persistent lack of expanded black characterizations within popular culture as a whole.

Sex as a Weapon

In traditional Hollywood fare, the gangster genre's "virgins (mothers, sisters)" stand in stark contrast to its molls, its "broads who 'put out.' "[10] Putting out means to have sex with a man without the benefit of marriage, which defies the strict taboo that maintains the social order by containing women's sexuality. In contrast to the mythologized virtue of the gangster's female relatives, molls are fetishized in traditional Hollywood for the very sexuality denied other women. Both female types are enclosed within the Madonna-whore binary—reduced to their sexual utility, whether for procreation or recreation. Ideally, the border between good girls and bad girls, or homemakers and homewreckers, is policed onscreen not only by a marriage license but also by the rewarding and punishing of specific behaviors. The line separating virgin from tramp in classic cinema is usually wafer thin and, once crossed, puts the "manhandled" gals on a slippery slope that eventually dumps them onto the wrong side of the tracks where the rest of the vamps, tramps, trollops, hussies, and whores live. It is within these dimly lit streets, shadowy alleyways, seedy motels, and sleazy saloons that the sisters in sin strut their stuff.

In gangster films, good girls who get married, and are supposedly permitted a sexualized nature, find themselves on the margins as well. First, because wives in traditional stories are supposed to have sex only to become mothers, not for pleasure's sake. Second, because sex in classic cinema, even when sanctioned by marriage, is given limited screen time, further restricting these women's sphere of influence. One effect of this sexless characterization for wives and mothers is to make them appear dull and irrelevant. They act as synthetic foils for gangsters who appear more virile and dynamic by comparison. As Rupert Wilkinson notes, "By using femininity as a defining opposite, the tough-guy tradition put pressure on women to be wholesome, sweet, and ultimately submissive, whether as Victorian wives and mothers or as cute majorettes."[11] Similarly, molls must be clearly marked as manhandled to further enhance the goodness of the wives and mothers. Molls also are caught up in classic Hollywood's taboo against overt sexuality, even though they existed in part *for* their sexuality. Thus, the molls had to display signifiers that clearly marked them as cheap imitations of virtuous women, donning "loud" clothes and clunky rhinestones, putting them at odds with "good" girls who aimed for dainty pearls and understatement. Another way to indicate the moll's breach of social mores was to have her "perform" toughness, making it clear she has "been around the block," smoking, cursing, flirting, and, in general, behaving badly. With modern cinema now able to depict sex onscreen, sometimes graphically, there would seem to be less of a need to perform many of the same signifiers of toughness. Yet Judy Holiday's performance as a tough-talking (albeit comic) moll in *Born Yesterday* (1950), with her wisecracks and bawdy shouts across a room, consistently reappears in contemporary characters, such as Sharon Stone's moll in *Gloria* (1999) or Edie Falco's Mob wife, Carmela, in *The Sopranos*. Their brand of toughness still indicates their betrayal of idealized femininity and embrace of masculine tropes, which, traditionally, "have been constructed through a process of mutual exclusion."[12] Classic molls and recent Mob wives like Carmela are pitted against "bland," soft-spoken women who can further indicate "difference."

It remains difficult to define what exactly is meant by "toughness," whether a performance or a deeply internalized quality.[13] Aspects of our understanding reek of masculinity and, more often than not, exclude women. Change the word "guy" to "woman," and feminize the related pronouns, in the following description of toughness and see if the changes transcend convention: "The tough guy is masterful. He can manage situations. . . . Calculation and self-control increase his effectiveness. . . . A tough guy is dynamic. His style celebrates action, impact, and the power of speed"; most important, a tough guy is not afraid to "face down rivals and aggressors; he sees almost everyone as a potential adversary."[14] Even if a female character within conventional stories fits the above description, rather than seem admirable, she appears unfeminine. Such "dynamic" women haunted 1940s film noir stories and appeared to be downright dangerous. Noir's lethal black widows did not merely face down rivals, they behaved like predators on the prowl for victims. They were not women who took care of themselves but castrating apparitions who gave men nightmares. In their heyday, they offered revealing testimonies about the social anxieties affecting postwar America, including worries over the era's changing gender roles. Sylvia Harvey argues that noir women reflected an acute angst about "important shifts in the position of women in American society," including the "temporary but widespread introduction of women into the American labor force during World War II and the changing economic and ideological function of the family."[15] In noir films, women who tried to transcend, if not openly sabotage, the cult of domesticity were insidiously punished. Perhaps a soothing image for traditionalists, but such films also offer glimpses of female aggression in action, which, for some, is empowering while it lasts. The same revelatory clues can be found among representations of women in gangster films; arguably, they are just as threatening to idealized notions of domesticity. In fact, they present even richer case studies because they remain in play. Their longevity suggests their links to history as participants in social upheaval and as agents in cinema's reflection of key cultural shifts.

Of Molls and Men

Gangster films were wildly popular and among the biggest moneymakers in Hollywood in the 1920s and early thirties. James Cagney and Humphrey Bogart were among the brightest stars.[16] Such films are basically studies of degenerate men who are ambitious but doomed, a fate echoed in their inability to have stable relationships with good girls. Thus, they keep company with molls. Unlike a good girl, a moll is not courted but paid for like an acquisition.

She can come as cheap as a pair of spats and is often as easily replaced. As a marker of his status, the gangster must keep her in fur coats and jewels as proof of his ascension. Still, despite her limited role and armed with only a sexy swagger and some wisecracks, the movie moll frequently steals the show: She often speaks her mind and dampens any notion that she is a submissive, platinum doll who will always do what she is told.

In the classic era, the platinum blond Jean Harlow played some of the best molls, including Gwen in *The Public Enemy* (1931), which made superstars of her and Cagney. Harlow's molls were as potent a symbol of women's liberation as the suffragists of a decade earlier, according to Molly Haskell. Moreover, while suffragists and reformers are shown being obsessed with the vote and antiliquor campaigns (eventually bringing about the unpopular era of Prohibition), flappers and molls, who keep company with bootleggers, asserted the "right to drink and smoke and party alongside men, to challenge the double standard."[17] Of course, if the moll too flagrantly thumbed her nose at social conventions, she was treated less sympathetically, even brutally. Appearing with Gwen in *The Public Enemy* is Kitty (Mae Clarke), who gets a halved grapefruit smashed in her face for stepping out of line.

The most complex moll of the classic period appears in the era's most notorious film, *Scarface* (1932), whose violence helped to bring about enforcement of the Hayes Code. The moll Poppy (Karen Morley) is a no-nonsense character who maintains her tough demeanor no matter how much gunfire crackles around her. When the gangster Tony enthusiastically shows off his new Tommy gun, shooting a stream of bullets into a nearby wall, she gapes "with an ecstatic look on her face, almost as though she were enjoying the sex act."[18] By never being too greedy or too attached to anything, Poppy is the only outlaw left standing by the end of the film—the men having been destroyed by greed, paranoia, and sloppy violence.

The classic moll's initial arrest occured when the Hayes Code was vigorously enforced in 1934; gangster films and their smoking, swearing, and sexually slack molls were among the first to show the effects of the morality crackdown.[19] Gangster films continued to be made, but the code tempered their most offensive displays, including their molls. In the post-code environment, although the moll survived, she slumped in the shadows and was supplanted by mealy mouthed do-gooders, misty-eyed virgins, and more expendable whores.

Although the code was finally dismantled by the social upheavals of the late 1960s, surprisingly, molls did not fare much better in the sexually permissive screen environment that followed. When *Scarface* was updated in 1983 by director Brian de Palma and screenwriter Oliver Stone, so was Poppy, but she hardly represented progress. The filmmakers may have thought it a promotion to have Tony (Al Pacino) marry his moll Elvira (Michelle Pfeiffer), yet the move hardly uplifts her character. Rather than smarting off to stand up for herself, she lips off to wound him. She deteriorates into an embittered drug addict with the self-esteem of an empty bullet casing. Rather than accept the money and risks that come with keeping company with gangsters, as Poppy did, Elvira hypocritically insults Tony for how he earns the money she spends. Worse than a leech, she is a complainer. In a particularly vicious scene, Elvira endures a public humiliation Poppy would never have stood for, as Tony berates her in a crowded restaurant for having a womb so polluted that she cannot bear him a child. In the remake, Tony is made Cuban, rather than Italian, and a drug dealer instead of a bootlegger, but he largely remains the same self-destructive thug who spectacularly rises and falls. The question remains, though, why remake the story and so degrade her? Susan Faludi offers one theory: The 1980s prompted a conservative backlash that took aim, in part, at encouraging women to reinvest in traditional gender roles, neutralizing some of the forward motion begun by the women's movement a decade before.[20] Like the "backlash" of the 1930s, when the code was put into action, popular-culture images of the 1980s often showed "nontraditional" females, like Elvira (also women in *Dressed to Kill, Fatal Attraction, Body Double*), being punished for their sins.

A veritable glut of gangster films was churned out in the 1990s, and with it, a new crop of molls. In my prior book, *Pump 'Em Full of Lead: A Look at Gangsters on Film* (1998), I speculate that the resurgence reflected concerns at the time over intensifying political and social upheavals: an increasingly unstable economy, a mini stock market crash, and an ever-expanding illegal drug trade.[21] However, contemporary molls were downgraded while Mob wives were given the limelight. Such a superficial model of a moll surfaces in *Bugsy* (1991), a film about the gangster Bugsy Siegel (Warren Beatty), who invented Las Vegas in the late 1940s. But it is Siegel's tempestuous relationship with the stunning, tough-talking moll Virginia Hill (Annette Bening) that lies at the heart of the story. The real Hill, who embezzled $2 million of Mob money, which she later wisely returned, was well known in the Mob world, having played bed partner to several top gangsters, none of whom she betrayed during her colorful performances before the 1950s-era Congressional committees investigating organized crime. Despite having more screen time than Harlow ever had, Hill here remains at the service of a plot that privileges only Siegel's perspective. In real life, Hill committed suicide while living in Europe, broken and alone.[22] In the film, she simply disappears. Her dismissal demonstrates that despite the film's modern release date and perhaps because of its fit with neoconservative impulses and the prevailing nostalgia for bygone eras, the gangster himself remains the only character worthy of a finale.

Another film that shows a contemporary contempt for the once-vital moll is a remake of *Born Yesterday*, which garnered Judy Holiday a best actress Oscar in 1950. The film was updated in 1993, featuring Melanie Griffith in the title role. In both versions, Billie's thuggish "sponsor" hires a bookish reporter to "enlighten" her because he is convinced he is being held back from access to corruptible Congressmen by his less-than-classy moll. The best bits in the original film are those that showcase Billie's fearless (and comical) taunts of her bad-tempered thug. She also struts her sexuality in front of the reporter, offering to educate *him*, if he agrees to be her lover, as she already has a sponsor to take care of the bills. She is, at her core, a street-smart survivor who may be shameless but is nobody's fool. As Maria Di Battista notes of classic molls like Holiday's Billie, "when befuddled, bewildered, or simply bamboozled by the world, [they] knew how to speak up for themselves. They were certainly not born yesterday."[23] In other words, Billie's brand of toughness becomes one of the cornerstones of the more self-empowering toughness that is present in today's Mob wives but that is lacking in contemporary molls. Given the era, the 1950 Billie took care of herself but was careful to avoid serious challenges to patriarchy; she had to play dumb to be smart. Griffith's remake, despite its 1993 release date, fails to include Holiday's spark of defiance. Griffith is too tentative, too "soft" to match the belligerent Harry; their once-famous match-ups now favor the hard-nosed mobster. Griffith's Billie has lost touch with her toughness and, with it, most of her strength. Such a characterization is indicative of the conservative mood of the 1990s, and the moll's devolution from sassy dame to damsel in distress speaks volumes about the mood's infiltration of popular culture.

Another Hollywood blond who often appears in hard-nosed roles is Sharon Stone. Despite Stone's tough persona, her *Gloria* (1999) is a pale comparison with the original starring Gena Rowlands (1980). Both versions tell the story of a seasoned, middle-aged moll who redeems her life by protecting a dead Mob accountant's six-year-old son now in possession of incriminating files that the Mob wants back. In the 1980 version, Gloria, once the girlfriend of a Mob boss, knows how gangsters think and how they kill. She runs off with the boy and outsmarts and kills some of the thugs chasing her, until finally she escapes and starts a new life.[24]

Stone's Gloria is regressive. The film reflects a prevailing conservatism that purports to believe in "family values" but that translates into urging women to reinvest in their roles as nurturers at the expense of other identities. Stone's Gloria lacks Rowlands's lived-in face and toughened interior, performing more surface markers of toughness, like cursing and pointing guns at men (but never firing them like the original Gloria). And she frequently bursts into tears when the going gets rough.[25]

Molls seem to have outlived their usefulness as cultural emblems and symbols of rebellion. Meanwhile, the once meek and mousy wives, mothers, and sisters of the screen underworld have emerged as the trailblazers of new portraits of feminine strength. They may recall the moll's sass and swagger, but their toughness borrows more from the gangster than from most female characters who preceded them. These new tougher Mob women have managed to escape conservative scorn and evade criticism because nobody has paid much attention to these women, never figuring they could mount any real threat to patriarchy. After all, they remain largely confined to the home, which still invites the patronizing dismissal that anything involving homebodies and the homefront is tame and irrelevant, especially in a gangster story. Yet, thanks to *The Sopranos*, which has become a cultural phenomenon in the last few years, a bright light is shining on these dynamic women. Their modern transformation began with the gangster genre's rebirth with Francis Ford Coppola's *The Godfather* (1972). This landmark film not only revamped the gangster but also put him into the home, where the Mob's women live. The Corleone women were not always static figures but characters reflecting definitive cultural shifts, including the progressive steps of feminism. In the new "domesticated" gangster films, the women start sharing the spotlight.

Wives, Mothers, and Partners in Crime

In the first *Godfather* film, the female characters largely keep to familiar stereotypes, but the added emphasis on the domestic nature of the Corleone family provides space that invites play within these characterizations. Connie Corleone (Talia Shire) is the character who undergoes the most telling changes throughout the *Godfather* films, which span 18 years. In the first film, she is the epitome of the good girl trapped in a bad family. As the unwitting daughter and abused wife of Mafiosi, her fate is blamed on blood ties instead of errant personal choices. During the first film, though, she loses her innocence, having been beaten by her husband and then surviving his murder at the hands of her brother. In the first sequel, she responds by becoming a promiscuous divorcee who defies her brother's pleas to return home. By the end of the sequel, though, she reforms, vowing to redevote herself to taking care of her children and her brother, the new don. However, in *The Godfather, Part III* (1990), Connie undergoes a radical change. It is while performing her duties as a dutiful mother and sister that she toughens up and sinks deeper into the underworld, while her brother Michael struggles to unsuccessfully leave the Mob. As Douglas Brode observes, Connie is now "a wild-eyed combination of Lady Macbeth and [Lucrezia] Borgia; she manipulates, controls, and kills with the ruthless effectiveness once demonstrated by her brother and, before that, her father."[26] At one point, after hearing Connie plot a revenge on one of the family's enemies, Michael aptly notes, "Maybe they should fear *you*," referring to his sister's increasing involvement as more an underboss than a "civilian." It is Connie who gives Vincent the order to kill a family rival and, later in the film, poisons another mafia chieftain with tainted cannolis; a homemaker gone awry, for sure. Unlike the men, though, Connie never resorts to waving a gun around or to threaten physical violence in order to yield her power. She relies on an internal toughness learned from years of living and working with mobsters but still inscribed with traditional feminine protocol; she keeps her demeanor soft and never becomes too obvious about deploying power. In this way, Connie lays the foundation for Carmela, who will shed more of the traditional feminine packaging in favor of more naked displays of a woman exercising power—still without having to wave a gun around.

To bring in guns would mean risking the protection women like Connie Corleone are customarily afforded, as supposed civilians and noncombatants. As such, they are usually spared the customary bloodletting associated with gangster films. Like molls, Mob wives enjoy the rewards of crime without taking any risks to earn them. Unlike molls, their special status as wives not only exempts them from the Mob's workplace violence but also keeps them from being viewed as gold diggers. As homemakers, it is assumed they work for their end of the family's income. The underworld and its domestic arrangements, though, have changed like most others, and the rules for women who partner with mobsters have become just as murky in actuality as onscreen. As Anthony Bruno reports, "Every member of law enforcement . . . [knows] Mafia wives are not as innocent of their husbands' doings as they often claim," especially in light of what government wire taps are revealing about the conversations within mobsters' homes.[27] Their complicity in crime becomes the first chink in their protective armor, moving them one step closer to the line that safeguards them from the discarded women closer to the action, formerly the turf of molls.

A further demystification of the Mob wife was explored by Martin Scorsese, the other preeminent Hollywood filmmaker making gangster films. His *GoodFellas* (1990) includes a fundamentally new portrait of a Mob wife—one who is also a partner in crime. Inspired by a true gangland account, the film tells the true story of Henry and Karen Hill, who first thrive then run from the underworld, ending up in the witness protection program. Karen Hill (Lorraine Bracco) overturns many of the conventions embodied by previous female characters by, first, being allowed to talk in voiceovers to help narrate the story, an empowering position never before accorded a female character in a gangster story. Her voiceovers put her in the subject position, and we hear the same intoxicating greed in her that we find in Henry (Ray Liotta) and the other wiseguys. We witness the underworld as she does. After Henry bloodies a guy's face with the butt of a gun, he hands the gun to Karen to hide. Rather than being repulsed, like Poppy, she admits, "It turned me on." While Kay Corleone pretended too often to know nothing about Michael's criminal affairs, by contrast, "Karen revels in it."[28] By doing so, she transgresses the customary codes that contain (and discourage) female deviance and potential criminality. But Karen, like Poppy, remains with a gangster not to simply stand by her man but to demonstrate her own darker nature and willingness to live a dangerous life.

Eventually, the character Karen participates in Henry's criminal activities. She begins as a "bad girl who enjoys danger, sex, and drugs,"[29] but soon the film shows her assisting in his drug trafficking operation. Karen manages to subvert most traditional portrayals of Mob wives, which paint them as victims whose toughness cannot be deployed to serve a personal agenda, only to protect their family. But Karen proves otherwise, laying the foundation for the Soprano women, who will further expand the range of behaviors permitted such female characters.

An Expanding Range for a Few Sopranos

The domestic side of the criminal life had been creeping into gangster films since *The Public Enemy*, and the *Godfather*s and *GoodFellas* greatly elevated its importance. Coppola showed how a crime family's problems often spilled onto the blood family's dinner table, and Scorsese featured the Hill home as a makeshift drug factory. But *The Sopranos* positions the domestic sphere as the equal to the Mob's workplace, transforming the Soprano home into as active and perilous an environment as any crime scene. The show revels in detailing how workplace and home are insidiously interdependent, just as "family" has a duality here that describes both a collection of relatives and a criminal organization. Mob boss Tony Soprano (James Gandolfini) sits at the top of both family structures, purporting to run a waste management business to justify his lavish home in suburban New Jersey. His duplicity about his work, though, often poses less of a problem for him than his domestic woes, provided by Carmela, their daughter Meadow, and their son A. J., along with other assorted relatives.

This privileging of the domestic realm also elevates the role of women while reflecting the effects of feminism, even within the underworld. Before feminism, the home, like the workplace, was the domain of men. Although women worked in the home, they were not the "heads" of the households, and their "work" was not recognized as formal wage labor. After feminism, women not only gained empowerment in the workplace but also earned the right to have a voice in their homes. *The Sopranos* reflects both these cultural shifts, making the Sopranos' home more significant than in previous gangster stories and also showing the women there to be stronger than ever before. This newly discovered domesticity is enough to earn the show mention as a major contributor to the gangster genre's further evolution. But added to that is the show's immense popularity (among critics and viewers alike), indicating an acceptance of its depictions of such social changes and reflecting the ability of a popular culture product to tap a cultural truth that successfully resonates with viewers. In December 2002, the HBO series completed its fourth season, earning more than $75 million in video and DVD sales since its debut in 1999 and garnering the highest ratings for any show in cable history.[30] The increased attention on domestic issues and the problems of women is one of the reasons for the show's popularity. The show's success reflects the subtle transformations within audiences that enable them to endorse such representations. These tough women are active partners in this gangster saga and are menacing without having to deploy physical threat or fire a gun (unless it is absolutely necessary).

The show's patriarch, Tony Soprano, is not a tired stereotype of a brutalizing male figure; he is softened, made more vulnerable, representing the erosion of once-strict rules defining masculine behavior, especially the exaggerated male figure the gangster represents. Moreover, he seems most disturbed not by the stresses of a dangerous profession (trying to avoid being killed while having others killed) but by his fractured relationships with the women in his life. These wives, sisters, mothers, daughters, and occasional molls represent a fascinating blend of admirable and despicable qualities, including a toughness that is equal to that of the males. As Regina Barreca notes, these women are both "familiar" and "unpredictable," but those "two elements are rarely paired in the development of women on television and film." With the Soprano women, there is a "full menu of behaviors."[31] As Molly Haskell writes, women want to see themselves onscreen being "strange, loud, impolite, enigmatic, baroque, beautiful, ugly, vengeful, funny. We want nothing less, on or off the screen, than the wide variety and dazzling diversity of male options."[32] *The Sopranos* provides women within the Mob universe that rare range of representations.

The show's second-billed actor, Lorraine Bracco, portrays Tony's psychiatrist, Jennifer Melfi.[33] She shows him her tough, impenetrable veneer, yet we are privy to the contradictions beneath the surface as she seeks help from another therapist to deal with her own troubled life. By being drawn to Tony and his problems, despite warnings by colleagues to avoid him, she discloses her attraction to the dark side. No matter what happens to her, even, in one episode, being brutally raped and understandably traumatized, she retains her flintiness—her toughness testifying to her complexity and defiance of stereotypes concerning Italian women, especially in gangster stories. Tony picked Melfi over a Jewish male therapist, believing an Italian woman would be more sympathetic to him. Instead, she fearlessly digs into his wounded psyche, risking her safety in the process; he often shouts back and seems on the verge of assaulting her. But she is able to subdue him, since, Bracco says of her character, "I am his equal. . . . I'm as powerful as he is."[34] What seems to most unnerve Tony is her ability to control her emotions, to check her anger and fear—a quality Tony and his fellow male gangsters cannot grasp. It is what gives Dr. Melfi (and

Carmela) the edge over the men. And it is Tony's frustration over women's indirect but compelling power over him that Melfi uncovers when she asks him: "What's the one thing every woman—your mother, your wife, your daughter—have in common?" He replies, without blinking, "They all break my balls."[35] Simply put, they resist his authority and defy his usually effective and terrifying methods of coercion. He cannot simply physically terrorize these women nor simply point a gun at them to make them behave. They may be largely unarmed with conventional weaponry but are fortified with an inner resolve and fearlessness that he cannot understand or efficiently overpower. His therapist's professional cool, in particular, undermines Tony's confidence; it allows her to undermine somebody who is used to being a physical bully but is unable to defend himself against her psychological battering.

In contrast, Tony's mother, Livia (now deceased, following the death of Nancy Marchand, who portrayed the character), represents a more conventional but no less potent form of female toughness: the ability to emotionally batter. As one critic explains, "Not since *I, Claudius* has there been such a horrible example of Italian motherhood. Her deranged maternal instincts are what drove mobster son Tony to see a shrink—and when she found out, she tried to have him killed."[36] Tony says it best when he tells Livia in an early episode, "Everybody thought Dad was the ruthless one but I gotta hand it to you, Ma, if you'd been born after these feminists, you would've been the real gangster."[37] Ruthlessness forms the basis of Livia's toughness.

Tony's sister Janice (Aida Turturro) is a new figure in a gangster narrative. She blends old-fashioned passive aggressiveness with new-style toughness informed by feminism. First, she breaks with mother discourses embedded in past gangster stories by being a divorced mother of a son, whom she has lost track of. It is a small detail but effectively contradicts the stereotype of Italian mothers as selfless saints who live solely for their children. She is part hippie and part sociopath; she only acknowledges her aggressive tendencies when she thinks she is being threatened, and then she takes swift and brutal action. One storyline depicts her bizarre sex life, demonstrating a daring once permitted only molls. Janice allows her mobster boyfriend to hold a gun to her head during sex (filled with blanks, she assures a shocked Carmela), but after he belts her across the mouth and orders her into the kitchen, she returns with a loaded gun and kills him. During the 2002 season, after Janice loses patience with another troubling boyfriend, she physically thrashes him, leaving the gangster cowering on the staircase before ordering him out of her house. She defies the image of a woman as a victim, or one who needs a man to protect her. She is tough enough to fight her own battles, even to kill, when enraged. Like the other hybridized women in *The Sopranos*, Janice usually exercises power and manipulates circumstances to her advantage without having to resort to physical violence. However, when pushed, she proves capable of being able to kill if she has to.

Standing in sharpest contrast to Livia's vindictiveness and Janice's unleashed fury is Carmela, the show's character who best represents a new model of female toughness. At its core, this toughness is more about coping than wounding. Carmela is a capable and multifaceted woman who is also a wife and a mother. However, those identities do not carry their usual baggage or make her seem out of place in a gangster story. She remains an edgy character who can curse, hang out with criminals, *and* yell at her kids to do their homework. She can be caring and callous, tough and tender, combining the best of a moll's fearlessness and the most earnest traits of a traditional wife and mother. At the same time, she manages to demystify the assumptions and limitations of both character types. "Far from being trapped by the all-embracing patriarchal structures she finds herself in, she finds ways to work them to her advantage. . . . Carmela is no archetypal mafia wife. Unlike her predecessors, she makes full use of the social advantages of being married to the Mob," note Kim Akass and Janet McCabe.[38] NBC's Katie Couric asked Falco if she liked her character, "this tough pragmatist." Falco answered, "She's not a victim. . . . And I love the fact that she's . . . forceful and outspoken."[39] Carmela's empowering toughness enables her to be forceful without having to use a gun or resort to physical violence. She both performs tough, like a classic moll or Dr. Melfi, but also lives tough, struggling daily to work through her contradictions and maintain control of her life and that of her family. As the series progresses, though, she increasingly focuses on her own survival, a radical impulse for a screen gangster's wife.

In the 2002 season finale, after one of Tony's mistresses calls the Soprano home and harasses Carmela, who, in turn, threatens to kill the woman, a bitterly angry Carmela throws Tony out of the house, promising to end their marriage no matter how much her children oppose the breakup of their home. If Carmela continues to strike out on her own, she will strip away more of the traditional trappings associated with her character type, becoming even less concerned with the welfare of others and more focused on her own agenda. As the season finale demonstrated, she dispensed with her usual covert approach to exercising power and more nakedly displayed her iron will. She challenged Tony's (as well as her children's) grip on her life, refusing to continue suturing together their fragile family ties. She confronted both her family's and the genre's assumptions about the acceptable limits of female behavior, especially for a married woman with children.

David Chase, the show's creator, explains that he includes Carmela's problems because such female characters were rarely given much dimension, and he was frustrated with their inclusion only as superficial elements, seen "stirring the . . . pasta, or crying at funerals and weddings. I began to think what it would be like to flesh out these characters."[40] Carmela is shown spending lots of time in her designer kitchen but also venturing out into public spaces, where her most clear-eyed displays of toughness occur. In one episode, she visits a university professor and works her over, insisting she write a letter of recommendation for Meadow. At first, the professor refuses, prompting Carmela to say, in a level voice, "I don't think you understand. I want you to write that letter." When the woman asks if she is being threatened, Carmela does little to disabuse the woman of the idea. In this case, she uses "silent intimidation" and the Mob's terrifying stereotype to her own advantage.[41] She later pushes Tony into donating $50,000 to Columbia University to ensure Meadow's acceptance there—a move Tony sees as a "shakedown," shouting, "I won't pay. I know too much about extortion." But Carmela shows the same resolve she did with the professor, refusing to back down, and in the end, Tony pays. Again, she is depicted as an active agent who deploys her toughness, both a performance and an inner quality, to get what she wants. She may have to invoke Tony's lethal reputation on some occasions, but usually Carmela's metallic stare is enough.

By the 2002 season, she began laying out a possible exit strategy not only from her domesticated world but also from her dependency on Tony and his underworld. She stole $40,000 worth of Mob-earned money from Tony's hiding place in the backyard and deposited the cash in discrete amounts, careful to stay below the $10,000 mark, as that would, by law, have required the bank to notify the FBI. By doing so, Carmela knowingly committed a crime and shattered many of the static images that previously limited women within gangster stories. She demonstrated the same rich array of impulses that underwrite the genre's best men, being rational and reckless, decent and scandalous, vulnerable and tough—blends rarely found in female characters.

A Tough Act to Follow

Carmela and the rest of the Soprano characters are based on existing Hollywood types but are pushing the boundaries of their fictional limits and, in the process, opening up new spaces for women, and perhaps men too. "Unlike more ordinary heroines, most of the women in The Sopranos do not offer up a gooey reservoir of sympathy, vulnerability, and virginity but instead offer in their place a sense of intelligent awareness, emotional skill, and a sense of shamelessness about their own competence."[42] The Soprano women introduced into the realm of popular culture new female subjectivities that are novel examples of capable, tough-minded women. These character types are earning acclaim and wider acceptance. More important, they are not doing so by beating men at their own game, which in a gangster film often means out-shooting or out-brutalizing an enemy. Rather, these women, despite the violent misogynistic environment in which they are operating, stand their ground, protect their turf, and help to rewrite the rules behind power plays without having to fire a shot. Moreover, these menacing Mob women are still stirring the pasta and taking care of their kids.

In a statement that remains true today, E. Ann Kaplan notes that the 1990s were part of "a painful transitional period, as indicated by the plethora of contradictory mother-discourses. . . . If we can begin to glimpse the possibilities of new female subjectivities, of female as well as male desire, . . . we will have achieved a lot."[43] The Soprano women, like the molls before them, have contributed to the newly emerging picture of what female desire looks like, including its hazardous consequences. By conflating notions of masculinity and femininity, they are helping to create characterizations that project alternative images onscreen, which are also leaving indelible marks on the genre's legacy. More important, rather than reflect exaggerated portraits of women getting tough to solve a fleeting crisis, these characters portray toughness as a quality woven into the fabric of their everyday lives. They have moved beyond "performing" toughness to being tough, not to act more like a man but to reflect the formidable women whom they have become.

These potent women holding their own in a man's world have evolved from the once daring molls who were the only female characters allowed to lust after sex and danger. They also can trace their lineage to once passive, apron-clad Mob moms who existed only to make the gangsters look bad. Today's Mob women are demonstrating feminist assertiveness that is not necessarily tied to their sexuality and a toughness that borrows the cockiness and emotional cool of the traditional tough guy, but most often rejects his reliance on a smoking gun. Rather than simply beat a man at his own game, such women are helping to change the rules of the game itself. The gangster story is being transformed by these new Mob women, who are having to operate in one of the most masculinized and misogynistic turfs in popular culture. Finally, they brought toughness into the home, which is, more and more, where the action is in a gangster story. And at home, these women are not always armed but are certainly dangerous.

Notes

1. Yvonne Tasker, *Working Girls: Gender and Sexuality in Popular Cinema* (London: Routledge, 1998), 69.
2. Tasker, 82.
3. See Marilyn Yaquinto, *Pump 'Em Full of Lead: A Look at Gangsters on Film* (New York: Twayne Publishers, 1998); David E. Ruth, *Inventing the Public Enemy: The Gangster in American Culture, 1918–1934* (Chicago: University of

228 Marilyn Yaquinto

228 Marilyn Yaquinto

228 Marilyn Yaquinto

228 Marilyn Yaquinto

228 Marilyn Yaquinto

228 Marilyn Yaquinto

228 Marilyn Yaquinto

Chicago Press, 1996); Robert B. Ray, *A Certain Tendency of the Hollywood Cinema, 1930–1980* (Princeton, NJ: Princeton University Press, 1985).

4. Bob Simon, "The Two Mobs," *60 Minutes II*, Columbia Broadcasting Company, October 2, 2002. (Simon interviews a Mob wife who was arrested by federal agents and turned state's witness against her husband.)
5. See Laura Mulvey, *Visual and Other Pleasures* (Bloomington: Indiana University Press, 1989).
6. Teresa de Lauretis, *Alice Doesn't: Feminism, Semiotics, Cinema* (Bloomington: Indiana University Press, 1984), 39.
7. Judith Mayne, "Feminist Film Theory and Criticism," in *Multiple Voices in Feminist Film Criticism*, ed. Diane Carson, Linda Dittmar, and Janice R. Welsch (Minneapolis: University of Minnesota Press, 1994), 57.
8. See bell hooks, *Black Looks: Race and Representation* (Boston: South End Press, 1992); Stuart Hall, "The Spectacle of the 'Other,'" in *Representation: Cultural Representations and Signifying Practices*, ed. Stuart Hall (London: Sage Publications, 2000); Cornel West, *Race Matters* (Boston: Beacon Press, 2001); Sander L. Gilman, *Difference and Pathology: Stereotypes of Sexuality, Race, and Madness* (Ithaca, NY: Cornell University Press, 1985).
9. hooks, 65–7.
10. Kim Akass and Janet McCabe, "Beyond the Bada Bing! Negotiating Female Narrative Authority in *The Sopranos*," in *This Thing of Ours: Investigating the Sopranos*, ed. David Lavery (New York: Columbia University Press, 2002), 147.
11. Rupert Wilkinson, *American Tough: The Tough-Guy Tradition and American Character* (Westport, CT: Greenwood Press, 1984), 8.
12. Susan Bordo, as quoted in Sherrie A. Inness, *Tough Girls: Women Warriors and Wonder Women in Popular Culture* (Philadelphia: University of Pennsylvania Press, 1999), 21.
13. Inness, 12.
14. Wilkinson, 7.
15. Sylvia Harvey, "Woman's Place: The Absent Family of Film Noir," in *Women in Film Noir*, ed. E. Ann Kaplan (London: British Film Institute, 1998), 38.
16. Robert Sklar, *City Boys: Cagney, Bogart, Garfield* (Princeton, NJ: Princeton University Press, 1992). See also Yaquinto, Ruth, and Ray.
17. Molly Haskell, "Swaggering Sexuality Before the Mandated Blush," *The New York Times*, May 13, 2001, sec. 5.
18. Jay Robert Nash, *The Motion Picture Guide* (Chicago: Cinebooks, 1986), 2760.
19. See Raymond Moley, *The Hays Office* (New York: Bobbs-Merrill, 1945).
20. See Yaquinto and chapter 11 of Steven J. Ross, *Movies and American Society* (Malden, MA: Blackwell Publishers, 2002).
21. See Yaquinto, chapter 12.
22. Yaquinto, 204–5.
23. Maria Di Battista, *Fast-Talking Dames* (New Haven, CT: Yale University Press, 2001), 332.
24. Her moll is one of the first to investigate the character's conflicting feelings about how she uses her body, as a moll, as a site of commodity exchange. Part of the character's transformation can be tracked by watching her increasing willingness to be touched, which indicates her attempts to reclaim her body as her own.

See Gilles Deleuze, *Cinema2: The Time-Image* (Minneapolis: University of Minnesota Press, 1989), 192–3.

25. Stone's handling of the character, reinscribing her with displays of conventional femininity, is surprising since she is the same actor who portrays the lethal ice queen in *Basic Instinct* (1992) and the forceful but self-destructive Ginger in *Casino* (1995).

26. Douglas Brode, *Women, Money, & Guns: Crime Movies from Bonnie and Clyde to the Present* (New York: Citadel Press, 1995), 173.

27. Anthony Bruno, "Married to the Mob: Mafia Wives and Mistresses" in *The Crime Library*, database online, Courtroom Television Network, cited November 20, 2002: available at crimelibrary.crime.com/gangster_outlaws/mob_bosses/wives.

28. Cindy Donatelli and Sharon Alward, " 'I Dread You?' Married to the Mob in *The Godfather*, *GoodFellas*, and *The Sorpranos*," in *This Thing of Ours: Investigating the Sopranos*, ed. David Lavery (New York: Columbia University Press, 2002), 62.

29. Donatelli and Alward, 63.

30. Robert Bianco, *USA Today*, September 13, 2002, 2a.

31. Regina Barreca, "Why I Like the Women in *The Sopranos* Even Though I'm not Supposed To," in *A Sitdown with the Sopranos*, ed. Regina Barreca (New York: Palgrave Macmillan, 2002), 29–30.

32. Molly Haskell, *From Reverence to Rape: The Treatment of Women in the Movies* (Chicago: University of Chicago Press, 1987), 402.

33. Bracco, who also portrayed Karen Hill, recognizes the progressive nature of her two roles, as she explains, "The whole thing about *GoodFellas* was that in showing Karen and the kids . . . it was much more than the stereotypical mama-in-the-kitchen kind of Mafia film. Part of *The Sopranos*, too, is that it shows the humanization" of such characters (quoted in Akass and McCabe, 148).

34. Quoted in Glen O. Gabbard, *The Psychology of the Sopranos: Love, Death, Desire, and Betrayal in America's Favorite Gangster Family* (New York: Basic Books, 2002), 68.

35. Barreca, 42.

36. Bianco, *USA Today*.

37. Barreca, 33.

38. Akass and McCabe, 154–156.

39. Edie Falco, interview by Katie Couric, *Today*, National Broadcasting Company, September 13, 2002.

40. Donatelli and Alward, 70.

41. Akass and McCabe, 156.

42. Barreca, 32.

43. E. Ann Kaplan, *Motherhood and Representation: The Mother in Popular Culture and Melodrama* (London: Routledge, 1992), 219.

Chapter 9

"Tough Enough": Female Friendship and Heroism in *Xena* and *Buffy*

Sharon Ross

Over the past three decades, female action heroes have risen to the surface of American television as well as other media and captured the attention of viewers and feminist scholars. Two shows that have garnered much attention are *Xena: Warrior Princess* and *Buffy the Vampire Slayer*. These series and their heroines have offered new visions of heroism by inflecting the concept of toughness with the notion of flexibility. While traditional heroes of the past have been made tough via their individualism and their ability to confront obstacles by themselves, these women grow as heroes because of their female friends. Xena and her friend Gabrielle and Buffy and her friend Willow encourage each other to push the limits of what it means to be a hero, emphasizing the importance of flexibility. In particular, both television series stress that a woman can be "tough enough" to fight patriarchy when she learns to listen to other women's perspectives on the world and when she values her emotional bonds with other females as a source of strength.

In both *Xena* and *Buffy*, each lead woman finds that, increasingly, her sense of purpose is enmeshed with her friend's. The primary purpose of both Xena and Buffy is to be heroic and tough enough to fight evil forces, and because this becomes inextricable from their best friends' purposes, Gabrielle and Willow become heroes, too. This is a fundamental challenge to traditional notions of heroism in two ways. First, traditional heroism emphasizes the *lone* hero, able to stand apart from the communities for which he or she (usually he) is heroic. The interdependency of these series' titular heroines with their best friends refutes that heroes work best alone; rather, women need other women. Second, in these series, Gabrielle and Willow shift from "sidekick" status to heroes themselves, refuting a longstanding notion that female heroes are "exceptions to the rule" of what women are able to do. In effect, *Xena* and *Buffy* demonstrate that many women can be tough and heroic when women come together in a supportive community.

These four friends encounter other women as they seek to fight evil; the interactions that occur serve to legitimate females redefining their roles and status in society, so that women achieve a measure of authority in the world. Females who seem unheroic or passive initially learn heroism from Xena, Gabrielle, Buffy, and Willow. Just as often, the women to whom these lead characters offer assistance share new perspectives on heroism and action and teach that what is "tough" can vary depending on the circumstances. Thus, a critical element of heroism in these series involves Xena, Gabrielle, Buffy, and Willow being flexible with how they approach the situations with which they become involved. They learn to listen before they speak, converse before they act; many times, the solution to a problem is not easy to find, and it is the other women whom they are helping who can provide the best ideas.

The exchanges that such teaching and learning requires are rooted in "epistemic negotiation," a process of building knowledge in which individuals come together as a community to discuss what they each know and then debate how best to address the situation at hand.[1] The four friends are not heroes *for* other women so much as they are heroes *with* them; everyone involved has her say and everyone's thoughts and feelings are respected. *Xena* and *Buffy* emphasize the value of talking together as a method useful for women to understand how their experiences are rooted in patriarchy, so that they may take action to improve their lives as women. Lorraine Code argues that talking in the form of storytelling is a particularly viable way for women to exchange knowledge: "Stories make audible the multiplicity of voices of which knowledge . . . [is] made . . . contesting the hegemonic claims of the dominant."[2] Storytelling among the females in these programs includes qualitative inquiries from listeners as well as demands for descriptive evidence that provides context. Such processes honor differences of opinion that emerge when people with varying experiences meet, requiring participants to be flexible about what they think is "the truth" as women relate their varying experiences and perspectives.

Shows that feature a community of women demonstrate the viability of female bonding as a site of unorthodox modes of communication and action, particularly when women talk with other women.[3] This chapter examines how *Xena* and *Buffy* privilege epistemic negotiation as a productive means to being heroic. The strategies involved favor communal action, interdependency, and emotional knowing. Women listen to and argue with each other as they attempt to learn how to be tough enough to fight what goes wrong in their lives. The lead characters must be strong enough psychologically and emotionally to change their approaches to being heroic; they learn that the toughest hero is a flexible one who relies on others. Many patterns emerge throughout these shows in support of such interactions. This chapter focuses on (1) women coming together to resist patriarchal attempts to separate them from each other, and (2) women exploring the strength that lies in emotional knowing. *Xena* and *Buffy* offer a worldview in which women cannot be tough without female support and without learning to communicate and trust their feelings.

Female Friendships and Action Adventurers

Friendships between females are an important element of popular culture in the United States. While many depictions of female friendships have been presented as secondary in narratives concerning the nuclear family or the workplace, shifts within visual media industries have encouraged the viability (in terms of popularity and profit) of films and television shows focused on female friendships. Scholars have noted a recent increase in this trend with the rise of niche marketing's attempt to appeal to the highly lucrative female audience, whether teens, young adults, or adults.[4]

In spite of these media's long history of targeting female viewers, focusing stories on female friends has been a more recent trend.[5]

The representation of female friendships is deeply indebted to the "women's films" of the 1930s and 1940s, which often had female friendships incorporated marginally into their narrative framework. Still, these films featured competition among women. The independent women's films of the 1970s eventually lent support to the viability of female friendship films in the 1980s and early 1990s—a move intimately connected to the increasing visibility of feminism in mainstream culture and society.[6] Some feminist scholars note that a backlash occurred in the 1980s, when many films returned to representations of women fighting with each other rather than fighting together to achieve change.[7] Films such as *Fatal Attraction* (1987) and *Working Girl* (1988) pitted women against each other, "put[ting] into question the possibility for any sense of unity of women, of sisterhood."[8] Thus, the women of these films survived because they could best other women who stood in their way. Men were rarely the problem; other women were.

While many television shows featuring female characters have been popular and successful in the United States, the trajectories of these shows follow patterns similar to those found in film: Female friendships are marginalized or centered on heterosexual relationships with men, and frequently the potential for friendship is squelched by an emphasis on female rivalry. Only a handful of series from television's past have highlighted women bonding together successfully; some of these were *Laverne and Shirley* (1976–83), *Cagney and Lacey* (1982–88), *The Golden Girls* (1985–92), and *Designing Women* (1986–93). *Cagney and Lacey* has been noted for its representation of female friendship as a critical force in the lead characters' ability to survive in the male world of police work. However, the show faced considerable pressure from CBS to maintain the women's "femininity" and plots often revolved around their interactions with men.[9] This history makes the appearance and popularity of *Xena* and *Buffy* all the more noticeable, particularly since the shows also represent women as tough action adventurers who become heroes on their own terms.

In the past, and in the realm of action adventure in particular, strong female heroes have been represented as isolated from other women socially, such as in the films *Blue Steel* (1990) and *La Femme Nikita* (1991) and also the television series *Police Woman* (1974–78), *The Bionic Woman* (1976–78), and *Wonder Woman* (1976–79). In order for a female lead character to demonstrate even momentary control over story events, she had to be curtailed through punishment or demonstrations of excessive sexuality. For instance, the characters Sheena (1984), Red Sonja (1985), Pepper Anderson (1974–78), and Charlie's Angels (1976–81) have been noted more for their bodies than their actions. Another trend is to temper toughness with maternal motivation. In *Alien* (1979), *Terminator 2: Judgment Day* (1991), and *The Long Kiss Goodnight* (1996), the female heroes were kept isolated from other women because their loyalty resided ultimately with children's well-being. Such narrative controls kept strong female characters distant from "normal" women who might serve as friends or even eventual cohorts in community-oriented action. Instead, tough women of the past were strong because they could withstand loneliness, or stories about tough women made it a priority to represent them as not so tough that they might forsake heterosexuality and family. Further, many of the tough females cited above learned their toughness from men. Other adult women could not function to bring them emotional sustenance or support.

Feminist scholars studying action adventure on television note that this genre poses difficulties for the representation of powerful women.[10] Dominant society's desire to maintain distinct categories of masculinity and femininity leads to problems when a television producer wishes to place a woman in an action-adventure setting.[11] To be tough is to be unfeminine by normative standards, and for decades such a heroine was unthinkable. The "solution" was to position tough women as appropriately feminine by making them not as tough as men, who would inevitably save them or help them to save others. This restrictive definition of "tough" began to shift slowly as feminism gained a stronger hold in culture and society. Today there is room in popular media for different types of heroic action—a space has been carved out for different kinds of tough women. Feminism has created a cultural environment more receptive to female characters demanding power within their narrative worlds.[12]

Still, it is notable that one of the tough female action adventurers with the biggest ratings on a major network in 2001 was Sydney Bristow of *Alias* (2001), a woman whose bonds with other women are rooted primarily in deceit and danger.[13] Sydney is tough, but frequently her emotions create rather than help her solve problems. The tendency to portray female heroes as necessarily lonely has been resisted strongly in *Xena*, a show that Sherrie A. Inness argues demonstrates that "toughness in women does not have to be antithetical to friendship."[14] *Buffy* resists the vision of the isolated female hero as well: "In many of its strongest moments, [it] is a show of friendship, not single combat" (see figure 9.1).[15] In my own analysis of both series elsewhere, I argue that one of the most appealing aspects of these two shows for fans is this coexistence of toughness and female friendship; the importance of interpersonal bonds to the heroines encourages them to see toughness as something that can include caring for and about other tough women.[16]

From the beginning, *Xena* and *Buffy* highlight female bonding as supportive of an environment in which women can question and

Figure 9.1. Over *Buffy*'s seven seasons, the show's community of heroes expanded to include many women and men

usurp patriarchal authority. The primary female friendships depicted are integral to the stories and reexamine continually what it means to be an effective, tough woman. When Xena, an evil warlord, decides to devote her life to atoning for her past atrocities, she meets Gabrielle, who insists on accompanying her on her journeys. Gabrielle leaves her village (and an impending marriage) because she wants to be tougher—"like Xena," she tells her sister. With her story-telling skills (she is a bard) and personal philosophy of pacifism, Gabrielle brings into Xena's life new traits for toughness and heroism. In turn, Xena offers her a vision of pacifism that can incorporate physical strength and aggression. When Buffy, a former cheerleader, is called through her lineage to a life of slaying vampires in Sunnydale, at first she does not want to slay and tells her male Watcher that she is done working for others. After she meets Willow, however, Buffy finds that the support of friendship provides her with new ways to handle being a tough hero. Willow, with her computer skills and later her skills as a developing Wicca, brings into Buffy's life the power of intelligence and female unity. In turn, Buffy offers her new friend a vision of herself as someone capable of learning new skills and achieving heroism suited to her own unique identity.

This questioning of official patriarchal authority is in line with other television shows of the 1990s. From Patsy and Edina's law-breaking antics in *Absolutely Fabulous* (1994–98) to the raucous rebellions of Roseanne and Jackie and their female friends in *Roseanne* (1988–97), television in this decade offered rebellious women working together in a variety of ways. However, the fact that the women of *Xena* and *Buffy* are tough action heroes rather than only funny protagonists is a welcome development in television.[17] The representation of collective action supported through female friendship in both of these shows allows for a redefinition of tough heroism as communal, respectful of emotions, and something to be taken quite seriously.

Divided We Fall: Women Resisting Separation

Through the presence of a community of mostly women, *Xena* and *Buffy* suggest that a tough hero functions best when she is willing to be flexible. In her work on feminism and knowledge, Code relies on a model of epistemology that depends on people coming together to produce knowledge collectively, discussing and debating the meaning of the events and people around them.[18] In such a framework, productive knowledge building among women requires an awareness of the context within which different women live and a commitment to interdependency rather than individualism.

Code argues that communication must be rooted, therefore, in community. When women come together to share stories and experiences, they promote an environment in which productive change and growth can occur. When individuals are bound to each other, rather than existing solely independently, empathy emerges as a necessary component of decision making. These criteria for comprehending situations thoroughly enough to take action are similar to what one sees in soap operas; women talk with each other repeatedly about one event until they achieve an understanding of that event. *Buffy* and *Xena* have narrative structures that resonate with those of soap operas in that the series emphasize how individuals' lives weave together through webs of constantly renegotiated relationships.[19] Code argues that such forms of communication and knowledge production exemplify an "epistemology of everyday life" that values aspects of women's experiences that society typically devalues and discounts as trivial.[20]

Both shows represent women's interdependence as a healthy means of developing mutually beneficial heroism. Code argues that epistemic negotiation has traditionally been the domain of women, traceable to women's reliance on oral culture when other modes of communication were not open to them.[21] Legitimate knowing in Western patriarchal cultures has for centuries situated the ideal knower as an autonomous individual (typically a white male), able to understand morality and ethics enough to be a hero.[22] No room for interdependence exists within what is seen as proper moral reasoning and heroic action. The essence of heroism rests on a moral toughness, man's ability to remain true to what he knew to be right and wrong, regardless of the circumstances. This might result in a man having to ignore his personal bonds with others in the name of truth and justice, but such isolationism only proves further how strong he is.

Ironically, it is within traditional studies of ethics and morality that alternatives to normative epistemological assumptions have emerged—alternatives that, while still defined by men, open a door for the validity of ways of knowing that have been associated historically with women. For example, Maurice Merleau-Ponty stresses the importance of emotions and personal experience in establishing ethics, and Oliver Sacks's work on morality suggests that storytelling and conversation can enhance decision making.[23] Feminist scholars have turned to Merleau-Ponty, Sacks, and others to produce feminist epistemologies that allow for notions of care and nurturing. For example, Gail Weiss traces the work of such theorists to the development of Carol Gilligan's concept of an "ethics of care," a term Gilligan uses to describe how women evaluate events and circumstances morally by attending to context and emotions.[24] Code uses Sacks's theories to argue that "imagination is essential to the openness that seeing things from someone else's point of view requires."[25] These feminist scholars have emphasized that a place exists in both morality and epistemology for "women's ways" of knowing that accord value to the role of context, community, and interdependence. What is right or wrong has in part to do with what the given circumstances are, including the histories (both personal and social) of those involved.

The fictional example that Code uses to exemplify such strategies of knowledge and morality is the play *A Jury of Her Peers*, in which local women gather to discuss whether a neighbor woman is guilty of murder when the victim in question is an abusive spouse. The women examine the scene of the crime and collectively decide that, in fact, no crime was committed; one woman goes so far as to remove evidence from the house that might incriminate the wife.[26] Through activities as mundane as talking and gossip, the female neighbors prompt each other to ask questions and make clarifications, checking their individual knowledge against each other's to produce a collectively agreed upon knowledge that can include an acceptance of paradoxes and contradictions. (The wife killed her husband, but she did not act immorally.) The women resist what patriarchal law and ethics inform them is true; together, they give each other strength to defy those in positions of authority.

Similar moments of forming knowledge occur repeatedly in *Xena* and *Buffy*. In order for the lead females to be tough heroes, they must be flexible in how they understand the situations they face. This requires the ability to imagine possibilities they themselves may not have considered; collectively, Xena, Gabrielle, Buffy, and Willow work to integrate these differing possibilities. If Xena or Buffy were to dominate all decision making and if their toughness were to depend on a set of hard-and-fast rules of action, their heroism would be weakened. Indeed, Brian Wall and Michael Zryd argue that *Buffy* (and, I would add, *Xena*) offers a "radical utopian alternative [to knowledge]: a non-alienated way of working together" in which Buffy and Xena almost always consult with their friends before taking action.[27]

The primary strategy of knowledge building (and the determination of what actions to take based on that knowledge) in both series is epistemic negotiation. Women meet and examine the context of the situation. They discuss what they each know, with a successful course of action dependant on those involved honoring their bonds with the other women. For example, in "A Necessary Evil," Xena and Gabrielle decide that they have to work with their enemy Callisto if they want to stop a rogue Amazon from becoming a vengeful goddess. Although they both deplore Callisto, the moral need to defeat the Amazon determines the course of action they must take. Xena and Gabrielle must be tough enough to resist a normative logic telling them that Callisto can do no good; this flexibility allows them, ultimately, to defeat the Amazon. "Graduation Day" in *Buffy* emphasizes the importance of context similarly. In the two-episode story, Buffy alternates between different ways of knowing and acting morally. She has no qualms about deciding to kill her enemy Faith, even though only a few episodes previously she had found killing a human to be immoral. Because Faith's blood would save the life of Buffy's lover, Angel, and because Faith is responsible for his illness, Buffy will spill Faith's blood if she can. Buffy is flexible enough to assess killing differently, based on the situation at hand; this flexibility allows her to be tough enough to attempt actions (killing) that she would not under other circumstances.

These episodes emphasize the importance of heroes being flexible about morality and truth and stress that different methods and strategies should be available for women to use depending on the context. *Xena* and *Buffy* create alternative ways of knowing that can best be sustained through communities in which leadership and heroism shift from person to person as necessary.[28] Xena and Buffy need other people's input and assistance to make many of the most important decisions in their lives, and, at times, they must let Gabrielle and Willow make decisions and take action instead. The women in these programs share power with each other whenever they can, rather than relying on a patriarchal model that organizes power and leadership linearly and hierarchically. Further, when they must make difficult and risky decisions, the support of other women around them helps them to do so. Thus, women's interdependency brings them the resources they need to fix problems in their worlds.

Episodes in both series that feature females helping other females are most effective in demonstrating the value of women coming together to fight patriarchal injustices. Xena, Gabrielle, Buffy, and Willow intervene in other women's lives in attempts to help them become tough enough to resolve patriarchal problems, and they learn from these women while doing so. These interventions occur typically after a good deal of talking; those involved exchange their perspectives on the situation with each other so that the heroines can offer assistance that will be of real value. For example, in "Here She Comes, Miss Amphipolis," Xena talks with beauty pageant contestants, trying to encourage them to disassociate themselves from men who are using their bodies for monetary and political gain. In turn, the contestants offer her their own thoughts on why they are doing what they are doing, explaining that economic need and concern for their families and communities are factors in their decisions to be part of the pageant.

Through conversation and gossip, Xena learns to respect the choices these women have made; she turns her attention to the men who have created those circumstances instead of dismissing the beauty contestants as "underdressed, overdeveloped bimbos" (how she and Gabrielle initially assessed the women). Similarly, in "Beware Greeks Bearing Gifts" and "Many Happy Returns," Xena and Gabrielle talk to Helen of Troy and the virgin Jania about the dangers of living one's life exclusively for men and their desires; these women explain how hard it is for them to change their lives when they have so little power in their specific patriarchal contexts. In these episodes, epistemic negotiation helps the two friends to first empathize with the difficult positions of Helen and Jania and then strategize ways to assist them. All of the women work together to help each other understand what is occurring and determine how they can best improve the situation. In the end, Xena and Gabrielle demonstrate to their friends that a woman can be tough without a man by her side; Helen leaves Paris and decides to travel the world, and Jania leaves her misogynistic religion and opens a shelter for abused women.

By demonstrating an alternative to living under patriarchal rules, Xena and Gabrielle encourage many of the women whom they meet to strike out on their own. In turn, the two friends come to understand more fully the difficulties of escaping such situations. Comparable examples can be found in *Buffy*. For example, in "Beauty and the Beasts," Buffy and Willow reach out to a female classmate whose boyfriend is abusing her physically. In a classic intervention scene, the two friends tell the girl that absolutely no excuses exist for abusing a woman, even when the abuse can be linked to a magical potion (as is the case in this episode). In "Made to Love You," Buffy is able to tap into her increasing capacity for empathy and learning and extend her help to a female robot whose male creator/boyfriend has abandoned her. As in *Xena*, Buffy and Willow work to help other women become tough enough to survive without men, encouraging females to turn to a community of women for support. In addition, these two friends learn from the women with whom they come into contact, understanding the reasons someone their age might believe an abuser could change and learning how even human girls can behave like robots at times when it comes to men. Situations are not always as clear-cut as they appear, and a strong hero accepts this and learns to embrace the idea that what is true and moral depends on the context.

Both series are at their most effective when they offer stories of the primary female friends resisting men's attempts to keep them apart. Such episodes offer examples of not only how epistemic negotiation can be fruitful for women but also of how strong female friendships can be a source of resistance. Interdependency is not a sign of weakness; rather, it is the heart of toughness. An example of this occurs in *Xena*'s "When Fates Collide," in which Caesar (a long-time foe of Xena and Gabrielle) alters history. In his patriarchal fantasy-come-true, Xena is his passive wife, and

Gabrielle is a playwright whom Xena has never met. Nevertheless, when Gabrielle comes to Rome with her new play, she and Xena are drawn to each other inexplicably. The two "strangers" explore this attraction tentatively, and, through conversation, they come to understand that, as impossible as it seems, they are in fact connected with each other. In time, their faith in this "unprovable" knowledge allows them to set reality right, even though they must face death to do so. Both women question what they "know" (that Caesar is honest and a just ruler; that they have never met); their longtime friendship reaches through a spell to make them tough enough to create their own knowledge, defy the despot, and commit to their unique relationship.

Other episodes abound in which Xena and Gabrielle fight patriarchal attempts to separate them. In "Fallen Angel," the male archangels of heaven resist, initially, the women, who try to save each other during a war between heaven and hell. The friends refuse to abandon each other and do not rest until the archangels give them their way. Xena and Gabrielle also fight constantly against the Greek god Ares's attempts to keep the two women apart. In "The Reckoning," Xena must resist Ares's offer to make her a god, and in "Seeds of Faith" Gabrielle must do the same. Each of these episodes sustains the bonds between the two women and provides situations in which they learn that together they are tough enough to resist patriarchal oppression and help others. As Code argues, when women learn to rely on each other for strength, they are able to create their own spaces of authority, and "the creation of such spaces depends on the collective and mutually enabling efforts of women who can trust themselves to know, and to know that they know."[29] Xena and Gabrielle trust each other and their respective knowledge enough to challenge the "facts" that surround them, and thus they are able to reclaim their lives together as heroes.

In *Buffy*, patriarchal attempts to separate Buffy and Willow tend to occur in the realm of heterosexual dating. In "I Robot, You Jane" a digitalized demon talks Willow into withdrawing from her friend and arranges to have Buffy killed. Buffy follows her instincts and is tough enough to risk her best friend's anger when she argues that boys should never be put ahead of their friendship. In "The 'I' in

Team" Willow must intervene when Buffy's new relationship with a government soldier who helps them interferes with the two girls' friendship. She tells Buffy that it is not wise to ignore her friends for any man, no matter how wonderful. This romantic relationship allows Spike later to manipulate both women's feelings of separation from each other ("Yoko"). Spike knows that to create a distance between these friends will make them susceptible to attack; without each other, Buffy and Willow are not tough enough to fight evil. When the two friends figure out that Spike has been driving them apart, they work to repair the situation through talking with each other and recommitting to their friendship (see figure 9.2).

As with Xena and Gabrielle's patriarchal travails, these events help Buffy and Willow to reassess and strengthen their senses of identity and purpose as woven together. In "I Robot" and "The 'I' in Team," both women learn how to grapple with their sexual and romantic desires in relation to their desire to be friends with each other. They learn to prioritize their friendship and to be suspicious

Figure 9.2. Buffy and Willow share a conversation that keeps them in touch with each other's feelings

of any man who keeps them from spending time together. In "Yoko," Buffy and Willow learn that becoming distant from each other was in part their responsibility and that, when they neglect their friendship, they become weaker heroes. The show positions romantic love often as "noise" that disrupts communication between women.[30] More importantly, however, these examples support the idea that women together can overcome or transform such noise.

Such episodes in *Xena* and *Buffy* situate female friendships as integral to redefining heroism in several ways. First, the friendships contribute to each woman better understanding her purpose as related to her friend's. Second, the friendships are a source of protection against patriarchal attempts to separate these women from each other. Third, the friendships are a source of empowerment that helps these women resist and renegotiate their lives under patriarchy. Bonds between women are represented as a source of toughness; they provide the strength needed to resist oppression and effect change. One woman's heroism is connected to another's, and women's interlocking lives are critical to heroism operating effectively. Epistemic negotiation can help women disrupt the stereotype that their "normal" positions within patriarchal systems are more important than their relationships with other women.[31] These shows suggest that bonds between women are the first step in becoming tough enough to resist patriarchy.

Silence Is Not Golden: The Power of Emotional Expression

Many of the episodes discussed in the section above display a sense of emotional fragmentation when women are separated from each other, a state of being that induces fear and anxiety. Problematic situations are set straight often after the women come together to give voice to not only their view of events but also to their feelings about what is occurring; the emotional goal of each of these episodes is for the women to reconnect. Xena, Gabrielle, Buffy, and Willow come to value their feelings as a resource they can draw upon to help them make better-informed decisions as heroes. Emotions are not a sign of weakness, in spite of what patriarchy insists. Rather, women are less tough when they fail to communicate their feelings to each other (or are kept from doing so).

Some feminist psychologists and sociologists argue that women are pressured to remain silent and unobtrusive in patriarchal cultures and that this causes females to lose confidence, particularly in their right to express how they feel. These theorists suggest that female bonding and interdependency are useful elements for counteracting such pressures. For example, Lyn Mikel Brown's work demonstrates that adolescent girls encounter institutional resistance to the communication of their thoughts, feelings, and opinions.[32] Brown and Carol Gilligan's examination of female psychological development points out how patterns learned in youth extend to adulthood: "Women . . . speak of themselves as living in connection with others and yet describe a relational crisis: a giving up of voice, an abandonment of self, for the sake of becoming a good woman. . . ."[33] Hillary Carlip and Vendela Vida, in their respective examinations of the ways in which females from adolescence through early adulthood attempt to maintain bonds with other women, note that attempts to build communities of women strengthen females' abilities to resist patriarchy.[34]

Episodes in both series focus on females "losing voice" and self-confidence, examining what occurs when women hesitate to express their feelings. As each show develops, Gabrielle and Willow in particular face crises of uncertainty, but each time they face their fears and anxieties, they become less sidekicks and more central heroes. In "The Prodigal," when Gabrielle is still new to traveling with Xena, she begins to doubt her choice to leave home and marriage to take up a life of adventure and female companionship. Her feelings of incompetence and guilt, and her inability to explain how she feels, limit her ability to be tough. Gabrielle decides to return home without Xena, only to find that she is tougher than she knows: She saves her family and former neighbors from a warlord who has been attempting to take over the village. She then realizes that her feelings of inadequacy are unjustified; she may not be as tough as Xena yet, but she is more tough than she had been living a quiet life as a peasant girl. Early on in *Buffy* in "Halloween," Willow similarly feels that she is of no real value to her new friend in her work as a slayer. When Buffy is incapacitated due to a spell, however, Willow rises to the occasion and saves the entire town from being taken over by vampires and demons. Like Gabrielle, she discovers that she is tougher than she knew, and, as the series continues, Willow continues to grow as a heroine.

In these episodes, women's self-doubts and frustrations circulate around feelings of powerlessness, of not being "tough enough." In general, Gabrielle and Willow overcome anxiety and low self-confidence quickly; these two women are very much in touch with their emotions, and they learn that this character trait is an advantage when it comes to being tough. In fact, one of their primary jobs as friends is to teach Xena and Buffy to trust their emotions and embrace communicating their feelings. Gabrielle and Willow show the primary heroines that emotional knowing is critical to being effectively tough. Xena and Buffy, at times, struggle with communicating their thoughts and emotions; they are more likely than their companions to cling to traditional notions of toughness that demand a control of emotions in order to be heroic. Both women must relearn how to face what they feel and how to incorporate emotional knowledge into their ideas of toughness.

Xena comes to terms with her emotionally rigid past by voicing the feelings she has repressed and acknowledging the feelings of those her actions have affected. In "A Necessary Evil," she apologizes publicly for having killed Callisto's family when Callisto was a child. Eventually, in "Fallen Angel," Xena, Gabrielle, and Callisto are given a spiritually guided chance to know each other on an emotional level after they all die; this final knowing allows all the women to understand and forgive each other. Buffy similarly learns that when she denies her emotions she becomes less tough. In "Anne," she literally runs away from her pain and anger over Angel's death; when she returns in "Dead Man's Party," Buffy's mother and Willow force her to express her feelings and deal with theirs so that she can return to her former toughness. In "Weight of the World," Buffy suffers her own loss of confidence and slips into a catatonic state when she fails to protect her sister from a vengeful goddess; however, Willow's love and skillful emotional knowing help Buffy face her fear and guilt. Willow stresses to her friend that, together in their love for each other, they can handle anything.

Emotional connections with the women in their lives make Xena tough enough to fight the gods without religiously sanctioned power and Buffy tough enough to give her own life; both women find toughness in their love for friends and family rather than in traditional notions of heroism that demand emotional isolation. These examples from both series demonstrate the value of female friendship and female bonding in providing a space where women can express themselves and resist the self-doubt and lack of confidence they may have about their identities and purposes. More importantly, these women never stop with the expression of their emotional knowledge. Giving voice almost always leads to taking action; both *Xena* and *Buffy* suggest that communication among women should be but the first step toward resisting silence.[35] In these series, women validate each other's feelings and thoughts and *use* their new knowledge to help each other take action against people and institutions working to keep them silent, powerless, and lonely.

Both series are at their most effective in representing the benefits of emotional knowing when episodes feature each of the primary females weathering a mutual emotional crisis. Such stories offer examples of not only how understanding and expressing one's feelings can be fruitful for women but also how strong female friendships can become even stronger through emotional catharsis. When Xena, Gabrielle, Buffy, and Willow are able to maintain their bonds in the face of the extreme emotional stress that their lives as heroes creates, their relationships become firmer, and they themselves become better heroes. These series make a thematic connection between the communication of feelings and the ability to be heroes: The women learn that they lose some of their toughness when they shut each other out emotionally.[36]

Breaking New Ground

Xena and *Buffy* break through traditional patterns of heroic toughness that prioritize individualism, isolationism, and emotional withdrawal; these shows offer new visions of women coming together in harmony and community rather than in envy and competition. Processes of epistemic negotiation emerge as indispensable to the lead female characters making good choices or being tough enough to be heroic. The methods involved are unorthodox in relation to normative ways of knowing, but these methods are proven to be productive. Unorthodox, apparently nonmethodical ways of understanding operate especially well for people whose lived experiences are nonmethodical.[37] In the fantastic worlds of *Xena* and *Buffy*, the apparently illogical experiences in which these women consistently find themselves demand flexible strategies of knowing that value interdependency, community, and emotional knowing as much as logic. The bonds between women are the ground upon which such dynamics occur.

Through privileging female friendships, these shows are able to focus on women working together. This suggests there are productive possibilities when women share power and collectively resist patriarchy. Women can come together to be heroes. However, both *Xena* and *Buffy* set limits on what kinds of women can work together in such ways. For example, working-class females appear in both series in problematic guises, invoking stereotypes common in popular media. Working-class characters are often exoticized, demonized, or sexualized in ways that serve to marginalize them from the "proper" female communities within these shows. In *Buffy*, the character Faith represents a typical working-class figure; Faith thrives on sex, crime, and violence and looks down upon Buffy and her reliance on her friends. Faith is unable to communicate in any meaningful way with Buffy or Willow, and any expression of her anger results in problems rather than the beginnings of epistemic negotiation. As Elyce Rae Helford points out, while Buffy is able to communicate her anger in the show, in part this is because Buffy's middle-class status makes her anger "soft," something Faith's working-class status denies her.[38] In *Xena*, many peasant women also remain on the edge of the legitimate female communities at work in the show; characters such as the barmaid Meg and the peasant woman Minya serve as comic foils who can barely function without Xena or Gabrielle telling them exactly what to do. Incapable of communication, Meg and Minya are incapable of heroism, and Xena and Gabrielle must make all decisions with little consideration for these women. Ultimately, working-class women in both series are not able to operate effectively within the community of women these shows offer viewers.

Race is also a significant factor in terms of how both series set up criteria for who becomes a hero. *Buffy* and *Xena* both demonize and marginalize some women of color.[39] For example, in *Buffy*, the first slayer and another slayer (Kendra) are black; both females are traditionally tough in that they shun the idea of camaraderie and emotional bonding between women. Accordingly, the show shuns them.[40] Both shows feature women of color who embrace interdependency and emotional knowing as beneficial to women's toughness, but these characters serve in stereotypical fashion to support—never join forces with—the main female characters.[41] In *Xena*, the characters of Akimi and Lao Ma are both Asian; they teach Xena to be more spiritually in tune with herself, and both characters die quickly. Asian females in *Xena* easily fall into stereotyped representations of the lotus blossom (not tough enough to survive, as with Akimi and Lao Ma) and the dragon lady (too traditionally tough, in that she rejects other women, as with Lao Ma's evil daughter), as these guises are described by Jessica Hagedorn.[42]

Thus, while both shows offer modes of toughness significantly different from those of media past, they also follow a pattern of class- and race-based exclusion that dampens the flexible toughness the series champion otherwise. Still, *Xena* and *Buffy* transform toughness from a state of loneliness and separatism to a mode of heroism that embraces empathy and community. Code argues that it is important for women to take control of knowledge and to fight for women's ways of knowing to be revalued in society in order to combat damaging gender stereotypes.[43] Because females from such an early age constantly face patriarchal pressures to defer to men's toughness, and because this often results in women being separated from and suspicious of each other, the emphasis that both programs place on women coming together is important.

But, after all, why is it important that these television series show us the tough women that they do? In her book about female friendships, Sandra Sheehy interviews over 200 girls and women about the value of female friendship in their lives, discussing what is necessary in a healthy female friendship.[44] She suggests that fictional representations of females working together figure in how real women think about such bonds. This is valuable because the fantasy framework of these shows, for as much possibility as it offers, might just as easily suggest that productive female bonds can only emerge in the most fantastic of circumstances. Kathleen Karlyn, for example, points out that shows such as *Xena* and *Buffy* seem to be suggesting that "in order to even imagine female heroism, we're placing it in the realm of fantasy."[45] Do these texts offer visions of collective female toughness that resonate with actual women?

In my own research on fans of both shows, viewers indicated that Xena, Gabrielle, Buffy, and Willow can serve as role models and sources of inspiration for women. In particular, the bonds between the lead women appeal to female viewers; they enjoy seeing representations of tough women working with rather than against each other.[46] (See figure 9.3.) Sheehy stresses that adult women need female companions to help them with their "quest for [their selves] ... [a quest] that leads to stronger, more satisfying, more enduring friendships."[47] Gabrielle and Willow are involved critically in developing Xena's and Buffy's quests and vice versa. With the supportive environment of friendship, these television women come to enjoy

Figure 9.3. In Buffy and Xena, female bonding helps women resist patriarchal pressures

redefining what they know. Heroism especially is redefined; it involves community, interdependency, and emotions.

Xena and *Buffy* model ways in which women can come together to know and to take action in their worlds; these shows also offer a vision of female bonding as something powerful and resilient. Instead of one tough heroine, these programs offer communities of women involved in heroic action. While not every woman can wield a broadsword, every woman has the potential to rely on her friends for strength and courage when the going gets tough. In a world in which women (and men) are hungry for visions of females working together to create change, shows offering this are important. We cannot afford to ignore what television does and does not offer in terms of visions of women nor can we ignore how such visions resonate and interact with the world in which we live.

Notes

1. Lorraine Code, *Rhetorical Spaces: Essays on Gendered Locations* (New York: Routledge, 1995), 147.
2. Code, 160.
3. Bonnie Dow, *Prime-Time Feminism: Television, Media Culture, and the Women's Movement Since 1970* (Philadelphia: University of Pennsylvania Press, 1996).
4. Hilary Radner, *Shopping Around: Feminine Culture and the Pursuit of Pleasure* (New York: Routledge Press, 1995); Ien Ang, "Melodramatic Identifications: Television Fiction and Women's Fantasy," in *Feminist Television Criticism: A Reader*, ed. Charlotte Brundson, Julie D'Acci, and Lynne Spiegel (Oxford: Clarendon Press, 1997), 155–65; Karen Hollinger, *In the Company of Women: Contemporary Female Friendship Films* (Minneapolis: University of Minnesota Press, 1998).
5. Soo-Hyun Susie Parks, "Pleasurable Contradictions: Perceptions and Negotiations of *Xena*" (master's thesis, Ohio State University, 1997); Hollinger, 1–26.
6. Hollinger, 2–3.
7. Suzanna Walters, *Material Girls: Making Sense of Feminist Cultural Theory* (Berkeley: University of California Press, 1995); Hollinger, 207–35.
8. Walters, 136–37.
9. Julie D'Acci, *Defining Women: Television and the Case of Cagney and Lacey* (Chapel Hill, NC: University of North Carolina Press, 1994); Danae Clark, "Cagney and Lacey: Feminist Strategies of Detection," in *Television and Women's Culture: The Politics of the Popular*, ed. Mary Ellen Brown (London: Sage Publications, 1990), 117–33.
10. Yvonne Tasker, *Working Girls: Gender and Sexuality in Popular Cinema* (New York: Routledge, 1998), 67–88; Sherrie A. Inness, *Tough Girls: Women*

Warriors and Wonder Women in Popular Culture (Philadelphia: University of Pennsylvania Press, 1999), 6–8 and 166–75.

11. Aaron Spelling noted in a recent television special on *Charlie's Angels* that he had trouble convincing networks that women could carry an action-oriented series, delaying the start of the show until he gathered more support. *TV Tales: "Charlie's Angels" Behind the Scenes*, E! Television Network, January 6, 2003.

12. Inness, 10; Lori Landy, *Madcaps, Screwballs, Con Women: The Female Trickster in American Culture* (Philadelphia: University of Pennsylvania Press, 1998), 197–218.

13. *Entertainment Weekly* (May 31, 2002): 65–9.

14. Inness, 168.

15. Rhonda Wilcox, "'Who Died and Made Her the Boss?' Patterns of Mortality in *Buffy*," in *Fighting the Forces: What's at Stake in Buffy the Vampire Slayer*, ed. Rhonda Wilcox and David Lavery (Lanham: Rowman and Littlefield Publishers, 2002), 3–17, 6.

16. Sharon Ross, "Super(natural) Women: Female Heroes, Their Friends, and Their Fans" (Ph.D. diss., University of Texas at Austin, 2002).

17. For a more detailed discussion of the feminist underpinnings of *Absolutely Fabulous*, see Beverly Kirkham and Pat Skeggs, "*AbFab*: Absolutely Feminist?," in *The Television Studies Book*, ed. Christine Geraghty and David Lusted (New York: St. Martin's Press, 1998), 287–300. For an excellent discussion of *Roseanne*, see Kathleen Rowe, *The Unruly Woman: Gender and the Genres of Laughter* (Austin: University of Texas Press, 1995).

18. Code, 147, 158.

19. Roz Kaveney, "'She Saved the World. A Lot': An Introduction to the Themes and Structures of *Buffy* and *Angel*," in *Reading the Vampire Slayer: An Unofficial Critical Companion to Buffy and Angel*, ed. Roz Kaveney (New York: Tauris Parke Paperbacks, 2002), 1–36.

20. Code, xi.

21. Code, 150–53.

22. Gail Weiss, *Body Images: Embodiment as Corporeality* (New York: Routledge, 1999), 72.

23. Maurice Merleau-Ponty, *Phenomenology of Experience*, trans. Colin Smith (London: Routledge and Kegan Paul, 1962), 154–62; Oliver Sacks, *The Man Who Mistook His Wife for a Hat and Other Clinical Tales* (New York: Summit, 1985).

24. Weiss, 136–146. Carol Gilligan, *In A Different Voice: Psychological Theory and Women's Development* (Cambridge, MA: Harvard University Press, 1982) and "Moral Orientation and Moral Development," in *Justice and Care: Essential Readings in Feminist Ethics*, ed. Virginia Held (Boulder: Westview Press, 1995).

25. Code, 166.

26. Code, 145–46.

27. Brian Wall and Michael Zryd, "Vampire Dialectics: Knowledge, Institutions and Labour," in *Reading the Vampire Slayer: An Unofficial Critical Companion to Buffy and Angel*, ed. Roz Kaveney (New York: Tauris Parke Paperbacks, 2002), 53–77, 53.

28. Zoe-Jane Playden, "'What You Are, What's to Come': Feminisms, Citizenship and the Divine," in *Reading the Vampire Slayer: An Unofficial Critical Companion to Buffy and Angel*, ed. Roz Kaveney (New York: Tauris Parke Paperbacks, 2002), 120–47, 138.

254 Sharon Ross

29. Lorraine Code, *What Can She Know? Feminist Theory and the Construction of Knowledge* (Ithaca, NY: Cornell University Press, 1991), 215–16.

30. Amy Fifarek, "Mind and Heart with Spirit Joined": The Buffyverse as an Information System," *The On Line International Journal of Buffy Studies* no. 3 (June 2001); available at http://www.slayage.tv/theon-lineinternational journal ofBuffystudies.

31. Code, 214–16.

32. Lyn Mikel Brown, *Raising Their Voices: The Politics of Girls' Anger* (Cambridge, MA: Harvard University Press, 1998). Brown also explores in great detail how girls' loss of voice is transformed into justified anger that is then turned against other girls or adult women, unproductively (111).

33. Lyn Mikel Brown and Carol Gilligan, *Meeting at the Crossroads: Women's Psychology and Girls' Development* (New York: Ballantine Books, 1992), 2.

34. Hillary Carlip, *Girl Power* (New York: Warner Books, 1995); Vendela Vida, *Girls on the Verge: Debutante Dips, Drive-Bys, and Other Initiations* (New York: St. Martin's Press, 1999).

35. Dana Cloud argues that feminism's emphasis on consciousness raising sometimes leads to consciousness raising as the ends, rather than the means, to ending women's oppression, and both series resist this trap. If people will not listen to women when they speak, it is vital that women have the authority and collective power to change their situations if they find this necessary. Dana Cloud, *Control and Consolation in American Culture and Politics: Rhetoric of Therapy* (Thousand Oaks, CA: Sage Publications, 1998), 103–30.

36. Many fans of *Xena* read the bonds between Xena and Gabrielle as lesbian, adding a complex layer to how these characters are negotiating their emotional knowledge and decision making. In fact, the episode "You Are There" addresses this dynamic in relation to whether or not the two will publicly give voice to the "kind" of relationship they share. For a fuller discussion, see Sharon Ross, "Super(natural) Women: Female Heroes, Their Friends, and Their Fans" (Ph.D. diss., University of Texas at Austin, 2002), 239–333; Elyce Rae Helford, "Feminism, Queer Studies, and the Sexual Politics of *Xena: Warrior Princess*," in *Fantasy Girls: Gender in the New Universe of Science Fiction and Fantasy Television*, ed. Elyce Rae Helford (Lanham, MD: Rowman and Littlefield, 2000), 135–62; and Inness, 168–70.

37. Code, 144–53.

38. Elyce Rae Helford, "'My Emotions Give Me Power': The Containment of Girls' Anger in *Buffy*," in *Fighting the Forces: What's at Stake in Buffy the Vampire Slayer*, ed. Rhonda Wilcox and David Lavery (Lanham, MD: Rowman and Littlefield Publishers, 2002), 18–34.

39. Inness, 175–76; Helford, 21.

40. Kendra eventually embraces Buffy and Willow's form of toughness, but the moment she does, a vampire kills her. This is in keeping with tragic mulatta storylines within popular culture. See Lynne Edwards, "Slaying in Black and White: Kendra as Tragic Mulatta in *Buffy*," in *Fighting the Forces: What's at Stake in Buffy the Vampire Slayer*, ed. Rhonda Wilcox and David Lavery (Lanham, MD: Rowman and Littlefield Publishers, 2002), 85–97.

41. Feminist scholars have noted this trend within popular media in general. For example, see Tania Modleski, "Cinema and the Dark Continent: Race and Gender in Popular Film," in *Writing on the Body: Female Embodiment and*

Feminist Theory, ed. Katie Conboy, Nadia Medina, and Sarah Stanbury (New York: Columbia University Press, 1997), 208–30.

42. Jessica Hagedorn, "Asian Women in Film: No Joy, No Luck," in *Facing Difference: Race, Gender, and Mass Media*, ed. Shirley Biagi and Marilyn Kern-Foxworth (Thousand Oaks, CA: Pine Forge Press, 1997), 32–7.

43. Code, 87–102.

44. Sandra Sheehey, *Connecting: The Enduring Power of Female Friendship* (New York: Harper Collins Publishers, 2000).

45. Nadya Labi, "For the Next Generation, Feminism is Being Sold as Glitz and Image," *Time* (June 29, 1998): 60–62.

46. Ross, 618–84.

47. Sheehy, 212.

Chapter 10

Little Miss Tough Chick of the Universe: *Farscape*'s Inverted Sexual Dynamics

Renny Christopher

Farscape, an original series of the SciFi channel (1999–2003), has as one of its main characters an alien female, Aeryn Sun, brought up in a culture that practices no gender differentiation. She carries a big gun, a big attitude, and a big sex appeal for male and female viewers. The show tells the story of John Crichton, an astronaut with the International Aeronautics and Space Administration who gets "sucked down a wormhole" while flying an experimental mission. He ends up in a "distant part of the galaxy" filled with exotic alien beings and cultures. His journey is one of the most remarkable to appear in the annals of science-fiction film and television, not the least for the inverted ("alien?") and experimental sexual dynamics he participates in during his sojourn on the biomechanoid Leviathan ship, Moya, with her crew of escaped prisoners and ex-Peacekeepers. One of these is Aeryn Sun, whose relationship with Crichton plays out in remarkably gender-switched terms. She is the tough chick of the universe, a female terminator, an implacable soldier, and Crichton's love interest.

Farscape is a show with sex and gender as one of its central foci. Science-fiction novelist Caitlin Kiernan writes:

> But what newcomers to the show often find most surprising of all is *Farscape*'s willingness to deal openly, honestly, erotically, and often

very humorously with sex. Sexuality and sensuality are subjects traditionally deemed taboo by the producers of television SF, who have
perhaps imagined their target audiences as eternally prepubescent
males too timid to consider the reality and complexity of the role of
sex in human relationships (well, human and alien relationships).[1]

Kiernan is right that *Farscape* challenges how we understand
women, men, gender roles, and sexuality. The show enters into the
territory of queerness with its gender play, since, in earthbound
human terms, Officer Aeryn Sun has what Judith Butler would call
an "unintelligible" gender,[2] and, more remarkably, so does John
Crichton. As the two come together into first a sexual, then romantic
relationship over the course of the show's four-season development, the role reversal causes the relationship to play out in almost
homoerotic terms. Aeryn holds the homoerotic appeal of the kick-
ass female, a model of a woman who does not fear or need men,
that drew so many lesbian fans to Xena before her.

Science fiction possesses extraordinary freedom to explore gender roles and alternative sexualities, as Brian Attebery points out
when he writes that science fiction "began to be recognized in the
1960s and 1970s as a powerful tool for examining gender issues."[3]
Because science fiction can invent whole new universes, species,
and cultures, it is not limited to the representation of actual human
gender practices. Attebery is referring to print science fiction; film
and television have generally lagged far behind in their level of inno-
vation and exploration of gender. One marker of print science fiction's progressiveness in this area is the James Tiptree Award,
established in 1991 to honor "works of science fiction that explore
and expand gender roles";[4] the existence of this award recognizes
that many writers of science fiction are doing innovative work on
gender. Joan Haran's discussion of Melissa Scott's novel *Shadow
Man* in the context of queer theory illustrates some of the ways
print science fiction has participated in "rethinking apparently fundamental assumptions about what it means to be human."[5] In fact,
some writers even claim that fiction is ahead of theory in this area:
Veronica Hollinger, in her essay "(Re)reading Queerly," notes that
"complex and sophisticated inquiries into gender issues are by no
means new to science fiction, even if our theoretical representations

of these issues have not always kept pace with the fiction."[6] Fiction writers, through their inventions of alternate possibilities for gender practices and sexualities, Hollinger suggests, have made greater contributions to our culture's thinking than theory has made. The best science fiction takes nothing for granted, and in so doing, allows us to reinvent ourselves. And while print science fiction has led the way, television and film may be catching up.

Farscape is helping to bring television representations up to speed, although it is not doing so in a vacuum. During the last decade, many shifts in the representation of gender roles took place, and not exclusively within the science-fiction genre. In *The Frailty Myth*, Colette Dowling points out that women's attitudes toward their own appearance and physical ability have begun to change. She quotes one woman who suggests women should say, instead of, "I'm sexy," "I have a big intellect and bold spirit—and I can kick your ass."[7] Traditionally, women have been judged on their ability to display their femininity in appearance and in personality. Women have been told that they should be thin (but have large breasts), weak, soft, vulnerable, and deferential to men. The cultural trend that Dowling discusses is one in which women, especially younger women, reject the demand to look feminine and behave in a way that indicates weakness. Instead, women, such as the professional volleyball player quoted by Dowling, are asserting their power, rather than their weakness and vulnerability, both in terms of their personalities and their bodies. What Aeryn Sun and other tough women in popular culture do is to take this one step further, saying, in effect, "I can kick your ass, and you'll think I'm sexy because of it." This represents a major change in the way women are regarded; the popularity of figures such as Aeryn illustrates the wider range of possibilities for female behavior that are available.

Attitudes toward tough women have also shifted in genres other than science fiction. Timothy Shuker-Haines and Martha Umphrey write about the emergence of the "hard-boiled" female detective as having the potential "to destabilize radically" gendered oppositions within the detective genre,[8] and Timothy Shary writes in "Angry Young Women: The Emergence of the 'Tough Girl' Image in American Teen Films" that during the 1990s, "a distinct and interesting trend of portraying 'tough girls' emerged. . . . As more recent films have shown Generation X youth challenging notions of gender and power, these tough girl roles have become more complex and influential."[9] In Shary's view, these teen tough girls of recent films stand in contrast to the "twentysomething" female characters typical of "Generation X" films who are both cynical and disenfranchised; the teen tough girls, in contrast, "exhibit an increasing focus on their goals with minimal regard to propriety and social expectations."[10] These teen tough girls, according to Shary, have more agency than their older counterparts; they are strong enough to pursue their own goals and desires, rather than being deprived of their agency and responding to this lack of power with cynicism. This trend that Shary identifies is another way in which the range of behaviors that audiences are willing to accept as gendered female is widening. The images of women who act tough, who act independent, are images that contemporary audiences embrace.

But even while these steps forward in how women are presented have been taken, there has also been resistance, even within science fiction. Lee E. Heller focuses on backlash trends in popular media in his article on *Star Trek*, "The Persistence of Difference." He writes about "the postfeminist and New Traditionalist" opponents of change in gender roles "whose primary project is to reaffirm patriarchal heterosexuality and the gender roles associated therewith against the combined threats—as the discourse constructs it—of feminism and non-heterosexuality."[11] He argues that even while some *Star Trek: The Next Generation* episodes appear to endorse a progressive change in gender roles and sexuality, they in fact actually reinforce traditionalist roles. He demonstrates how *Star Trek: The Next Generation* retreats from alternative gender and sex roles; *Farscape*, in contrast, charges ahead to embrace alternatives. Heller traces how popular culture discourse in the 1980s and 1990s emphasized the difference between men and women, as exemplified by the very popular *Men Are from Mars, Women Are from Venus*.[12] As a measure of how gender roles have changed, he quotes a male-authored 1993 *Cosmopolitan* article in which the writer claims that more men "are in therapy today than twenty-five years ago, when feminism first gave women permission to be tough."[13] *Farscape*, in contrast to the earlier trends Heller cites, participates in the undercutting of gender difference. In the twenty-first century, judging from shows like *Farscape*, men are more likely to be propelled into bed than into therapy by tough women.

As we move into the twenty-first century, changes in popular culture's presentation of tough women have been decisive. Mary Spicuzza writes in a film review titled "Bad Heroines" that in *Tomb Raider*, Angelina Jolie

> leaps into action as the latest addition to an undeniable trend in the evolution of today's action hero, the butt-kicking babe. Other recent films like *Crouching Tiger, Hidden Dragon, Charlie's Angels* and *The Matrix* have all featured women who can not only hold their own, but prevail in combat. On television, female heroes have gone the way of undead-dueling *Buffy the Vampire Slayer*, genetically engineered *Dark Angel*, historic cult-hit *Xena: Warrior Princess* or cartoon animated superhero trio the *Power Puff Girls*. Movies and TV, combined with video games like "Tomb Raider," have launched a full-frontal, multimedia assault with visions of women warriors dominating male and female villains.[14]

She adds, significantly, "Producers wouldn't continue cranking out female action heroes if audience response wasn't overwhelmingly positive."[15] Shows like *Farscape* do build large and dedicated fan bases who respond specifically to the tough women in the shows. This can be clearly seen in the ongoing *Xena* fan culture, which continues long after the show has been cancelled. It is also apparent on the fan websites dedicated to *Farscape*, and especially in the responses recorded on those sites to the show's cancellation after its fourth season by the SciFi channel.[16]

Farscape is similar in structure to another science-fiction television series, *Space: Above and Beyond*, which was, like *Farscape*, produced in the late 1990s and explored alternative gender roles. Nickianne Moody, writing about *Space: Above and Beyond*, notes, "science fiction has always provided a narrative space that allows the reader to consider alternative ways of living."[17] She points out that *Space: Above and Beyond* "is part of a characteristic group of programmes which expresses great anxiety in the lived cultural experience of the contemporary period and explores this in fiction through drawn-out serial narrative." Like *Farscape, Space: Above and Beyond* explores gender dynamics; Moody examines the presentation of one of the female main characters, Shane Vansen, a military commander who takes what would traditionally be called a masculine role. Moody has a further insight into the structure of the series, which is applicable to *Farscape* as well. These television series have narrative arcs: linked episodes and storylines that span multiple episodes and sometimes carry over from season to season. As Moody observes, series such as these "produce demanding single episodes that rely heavily on the audience's knowledge of prior narrative accounts for their maximum emotional and intellectual impact."[18] This is the case with *Farscape*; the show even produced a special episode, "*Farscape* Undressed," at the beginning of its third season to fill in new viewers about its complex history. The importance of the show's structural form is that the characters undergo development, as they would in a novel, or over the course of a feature film, rather than have a series of disconnected adventures, that do not produce lasting changes in them.

The salient facts of the show are as follows. Officer Aeryn Sun was a member of the Peacekeepers, a much-feared military organization that stomps about in its jackboots through the part of the galaxy in which the disoriented astronaut Crichton finds himself. Raised aboard a Command Carrier, Aeryn has been trained all of her life to be a soldier and is part of a hypermilitarized culture in which people do not form serious emotional relationships. Among Sebaceans (her species), both males and females serve as Peacekeeper soldiers, and a person's rank has nothing to do with gender. Peacekeepers "recreate" with each other as a matter of convenience. The military hierarchy assigns reproduction. The institution of marriage or partnership does not exist. In traditional human terms, it is a masculinist culture, but women get to play too, on not only equal but undifferentiated terms. That is, not only is there gender equality between male and female Peacekeepers but there is no gender difference between them, although there is sexual difference and it is a heterosexual culture. But without gender difference, heterosexuality appears quite different from the form practiced in patriarchal culture.

Cyndy Hendershot, in her essay "Vampire and Replicant: The One-Sex Body in a Two-Sex World" writes, "the New Woman of the popular imagination [in the early twentieth century] placed sexual difference in peril, creating a vision of a new society not of men and women, but of men only."[19] This vision of a society of "men only," in which both males and females "act like men," is realized in Peacekeeper society, and it is exactly the kind of aggressive hyper- "masculine" society that might be projected based on patriarchal models, but its lack of a feminine gender role does not impede the enacting of heterosexual sex. It is only when Aeryn steps out of the disciplined Peacekeeper world that she, in effect, becomes queer. As Annamarie Jagose writes in *Queer Theory: An Introduction*, queer "describes those gestures or analytical models that dramatize incoherencies in the allegedly stable relations between chromosomal sex, gender, and sexual desire."[20] In Peacekeeper terms, Aeryn is not queer because her sex and her gender are not at odds. Her behavior follows Peacekeeper norms for both men and women; in Peacekeeper society, men and women have only one gender role, and she enacts it in keeping with the dictates of her society. In Peacekeeper terms, her gender is perfectly intelligible. In human terms, however, she is queer, since she is anatomically female but her behavior is not gendered female by human standards. The Peacekeeper gender norm for both men and women is the masculine norm for humans. Therefore, if one judges Aeryn in human terms, she is a man every way but physically.

Peacekeeper culture is presented as dystopian. It is the entry of the alien Crichton into this world that provides a catalyst for positive change and a vision of a different way of carrying out relationships. Peacekeepers solve all their conflicts through violence. The journey that Acryn goes on over the course of the show requires unlearning her military upbringing and becoming someone capable of thinking and feeling (read: unlearning her "masculinized" behavior and getting in touch with her "feminine"[21] side), and it is Crichton, the "feminized" man, who leads her on her way through this journey. Let me note again that Aeryn is not a human. Nonetheless, all the alien characters on the show, including not only those played by human actors (Aeryn, Ka D'Argo, Zhaan, Chiana, Crais) but those played by puppets[22] (Rygel, Pilot) can be read as humans, or stand-ins for humans, who have easily-understood desires, goals, and responses. The show makes no attempt to make the alien cultures truly "alien," and all their behavior is interpretable through a human lens. At the beginning of the twenty-first century, television can only present the kind of culturally experimental representations that we see in this show in science-fiction formats, disguised as alien. Just as the original *Star Trek* pioneered racial integration on television, giving us television's first interracial kiss between Captain Kirk and Lieutenant Uhura, contemporary science-fiction television is pioneering representations of gender and sexual possibilities that lie outside the norms of narrowly defined heterosexuality.

Gender in a Distant Galaxy

The main element in *Farscape*'s gender-bending is Aeryn, who is one tough chick, all right. On the special that described the series, "*Farscape* Undressed," the actor Ben Browder (Crichton) calls Claudia Black (Aeryn), "Little Miss Tough Chick of the Universe." She replies, "That's me," and it does seem to be her, both the character and the actor who plays her. Black played a hermaphrodite character in the Australian television series *Good Guys Bad Guys*. She also played an Amazon warrior in an episode of *Xena: Warrior Princess*. Black's screen name on the scifi.com *Farscape* bulletin board is "chickwithgun." From an article posted on a fan page:

> And what about the chick with gun ... ? Black does most of the fight sequences and stunts herself, and says, "My guns are getting bigger and bigger each episode—I'm loving it!"
>
> Claudia Black is clearly enjoying the journey. "I think, selfishly—this is biased—that Aeryn has the most interesting arc, because she starts at one polarity and crosses to another, and I get to fill in the gray areas, and that still interests me," she says. Season 1's "PK Tech Girl" is a signpost for her. "It expanded the world of *Farscape*, literally, and that made me jump up to the plate to create a more physical, broader character. I can have more fun with her and make her the female Arnie."[23]

The "female Arnie" designation is apt; Aeryn is a kind of Terminator, but, like Schwarzenegger in *Terminator 2: Judgment*

Day, she is learning to be a protector rather than a killer, learning how to nurture. As a "tough chick" she has many science-fiction predecessors including Xena, Tank Girl, Sarah Connor, Ellen Ripley, and Commander Susan Ivanova from *Babylon 5*.

The comparison to Ivanova is of particular interest. She, an explicitly bisexual character, was very much a "tough chick" in her own right. Sharon Ney and Elaine Sciog-Lazarov write of Ivanova that "her power ... [is] manifested so negatively ... [that] she appears masculinized and militantly feminist."[24] While I disagree with their claim that her power is manifested negatively, since she is one of the show's unambiguous heroes, they raise an important point by claiming that she appears "militantly feminist." They are correct about this because in the human world of the twenty-third century, in which *Babylon 5* is set, women have achieved positions of power and command, but the structure of that society is still patriarchal, so Ivanova needs to be a feminist. Officer Aeryn Sun has no need of feminism since, in human terms, she lives in a world that is post-feminist because it is post-patriarchal, and there is no need for feminism. (There is no evidence that the Sebaceans ever were a patriarchal culture, so it might be nonpatriarchal, instead of post-patriarchal.) Thus *Babylon 5* presents a world in which contemporary women can recognize their own struggles, while *Farscape* presents a purely fantasy world into which contemporary fans of the "tough chick" genre can project themselves as an alternative to the not-yet post-patriarchal world in which we find ourselves.

Aeryn's gender ambiguity is a major element of her characterization. There is never any ambiguity about her sex—she is clearly anatomically female—but her gender, that is, the set of behaviors assigned to persons based on their anatomical sex, is much more "masculine" than "feminine." Her name is ambiguous; it sounds like both "Erin" and "Aaron," and her surname, Sun, pronounced with the Australian/extra-Galactic accent given it in the show, sounds like "soon," but, given the usual American pronunciation, would be a homonym for "son." As a Peacekeeper, she has been trained to suppress her emotions. She has gone through the same social conditioning that men are given in traditional western culture. As Claudia Black remarks in "*Farscape* Undressed," "she is born and bred to be a soldier."

More surprising than Aeryn's "masculinization" is the extent to which the show is able to pull off Crichton's "feminization" without risking his status as an action hero. He is a hero who operates through brain, not brawn, while she, when we first meet her, acts only through brawn. He is placed in a "feminized" position at the beginning of the show when he finds himself lost among aliens. He is weak, and he is menaced. In the premiere, when he first arrives on the biomechanoid Leviathan ship Moya, he is injected with translator microbes—that is, his body is penetrated—and then D'Argo knocks him out with his phallic tongue. When Crichton awakens in his cell, he discovers he has been stripped, completing the symbolic rape. And he discovers he is in the cell with a figure in a dark and dangerous-looking spacesuit, a figure that Rygel refers to as "that," stripping it of a gender and investing it with menace. It turns out to be Aeryn. When she takes off her helmet, she is revealed as female, but this revelation does not alleviate the danger she represents since her first action is to throw Crichton to the floor, revealing that, by human standards, her gender behavior does not match her sex. She drops on top of him, a knee by each of his ears—a female-dominant position that suggests both sex and violence but with the female doing violence to the male, a reversal of the habitual patriarchal practice of heterosexuality.

Aeryn is always the superior fighter, and Crichton always unabashedly acknowledges her superior fighting abilities. In "*Farscape* Undressed," Browder describes Crichton's first meeting with Aeryn as "Boy meets girl; girl kicks boy's ass." And so it always goes between them. In "Unrealized Realities," a season-four episode, Crichton travels through a wormhole back in time to his first day aboard Moya, and we see his first encounter with Aeryn replayed. Because he knows what is coming, he blocks her attack and says, in explanation of his ability to do so, which he lacked the first time around, "I learned from the best—you." Then she attacks him again and pins him, just as she did the first time it happened. Their physical relationship remains the same—she is always capable of beating him up, despite their having become lovers in season three.

Unlike in many films and television shows, having sex does not weaken Aeryn or change the physical dominance between her and Crichton. Diane Dubois writes in " 'Seeing the Female Body

Differently': Gender Issues in *The Silence of the Lambs*" that in "habitual representations of women in film," women who "reject the role of passive object and choose to become active and inquisitive . . . are punished, often by death. If they become powerful in any way at all, they must be disempowered."[25] *Farscape* acts as a dramatic reversal of this "habitual" representation, in that Aeryn is never disempowered. Crichton and she are lovers and are shown as having an active, even rambunctious, sex life throughout seasons three and four, but their sexual involvement never results in a power reversal between them. She remains the better pilot, the better fighter, and the more physically powerful and impressive of the two. For her, engaging in sex is no form of surrender.

Aeryn beats up on Crichton fairly frequently. In "Throne for a Loss," when he refuses to go along with her plan, she punches him in the jaw, knocks him cold, and straps him, unconscious, into her warship to take him along on her mission. She beats up just about everyone, and she almost always wins; when she does not, there are extenuating circumstances. For example, in "Durka Returns," Durka, a former Peacekeeper commander, knocks Aeryn out with a surprise attack she does not see coming because she thinks he has been mind cleansed. This is the first time she is ever defeated by a male; she usually does the damage to others. While male characters sometimes overcome her through surprise or superior firepower, she is never bested in a one-on-one fair fight. In "Taking the Stone," Crichton says to her: "You are the pinup girl for frontal assault."

In contrast to Aeryn, Crichton, while he lacks her physical prowess, is always the one best able to use his head and to employ cunning (a "feminine" quality) to discover a way out of dangerous situations. In the premiere, he makes two escapes using brains, not brawn. First, he escapes from Peacekeeper soldiers when he preoccupies them with his puzzle ring, and, later, he figures out how to cause Moya to do an experimental gravity-sling maneuver to escape from the Peacekeepers. His "heroic action" in this instance is to get down on his knees and write equations on the floor. Although he does the figuring, Aeryn, the better pilot (a "masculine" skill), does the flying. *Farscape* posits a galaxy in which identity is not grounded in difference-based gender roles.

(Of course, Crichton's identity is based on a difference-based *species* role.) Aeryn's identity is more stable than Crichton's, in the sense that although she is undergoing changes, she undergoes them gradually, in an evolutionary sort of way. His identity, in contrast, is radically unstable, in that he often becomes altogether different people. In "My Three Crichtons," he is split into three versions of himself. During the entire second season, he is progressively taken over by the archvillain Scorpius's neural clone, which he carries in his brain; ultimately, he is temporarily transformed into Scorpius. Crichton is split in two in "Eat Me" and spends much of the third season as two versions of himself. The only time Aeryn undergoes any such transformation is when she is injected with Pilot's DNA in "DNA Mad Scientist," an early first-season episode. After that, Aeryn is always Aeryn, and Crichton is almost always someone else. In this, he is the more "feminine" of the two, since in terms of traditional gender roles, women are thought to be more changeable, to the point of being "flighty," whereas men are expected to be stable. *Farscape* takes changeability and vulnerability and makes them human, rather than "feminine" characteristics, since Crichton's identity and his difference from those around him are based on his species rather than his gender. But since we are watching a human male actor and a human female actor playing these roles, what we are watching on the screen is a man "acting like a woman" and a woman "acting like a man," offering us a vision of a world free of the constraints under which we, the audience, actually live. For this reason it is important that Sebaceans look just like humans. Claudia Black plays an alien without makeup or prosthetics, so we tend to forget that Peacekeepers are very alien.

Despite, or perhaps because of, their gender-role reversal, Aeryn and Crichton are attracted to each other from the start, although she denies that attraction at first because she thinks he is weak and hopeless. When he complains to Zhaan that with "Aeryn and D'Argo, it's like everything's a test," Zhaan replies, "John, they're soldiers. Win their respect." Zhaan thus classes Aeryn and D'Argo together in the ungendered category "soldiers." Nonetheless, in "I, ET," the second episode, the sexual tension between Crichton and Aeryn arises, and it builds slowly throughout the first season. It is maintained throughout season two, and season three brings the two together, finally, as lovers, with him being the partner who demands not just sex but emotional commitment, which she is reluctant to give. In the episode "Suns and Lovers," she reverses her earlier decision that they should not act on their attraction to each other because doing so could be disruptive to the crew as a whole. But he rejects her offer to have sex because she has offered only sex, not an emotional relationship. Her response to his rejection is to reiterate her own rejection of emotion and reinforce her offer of sex: "I don't need your emotions, but we can have sex if you want." She is perfectly comfortable being sexually aggressive but uncomfortable with love and commitment; the traditional roles are reversed.

Their role reversal is an integral part of their flirtation through seasons one and two. "PK Tech Girl" makes an explicit contrast between Aeryn, the former Peacekeeper soldier, and Gilina, a Peacekeeper technician who is very "feminine." Gilina falls in love with Crichton because of his kindness and compassion, which stand in contrast to Aeryn's anger and brutality toward her. Gilina flirts coquettishly with him.[26] When Aeryn walks in on them kissing, she lifts a very heavy piece of equipment over her head and walks off with it, expressing her jealousy with a show of physical ("masculine") prowess. He follows her, and Aeryn confesses her attraction to him for the first time. Much as he may be attracted to the "feminine" Gilina, he is more attracted to the "masculine" Aeryn who is taller than he is and at least as physically strong, if not stronger. Dowling, in *The Frailty Myth*, writes, "the idea that women are unable to achieve the same levels of physical development as men is today under question. The only reason some women don't perform at similar levels, suggest some sport sociologists and even physicians, is that women have been cast as biologically incapable for so long."[27] *Farscape* explores an alternate universe in which women have not been cast as "biologically incapable," and, as a result, the human male Crichton encounters a female who is his equal or even superior, physically. What is truly extraordinary is that *Farscape* further posits that he is able to accept her gender identity and still be romantically and sexually drawn to her, acting out a complementary gender role in which he plays give and take with being aggressor and pursued, rescuer and rescued. He is willing to play "girl" to her "guy." Later in this episode, Crichton is in a vulnerable position, being menaced by a fire-spitting Sheyang, and repeats quietly "Aeryn will be here," just like a damsel in distress tied to the railroad tracks and waiting for her male rescuer to arrive. Aeryn, her pulse rifle in hand, comes sliding down a chain like Douglas Fairbanks and rescues him, just as he knew she would.

Aeryn's Phallic Signifier

Aeryn and Crichton do not just enact complementary gender roles; the show reinforces their role swapping by giving them phallic and yonic signifiers. In "Thank God it's Friday, Again," Aeryn makes a try at English slang; she says of the character Volmae, "She gives me a woody." Crichton corrects her: Volmae gives her "the willies." But it is a pointed malapropism; Aeryn points to her possession of a symbolic phallus (her attitude, her pulse rifle), by making reference to the penis she does not have (a phallus cannot get an erection, can it?). In a gender-switched heterosexual (or is it lesbian?) context, a woman gives Aeryn an erection. In the same episode, while Aeryn speaks of her symbolic phallus, Crichton is symbolically penetrated, demonstrating his possession of a symbolic yoni,[28] when Skylarian dissidents put a worm into him. One of them shows him the very penile-looking worm while another holds him down with a hand over his mouth; then the worm burrows into Crichton's belly. This sequence is so blatantly obvious in its sexual symbolism that it could only occur in science fiction.

Cyndy Hendershot writes that the body "has traditionally been used as a means for representing masculine superiority and feminine inferiority. The confusion between phallus and penis has served to biologize masculinity as a visible plenitude: the erect penis symbolizes masculine superiority and virility while the hidden female genitalia have been read as inferior and impotent."[29] Neither Crichton nor Aeryn has a visible penis because of the medium (primetime television) in which they exist, but they both make reference to invisible and symbolic penises—when Aeryn says "she gives me a woody" and when, in response to her admitting that she scented her hair to see if he would notice, Crichton says he is "standing at attention."[30] The show carefully establishes that both have phalluses, but they both also sometimes act "feminine" (Aeryn far less frequently than Crichton), making them both ambiguously gendered, with her consistently taking the more "masculine" role and him taking the more "feminine." In one episode ("DNA Mad Scientist"), he says to her, "That makes us the odd man out." This is more than just a figure of speech. In many ways Crichton does relate to her as a man. The references to phalluses, and Aeryn's constant association with her pulse rifle, serve to underscore her masculinization, making their relationship seem almost like a same-sex pairing. He is a feminized man, and she is a masculine woman.

While Aeryn always remains masculine, she changes her style of masculinity as the show evolves. Part of her character development throughout the series is her need to learn to be emotional, to overcome her masculinist Peacekeeper conditioning, and it is Crichton, who is never afraid to reveal emotions, who teaches her, both explicitly and by example, to become more emotional, more "feminine." In "DNA Mad Scientist," Aeryn shows compassion, for the first time, for Pilot when Zhaan, D'Argo, and Rygel cut off one of his arms in payment for star maps to their home planets. That aligns Aeryn with Crichton, who also sympathizes with Pilot. Later in the episode, when Aeryn, injected with Pilot's DNA, begins to experience a genetic transformation, Crichton asks, is it "just your usual PMS? Peacekeeper Military Shit." His comment transforms the sexist notion of premenstrual syndrome[31] into a critique of the Peacekeepers' "hypermasculine" militarization, embodied in Aeryn's female body. She is seen as vulnerable and admits to fear for the first time in this episode—not because of physical danger but because her mind is being overwhelmed as she develops pilot's multitasking capabilities. She is single-minded (as males are traditionally thought to be) and when she has to think about more than one thing at once, she panics.

In "Rhapsody in Blue," Aeryn appears wearing Crichton's underwear. When he claims them as his, she denies that they are since they have the name "Calvin" in them. She is explicitly cross-dressing, and this episode is one in which the gender-role reversal is most clear. A group of deviant Delvians attack by making the crew see what they either want or fear. On the one hand, Crichton sees Alex, his girlfriend who in reality left him to pursue her own career but who appears in his delusion as his wife. He sees something he wants, something that re-enforces traditional gender roles. Aeryn, on the other hand, sees her worst fear—disarmament. She sees her pulse rifle, her phallus, fall apart in her hands.

As part of Aeryn's education, of learning to leave behind the hypermasculine callousness of her Peacekeeper upbringing, she has to face her past and come to terms with actions she has taken that conformed to Peacekeeper morality, which she has, under Crichton's influence, rejected. What she learns over the course of the show's four seasons is how to be tough without being brutal, how to be brave and strong without being devoid of emotion. In effect, she learns how to be an ideal man, by feminist standards. The learning is a hard journey for her, though. She has a dark secret, revealed in the season-two episode "The Way We Weren't." It turns out that she participated in the murder of Moya's original pilot in her former life as a Peacekeeper, when she was involved with a Peacekeeper officer named Velorek. When she tells Crichton that she and Velorek were "lovers," he says, "I don't think I've ever heard you use that word before." When he asks if she loved Velorek, she says, "I felt something for him I never felt for any of the other men I recreated with. I guess now I'd say that it was love." We see her with him in flashback. Velorek offers to arrange to have them posted together. He tells her that there is something special about her; she denies it. He says, "I know how I feel about you, and I think I know how you feel about me. When I leave here, I want you to come with me. You can be so much more." This last line is what Crichton says to Aeryn the day they meet, and it is his echoing of what Velorek had said to her before that sets her on her path of reform.

But when she was with Velorek, she betrayed his sabotage plan in order to get her prestigious flying Prowlers back, and Velorek is executed. And so we find out that Aeryn has had her former lover killed. She says, "I was a Peacekeeper then, and things were very different—my priorities, my values, and my relationships." At the end of the episode, she says to Pilot: "Do you remember when you first came aboard Moya? Velorek stroked your cheek like this to calm you. Back then I couldn't fathom why he'd do a thing like that. And now I couldn't fathom not doing it. We've come a long way since then, Pilot, and we've still got a long way to go." She is learning to become a sensitive new-age male, rather than a heartless, hyper- "masculine" Peacekeeper soldier.

In contrast to Aeryn's "masculine" nature, Crichton is consistently "feminine" in his character. He is openly emotional, sensitive, empathetic, and other-directed. In "Through the Looking Glass," the crew debates about abandoning Moya because of her pregnancy, which increases their chance of being captured. All but Aeryn and Crichton are in favor of abandoning her, but her motivation is a soldier's loyalty, while he expresses his sympathy for Moya and her baby. He says that she is just trying to protect her baby, and "can you blame her for that?" He is the only member of the crew who empathizes with—who practically shares—Moya's maternal instincts. When she offers to lose the baby in order to get them out of the interdimensional split they are in, Crichton reacts strongly against that thought, saying, "whatever happens, we go together. We keep the baby." In "A Look at the Princess," Crichton does not want to marry the princess and remain on her planet, but after he discovers she has already been made pregnant by him, he immediately volunteers to be turned into a statue for 80 years alongside her because the baby deserves a father. And when Aeryn becomes pregnant, he is willing to chase her all over the universe to be a parent to her child, even though it might not be his.

Crichton, put in a "feminized" position because he is a human among aliens, and therefore weak and vulnerable, is simultaneously an action hero in the traditional sense (he shoots bad guys, flies spaceships, and performs other heroic feats) and a character who embraces his "femininity" in that he values sensitivity, emotionality, and connectedness. He teaches these values to Aeryn, for whom they are alien because of her "masculinized" Peacekeeper culture. The two of them come together in a sphere where they can each enact behaviors that, in human terms, are gendered "masculine" or "feminine" but that lose their gender. Instead of understanding Aeryn and Crichton as swapping gender roles, it is possible, instead, to view them as reinventing behavior so that it is not gendered, and so that men and women can learn to value the same set of behaviors. It is significant, however, that though Peacekeeper society is already a society in which men and women enact the same behaviors, the set of behaviors that Peacekeepers value are negative and destructive because they represent only the most aggressive and coldhearted extremes of "masculine" behavior. When Crichton arrives, bringing "feminine" values with him, he and Aeryn create a new culture, which takes the best of the "masculine" (bravery, strength) and mixes it with the best of the "feminine" (emotionality, connectedness, openness) to create a culture of two in which "masculine" and "feminine" are mixed to create a possibility for interactions not based in gender roles.

Aeryn Comes to Earth

Despite Crichton's adoption of a "feminine" persona, he sometimes has traditional ideas about gender roles (his fantasies always take this form). This represents an inconsistency in the show, which is perhaps inevitable in series television, even in a show with such a tightly knit story arc as *Farscape*. Nonetheless, even when Crichton fantasizes about taking Aeryn to earth and placing her into a "feminine" role, his fantasies fail; her character has been too strongly constructed as "masculine" to make this shift even in fantasy.

Crichton's traditionalist ideas sometimes slip out in surprising ways. In "Family Ties," Aeryn remarks, "When I was very young one night, a soldier appeared over my bunk, battle-hardened, scarred," and he replies, "Cool. Your father." She says, "My mother." *Farscape* does something truly revolutionary with representations of maternity. The relationship between Aeryn and her mother, when put together with Crichton's attitude toward Leviathan and humanoid progeny, amounts to the show claiming that maternal instincts are not "natural" or exclusive to females. When her mother, Xalex Sun, enters the show, she has no maternal feelings for Aeryn whatever.[32] She is bitter and vengeful toward Aeryn. Xalex committed the indiscretion of having an unauthorized baby, which, like all Peacekeeper babies, was then raised by the State. But Xalex sneaked into her daughter's barracks in the middle of the night when Aeryn was a child to tell her that she had been born for love, not as an accident or assigned reproduction, and that that indiscretion cost Xalex her career. She is coldly willing to kill Aeryn, and Aeryn is willing, albeit reluctant, to kill her; Xalex possesses nothing we would recognize as maternal feelings. Crichton and Aeryn both have interactions with their same-sex parent, but while Crichton's father is nurturing and supportive, Aeryn's mother is a thoroughgoing "masculinized" Peacekeeper; these characters emphasize the gender-role reversals of Aeryn and Crichton's relationship. If there is anyone in the universe tougher than Aeryn, it is her mother.

While Crichton is more maternal in his feelings than either Aeryn or her mother, he does indulge himself in masculinist fantasies of Aeryn on Earth, in which he imagines her in a more traditional "feminine" role, and dressed in "feminine" clothes. One of the markers of Aeryn's tough-woman persona is in costuming. In the "real world" of the show, she is always dressed as a soldier, in masculinized clothes; we see her in Crichton's fantasies dressed in feminine human clothes, but it is not a good fit, even in fantasy. He puts her in drag in his fantasies, that is, and it does not fit. In the first episode, Aeryn is dressed in the black leather Peacekeeper unisex uniform; her femininity is marked only by her long hair, but Commander Crais also has long hair, worn in the same ponytail as Aeryn's, so in her world, even her hair is not a gender role marker. In one first-season episode, "Throne for a Loss," Aeryn is dressed in a sports bra, with a bare midriff, showing her well-muscled belly. But the show backed away from such displays of her body. In "Taking the Stone," an early season two episode, Aeryn and Crichton start dressing alike in a Peacekeeper unisex style, in long black leather coats, and they maintain that style for the rest of the series. This dress-alike serves to emphasize their gender-role reversals, since their clothing does not differentiate them. This clothing style therefore reinforces the universe of two that they create, the universe in which they can leave gender roles behind.

The series demonstrates that the ungendered universe they create together is the only one that works for both of them by showing Crichton's unsuccessful fantasies of bringing Aeryn to earth. These fantasies take her out of the unisex clothing they wear on Moya and put her into a femmed-out style that is a very jarring contrast to her rifle-toting black-leather-clad persona in the "real" world of the show (i.e., on the ship Moya). His fantasy attempts to make her into a human woman with human feminine behavior always fail. The episode "A Human Reaction" consists almost entirely of a fantasy of Crichton's; this is the first time we see Aeryn on Earth, in what will be a series of his fantasies that place her into his world. In this fantasy they escape from the captivity the human military is holding them in and break into a motel room. He opens the door, saying, "Ladies first," demonstrating how in his fantasies, their relationship is gendered in a standard human patriarchal mode. In the motel room, they sleep together, and it is very clearly he who makes the first move in the seduction, which is nothing like the way they mutually try to tear each other's spacesuits off in "The Flax," or the way, in the "real" world, she ultimately tells him, "We can have sex now." The next morning, she is dressed in a flower-print sundress. She is uncertain and awkward in it (even his fantasy grants her that), but the salient point is that in his fantasy, he changes her style from masculinized Peacekeeper soldier to femme. This is how he will always see her in his fantasies of her on Earth. In "Dog with Two Bones," Aeryn flirtatiously tries on a wedding dress, displaying her body in a way she never does on Moya. The unreality of his picture of a future on Earth with her is dramatically demonstrated in one cut in this episode in which we move from his fantasy Aeryn throwing her wedding bouquet to a scene of the real Aeryn, dressed in her habitual black leather, organizing repairs of Moya, and issuing orders to everyone, including him. Aeryn, in his fantasies, literally does not speak a human language. In the part of the universe she comes from, everyone has translator microbes and can understand each other's languages. She speaks her own language on Earth, and no one but Crichton understands her. Just as she cannot speak the language, she also cannot perform the gender Earth calls on her to perform.

For a relationship between the two of them to work, it must take place in the special universe they create for themselves, the place in which they can exist without having to conform to prescribed gender roles, where each can "act like a woman" or "act like a man" no matter what biological sex they have. It is this mixing of the traits usually considered to be "feminine" or "masculine" that is the hallmark of the show.

A Distant Part of the (Gendered) Universe

Farscape is set in a universe that is truly science fiction—a universe of experimental, alternative sex and gender roles that appeal to viewers who like their men to be women, their women to be men, their chicks to be tough, and their guys to be soft. This is a queer universe in which the lines between heterosexual and homosexual dynamics are blurred, where everything is alien, and anything is possible. Donna Haraway writes in *Simians, Cyborgs, and Women: The Reinvention of Nature*, "the possibilities for our reconstitution include the utopian dream of the hope for a monstrous world without gender."[33] The *Farscape* universe is not a world without gender, but it is a world in which gender is constructed in a much wider range of ways than a traditional human gender-role structure allows. It is not a monstrous world but a playful one.

In the *Farscape* universe, being born into a female or male body is not the major determinant of one's life possibilities. Women can be warriors or not; men can be emotional and maternal or not. Heterosexual men can exhibit "feminine" qualities and fall in love with tough women who are better fighters, better pilots, better at being all the things usually called "masculine." The *Farscape* universe is, measured by human terms, a remarkably queer universe. Hollinger suggests that using "the strategically powerful perspectives of queer theory . . . is one way in which feminist work can be mobilized to think against the grain of heteronormativity, so that we can also begin to think ourselves outside the binary oppositions of a fictively totalizing feminine/masculine divide."[34] What *Farscape* does in its gender play, in its role reversals, is to dismantle that "totalizing feminine/masculine divide" by showing us boys who will be girls and girls who will be boys. Or perhaps *Farscape* does not so much erase that divide as ignore it. The show creates a dystopic masculinist culture, the Peacekeepers, but the show also paints Earth as dystopic, in that Earth, with its narrowly defined gender roles and expectations, is not an environment in which the gender playfulness that characterizes the relationship between Aeryn and Crichton can exist. In Crichton's memories of Earth, there are no female astronauts. But out of these two dystrophies, these two characters, the "masculinized" woman and the "feminized" man, manage to create Haraway's world without gender, and in that world to love one another and to be loved by fans who want to participate in just such a world.

Farscape, by exploring a queer part of the universe, gives us an opportunity to explore where no one may have gone before. The show takes one step into a territory in which there will either be no gender, as Haraway suggests, or, perhaps, something even better than that: a territory in which gender is a free-for-all, completely severed from biological sex, and sexuality, too, then, is freed of heteronormativity. The relationship between Aeryn and Crichton is not heteronormative, even if it is heterosexual, because she is as much of a man as he is, and he is much more of a woman than she is. Their actual sexual practices cannot, of course, be shown on primetime television, but the openness of their gender play provides a free field of fantasy for fans attracted to alternative gender performances and sexualities.

Tough women in popular culture are leading the way into that territory by playing against longstanding gender stereotypes. By so doing, such women are easing our cultural fears of difference and of change in the realm of gender roles, accustoming us to the idea that biological sex and gendered behavior are separable. Cyndy Hendershot argues that the nineteenth- and twentieth-century texts that she examines (*Dracula* and *Invasion of the Body Snatchers*) represent a fear that "sexual difference may be a conceptual category and not a biological fact. Hence women may be able to perform masculine tasks . . . and men may expand the definition of masculinity to encompass feminine traits."[35] In *Farscape*, characters perform "masculine" tasks and exhibit "feminine" traits in ways not bound to biological sex, but, in the *Farscape* universe, this behavior is expressed not as a cultural fear but rather as a matter of play.

Viewers are attracted to Aeryn, the tough woman, as the fan pages dedicated to the show demonstrate.[36] She is one of the more complex characters to have been created in a science-fiction television series precisely because of the complexities the show constructs around her gendered behavior and sexuality. The degree of complexity this show is able to construct in its representation of gender is remarkable and operates as an indicator of the ways in which science fiction, especially in its depiction of tough women like Aeryn Sun, can play a role in the ongoing cultural discussion of women's place in our society.

Notes

1. Caitlin Kiernan, "*Worlds Glimpsed, Worlds Lost: Why Farscape Should Be Saved,*" accessed September 26, 2002, available at www.sfsite.com/09b/far136.htm.
2. Judith Butler, *Gender Trouble* (New York: Routledge, 1999).
3. Brian Attebery, "Science Fiction and the Gender of Knowledge," in *Speaking Science Fiction: Dialogues and Interpretations*, ed. Andy Sawyer and David Seed (Liverpool: Liverpool University Press, 2000), 131.
4. Joan Gordon and Madeline Scheckter, "Gender Resistance in the James Tiptree Award Anthology," *The New York Review of Science Fiction* 12, no. 11 (July 2000): 14.
5. Joan Haran, "Destabilizing Sex/Gender/Sexuality in Melissa Scott's *Shadow Man,*" *Foundation* 30, no. 82 (2001): 24.
6. Veronica Hollinger, "(Re)Reading Queerly: Science Fiction, Feminism, and the Defamiliarization of Gender," in *Future Females, the Next Generation: New Voices and Velocities in Feminist Science Fiction Criticism*, ed. Marleen S. Barr (Lanham, MD: Rowman & Littlefield Publishers, 2000), 197.
7. Colette Dowling, *The Frailty Myth* (New York: Random House, 2000), xxii.
8. Timothy Shuker-Haines and Martha M. Umphrey, "Gender (De)Mystified: Resistance and Recuperation in Hard-Boiled Female Detective Fiction," in *The Detective in American Fiction, Film, and Television*, ed. Jerome H. Delameter and Ruth Prigozy (Westport, CT: Greenwood Press, 1998), 71.
9. Timothy Shary, "Angry Young Women: The Emergence of the 'Tough Girl' Image in American Teen Films," *Post Script* 19, no. 2 (2000): 49.
10. Shary, 49.
11. Lee E. Heller, "The Persistence of Difference: Postfeminism, Popular Discourse, and Heterosexuality in *Star Trek: The Next Generation*," *Science Fiction Studies* 24, no. 2 (1997): 226. Heller uses "postfeminism" and "New Traditionalism" "to signify the conservative counterreaction—what Susan Faludi . . . calls a 'backlash'—against 1) the changing landscape of gender relationships. . . . 2)the disruption of traditional gender roles and identities, the implication of such terms is that 'postfeminism' does not just come after feminism—as if the feminist project were ended—but is an attempt to undermine and erase it" (243).
12. Heller, 228.
13. Heller, 229.

14. Mary Spicuzza, *Bad Heroines*, accessed November 5, 2002, available at www.metroactive.com/papers/metro/03.15.01/cover/womanfilm-0111.html.
15. Spicuzza, *Bad Heroines*.
16. Note: Xena fandom, commonly called the Xenaverse, can be seen at sites such as Dixie, "Xena Online Resources," accessed December 16, 2002, available at http://www.xenite.org/xor/home.shtml, Tom Simpson, "Tom's Xena Page," accessed May 31, 1996, available at http://www.xenafan.com, and Clio et al., "Xena," September 1996, accessed December 16, 2002, available at http://www.klio.net/XENA/. Fans of *Farscape* call themselves "Scapers" and have raised a protest over the show's cancellation following its fourth season. See, for example, "Save Farscape," accessed December 16, 2002, available at http://www.savefarscape.com, "Farscape Net Ring," accessed December 16, 2002, available at http://www.fortunecity.com/tatooine/uhura/270/, and "Message Center," accessed December 16, 2002, available at http://bboard.scifi.com/bboard/browse.cgi/1/5/984.
17. Nickianne Moody, "Displacements of Gender and Race in *Space: Above and Beyond*," in *Aliens R Us: The Other in Science Fiction Cinema*, ed. Ziauddin Sardar and Sean Cubitt (London: Pluto Press, 2002), 51.
18. Moody, 53.
19. Cyndy Hendershot, "Vampire and Replicant: The One-Sex Body in a Two-Sex World," *Science Fiction Studies* 22, no. 3 (1995): 378.
20. Annamarie Jagose, *Queer Theory: An Introduction* (New York: NYU Press, 1996), 3.
21. I put the terms "masculine" and "feminine" in quotation marks to indicate that I mean to refer to the collection of traits traditionally attributed to "masculine" and "feminine" behavior and learned by inhabitants of male and female bodies and not to any essentialist notion of biologically induced behavior. I do not believe, for example, that physical aggression is based in male biology, but rather in the socialization given to males. The show shares this viewpoint, since Aeryn, who is biologically female, has been socialized to be violently aggressive and is very good at it, while Crichton is thoughtful and sensitive, though clearly physically male. For an excellent discussion of the difficulties of defining "male" and "female," let alone "masculine" and "feminine," see Ann Fausto Sterling, *Sexing the Body: Gender Politics and the Construction of Sexuality* (New York: Basic Books, 2000).
22. The show is a Brian Henson production, involving high-quality puppets that give it a wider latitude in the representation of nonhumanoid aliens than any previous science-fiction television series has ever had. This is one of the aspects of the show that helps draw the audience into the alienness that this part of the galaxy represents for the human point-of-view character, who serves as the audience's surrogate.
23. Available at Claudiablackfans.Com/Inter_Articles/0800_Ign-Claudia.Html, accessed September 26, 2002.
24. Sharon Ney and Elaine Sciog-Lazarov, "The Construction of Feminine Identity in *Babylon 5*," in *Fantasy Girls: Gender in the New Universe of Science Fiction and Fantasy Television*, ed. Elyce Rae Helford (Lanham, MD: Rowman & Littlefield, 2000), 225.
25. Diane Dubois, " 'Seeing the Female Body Differently': Gender Issues in *The Silence of the Lambs*," *Journal of Gender Studies* 10, no. 3 (2001): 298.

26. It is notable that even the "feminized" character Gilina is a technician—a high-tech mechanic, in effect, not a profession that would have, during the twentieth century, served for a "feminine" character. The show undercuts gender stereotypes even while seemingly adhering to them.

27. Dowling, 204.

28. This show makes it necessary to invent a concept parallel to the phallus—as a penis is flesh, and a phallus a symbolic construct, I am construing that as a vagina is flesh, a yoni is a symbolic construct that represents female genitalia as a way of representing Crichton's feminization in a non-negative way. As Aeryn possesses an extra, strengthening dimension in her phallic state, so does Crichton in his yonic state.

29. Hendershot, 373.

30. Since Crichton makes this remark not while Aeryn is sitting on his lap in the module but after she has stalked off angry and he is following her across the hangar deck, presumably his reference is as metaphoric as hers.

31. For a discussion of the sexism of this "diagnosis" and a debunking of the "evidence" indicating its existence, see Ann Fausto Sterling, *Myths of Gender: Biological Theories About Women and Men* (New York: Basic Books, 1992).

32. Aeryn has her mother's surname, not her father's; this is evidently standard Peacekeeper practice.

33. Donna Haraway, *Simians, Cyborgs, and Women: The Reinvention of Nature* (New York: Routledge, 1991), 181.

34. Hollinger, 199

35. Hendershot, 375.

36. See, for example, Gigi, "An Unofficial Claudia Black Website," March 2002, accessed September 26, 2002, available at http://Claudiablackfans.Com/Inter_Articles/0800_Ign-Claudia.Html.

Notes on Contributors

Jeffrey A. Brown is assistant professor of popular culture at Bowling Green State University. His current research activities include gender and body issues in film, corporate media culture, urban ethnography, and comic book studies. He has published numerous articles about gender and film in journals such as *Screen, Cinema Journal,* and *The Journal of Popular Film and Television.* He also published an essay in the anthology, The *Reel Knockouts: Violent Women in the Movies.* He is also the author of *Black Superheroes: Milestone Comics and Their Fans* (University of Mississippi Press, 2001). He is currently working on a book about the changing representation of women as aggressive and sexualized media characters.

Renny Christopher is associate professor of English at California State University, Channel Islands. Her book, *The Viet Nam War/The American War: Images and Representations in Euro-American and Vietnamese Exile Narratives* (University of Massachusetts Press, 1995) was named Outstanding Book on Human Rights in North America by the Gustavas Myers Center for the Study of Human Rights in North America. She is working on an autobiography, *A Carpenter's Daughter: A Working-Class Woman in Higher Education,* which addresses her experiences as the first in her family to attend college. Her teaching and research interests focus on issues of race, class, and gender in United States literature and culture.

Sara Crosby received her Ph.D. at the University of Notre Dame. Her dissertation explores the role played by the female criminal in American political ideology from the Salem witch crisis at the end of the seventeenth century to the female poisoner obsession of the mid-nineteenth century. She also does research on gender in contemporary popular culture, Southern literature, and science fiction.

David Greven is assistant professor in the humanities at Boston University. He received his Ph.D. from Brandeis University, with a dissertation on the construction of masculinity in nineteenth-century American literature. He has written articles on Hitchcock, De Palma, myth in film and popular culture, and the sexual politics of teen comedies for journals including *Genders*, *Cineaste*, and *Cineaction*.

Dawn Heinecken is assistant professor of women's studies at the University of Louisville. Her research focuses on critical and cultural approaches to the study of gender representation in popular media, cultural studies, media audience reception, and feminist criticism. She published *The Warrior Women of Television: A Feminist Cultural Analysis of the New Female Body in Popular Media* (Peter Lang, 2003). With Vickie Rutledge Shields, she has written *Measuring Up: How Advertising Affects Self-Image* (University of Pennsylvania Press, 2002). She has authored book chapters and articles on Christian garage bands, romance novels, and science fiction television.

Claudia Herbst is assistant professor in the Department of Computer Graphics and Interactive Media at Pratt Institute, Brooklyn, New York. In her visual and theoretical work, she focuses on technology-inspired definitions of gender, media literacy, and on programming languages as culturally influential texts. She has published internationally on these topics. She is currently researching a book exploring the implications of women's absence from the production of programming languages.

Sherrie A. Inness is professor of English at Miami University. Her research interests include gender and cooking culture, girls' literature and culture, popular culture, and gender studies. She has published over a dozen books: *Intimate Communities: Representation and Social Transformation in Women's College Fiction, 1895–1910* (Bowling Green, 1995), *The Lesbian Menace: Ideology, Identity, and the Representation of Lesbian Life* (University of Massachusetts Press, 1997), *Tough Girls: Women Warriors and Wonder Women in Popular Culture* (University of Pennsylvania Press, 1999), *Dinner*

Roles: American Women and Culinary Culture (University of Iowa Press, 2001), *Nancy Drew and Company: Culture, Gender, and Girls' Series* (editor, Bowling Green, 1997), *Breaking Boundaries: New Perspectives on Regional Writing* (co-editor, University of Iowa Press, 1997), *Delinquents and Debutantes: Twentieth-Century American Girls' Cultures* (editor, New York University Press, 1998), *Millennium Girls: Today's Girls Around the World* (editor, Rowman & Littlefield, 1998), *Kitchen Culture in America: Popular Representations of Food, Gender, and Race* (editor, University of Pennsylvania Press, 2001), *Running for Their Lives: Girls, Cultural Identity, and Stories of Survival* (editor, Rowman & Littlefield, 2000), *Pilaf, Pozole, and Pad Thai: American Women and Ethnic Food* (editor, University of Massachusetts Press, 2001), *Cooking Lessons: The Politics of Gender and Food* (editor, Rowman & Littlefield, 2001), and *Disco Divas: Women, Gender, and Popular Culture in the 1970s* (editor, University of Pennsylvania Press, 2003).

Sharon Ross is assistant professor of television studies at Columbia College in Chicago. Her research focuses on representations of gender and sexuality in popular culture. She has published several articles, including "Talking Sex: Comparison Shopping Through Female Conversation in HBO's *Sex and the City*" (in *America Skewed and Viewed: Television Situation Comedies* [SUNY Press, 2004]), "Dormant Dormitory Friendships: The Continuing Saga of Race and Gender on *Felicity*" (in *Teen TV: Isolation, Inclusion and Identity* [British Film Institute, 2004]), and "Skeletons in the Closet: The HBO Family" (*"It's Not Just TV, It's HBO . . . "; HBO and the Reinvention of Quality Television* [forthcoming]).

Charlene Tung is assistant professor of women's and gender studies at Sonoma State University in California. Her current research focuses broadly on border transgressions. In addition to her research in gender, race, and sexuality in popular culture, she is currently preparing a manuscript on Filipina migrant careworkers in California and continues work on Taiwanese women's migration through the Americas.

Marilyn Yaquinto is a Ph.D. candidate in American culture studies at Bowling Green State University. Her research focus is on the role of popular culture on identity formations with regards to gender, race, ethnicity, and the policing of deviance within transcultural and transborder contexts. She has published two books, *Pump-'Em Full of Lead: A Look at Gangsters on Film* (Twayne, 1998) and (as co-author) *Sastun: My Apprenticeship with a Maya Healer* (Harper San Francisco, 1994).

Index